THE ARTISAN ROASTER

For Sebastian,

With my best wishes,

David Rau

2019.

First published in Australia in 2019
by The Artisan Roaster Enterprises

Copyright © David Rosa 2019

All rights reserved. No part of this book may be reproduced or utilised in any form or by any means, electronic or mechanical, including photocopying, recording, or by any information storage and retrieval system, without the prior written permission of the publishers.

Although all reasonable care has been taken in the preparation of this book, neither the publishers nor the author can accept any liability for any consequence arising from the use thereof, or the information contained therein. Every effort has been made to trace copyright holders and to obtain their permission for the use of copyright material. The publisher apologises for any errors or omissions and would be grateful if notified of any corrections that should be incorporated in future editions of this book.

The author has asserted his moral rights.

ISBN-13: 978-0-6485520-0-0

 A catalogue record for this book is available from the National Library of Australia

Design: Melissa Mylchreest, King Street Press
Cover photography: Todd Lopez
Printed and bound in China by 1010 Ltd.

For book trade enquiries, information on purchasing this book and media enquiries please visit: www.theartisanroaster.com

THE ARTISAN ROASTER

THE COMPLETE GUIDE
TO SETTING UP YOUR OWN
COFFEE ROASTERY CAFÉ

DAVID ROSA

PART A

GETTING STARTED

FOREWORD 9

INTRODUCTION 10

**A BRIEF HISTORY OF
COFFEE DRINKING** 14

**A BRIEF HISTORY OF COFFEE
ROASTING EQUIPMENT** 16

LIVING THE DREAM! 24

A-1 SETTING UP YOUR COFFEE ROASTERY/CAFÉ
1. Where do I actually start? — 30
2. Do your research — 31
3. Write your business plan — 32
4. Select your site — 33
5. Negotiate your lease — 34

A-2 DESIGNING AND BUILDING YOUR PERFECT RETAIL FIT-OUT AND ROASTERY/CAFÉ WORKSPACE
1. Functional work zone design and planning — 40
2. Approvals and permitted use — 44
3. Some shop equipment you will need – and some you won't — 45
4. Financing the setup of your roastery/café — 50
5. The importance of insurance cover — 52

A-3 PURCHASING YOUR COFFEE ROASTER
1. Coffee roaster designs and how they work — 56
2. Important features to consider when purchasing a coffee roaster — 61
3. The purchase protocol – avoiding common mistakes — 69
4. Buying used or rebuilt coffee roasters — 70
5. Installing and commissioning your coffee roaster — 71

PART B

ROASTING COFFEE

B-1 LET'S TALK ABOUT GREEN COFFEE

1. Coffee genealogy	80
2. What is a coffee bean?	85
3. Green coffee chemistry	87
4. Coffee origins and their typical characteristics	89
5. Green coffee processing methods	94
6. Coffee grading and identifying defects	98
7. Impact of processing methods on flavour	102
8. Seasonality, storage, shipping and packaging	104
9. Making sense of coffee certifications	108
10. Pros and cons of direct trade	109

B-2 LET'S START ROASTING COFFEE

1. Coffee roasting chemistry 101	112
2. Let's do a roast together	116
3. Planning your batch roast by roaster capacity	117
4. Airflow – what does it do?	118
5. Warming up your roaster and charge temperatures	119
6. Stages of the roast	120
7. Why development time is everything – and why you need to understand this	124
8. Two roast profiles to get you started	126
9. Roast levels and Agtron readings	128
10. Roasting techniques for achieving well-developed light roast coffees	131
11. The importance of cooling your roast fast	132
12. What to do in between roasts – being prepared	133
13. Some extra tips on achieving roast consistency	134
14. De-stoning your coffee – the last step	135
15. 'The last roast of the day' procedure	136

B-3 QUALITY CONTROL AND IMPLEMENTATION

1. Sample roasting – a different roasting technique/art	138
2. Cupping and sensory evaluation of your coffee roast batches	140
3. Fixing common roast faults	144
4. Packing and storage of your roasted coffee	144

B-4 SINGLE ORIGIN ROASTS AND BLENDING COFFEE

1. Single origin coffee v. blended coffee	147
2. The joy and art of coffee blending – a delicate balancing act	148
3. Putting together your first coffee blends	151
4. Some coffee blend recipes to get you started	152
5. What is decaffeinated coffee? The process and how to roast it	153

B-5 COFFEE ROASTER MAINTENANCE

1. Why you need to be OCD about cleaning your coffee roaster	157
2. Major breakdowns/technical specialist issues	158
3. What to do in a roaster fire situation	158

B-6 THE ECONOMICS OF COFFEE

1. Roasting to a quality/price point	163
2. Shrinkage!	163
3. Learning to cost coffee production and monitor margins	164

PART C

RUNNING YOUR BUSINESS

C-1 RUNNING YOUR ROASTERY/CAFÉ

1. Being a retailer	174
2. Staff – the face of your business	175
3. Customer service 101	178
4. How to sell coffee beans to non-coffee nerds	180
5. The roasted coffee beans display, stock turnover and freshness	182
6. Online coffee bean sales	184
7. A quick message on espresso and brew bar service	185
8. Financial accounting 101	189

C-2 MARKETING AND BUILDING BRAND VALUE

1. First steps in brand creation	194
2. Team up with a good brand design agency	195
3. Branding and packaging – getting it right	199
4. Digital and social media marketing	200
5. Attracting new customers and retaining them	204
6. Strategic marketing alliances	205
7. Websites and online strategies	206

C-3 EXPANSION OPPORTUNITIES

1. Opening more retail sites	209
2. Wholesale coffee – a whole new ball game	210
3. Idle capacity and its hidden costs	214
4. Contract roasters	215
5. Change management	220
6. Other approaches to expansion	222

C-4 THE END GAME – CASHING IN THE CHIPS

1. Plan the end game from the start	225
2. The red flags for potential buyers/investors	226
3. Five critical steps for getting your business sale ready	227
4. Are business brokers worth it?	237
5. A note on well-being for when you exit stage left	238

AN ARTISAN ROASTER'S DICTIONARY 240

BOOK, ARTICLE AND WEB REFERENCES 245

SUPPLIER DIRECTORY 246

INDEX 248

ACKNOWLEDGEMENTS 254

FOREWORD

It's a pleasure to preface this book about one of the most exciting and fascinating commodities in the world. For all too long there has been a lack of available knowledge about coffee roasting as our industry has evolved into what it is today. Who could have imagined the spectacular growth and diversity of the Australian coffee industry? From the seventies and eighties, when international and national roasters dominated the market, to the emergence of the artisan roasters in the early 2000s, it's a testament to the roasters, cafés and passionate coffee consumers.

Back then, for those starting up coffee roasting, learning the art wasn't easy. Invariably those with the knowledge saw no reason to share their hard-earned expertise with potential competitors. (Thankfully, though, there were generous exceptions.) The aspiring roaster could find few reference books, apart from those by Jobin and Bernhard Rothfos who were writing for the European market. Very little else existed that was instructive or, indeed, accurate.

As the artisan and specialty markets continue to grow and we have a proliferation of boutique and micro-roasters in all states, the need for information has become insatiable. Coffee roasting has a universal appeal, drawing in folk from every possible background and age. This book is written for those people – and it couldn't be better timed. David is certainly one of those generous exceptions, sharing his expertise on all aspects of establishing a roastery and the various pitfalls of running a successful business. This book covers every aspect, from coffee roasting through to marketing, branding and streamlining a coffee operation. What David shares is invaluable, informative and concise. It perfectly reflects his enthusiasm, honesty, thirst for knowledge and, not least, his sense of humour. I have no doubt this will be read, enjoyed and used as a guide for all new roasters as well as current roasters worldwide.

ANDREW MACKAY
DIRECTOR OF COFI-COM TRADING

INTRODUCTION

My first day in 1997.

It's September 9, 1997 and my then business partner and I open the doors of our new shop, Bay Coffee Roasters in Neutral Bay, for the first day's trade. All shiny and new, there had been a lot of interest in the neighbourhood prior to our opening day about what that strange machine in the window did: "You mean you roast coffee? I thought it just grew on trees like that!"; "Grind it for what, you mean it's not instant?"; "Good luck man, no-one will be interested with the Woolies across the road." Our first day's trade was $150 (a sum I'll never forget). I was 28 years old, my wife was expecting our first child and I had left my well-paid job as a Marketing Manager. WTF had I done?

From that first day it became apparent our retail marketing and sales strategy had to focus on educating our customers on the joys of freshly roasted "real coffee" and its benefits. Oh, and did I mention it was 1997? So being Mr Practical I figured it was time to pull out my trusty old Uni textbook on Basic Marketing. It was gonna be just like I'd studied at Uni, but scaled down to the local micro level, one customer at a time. Oh, God ...

Fast-forward 19 years and I am selling my company and its associated divisions. It's December 1, 2016 and I've just been handed the biggest damn cheque I'll probably ever hold in my hands. During those years I'd learned so much about coffee roasting, marketing and sales, consumer behaviour and, to a tiny extent, helped mould the industry in Australia into what it is today, a massive specialty coffee market known as the "Third Wave" that shows no signs of waning or running out of steam (pun intended). I feel very lucky and privileged to have been a part of this spectacular period of growth and change in the coffee industry.

It was a conscious choice to keep Bay Coffee small. We started as a micro-roastery, and while we grew considerably tonnage-wise through wholesale opportunities later on, I never lost sight of what we were about – a specialty artisan coffee roaster. I also didn't want the stress and headaches that went with being a larger brand. I loved my team, and we all had a great time doing what we did well.

Despite my years in the business I am not a household name. I chose not to name the brand after myself and, being the shy retiring type, I always kept a low (almost invisible) profile in the coffee industry, flying well under the publicity radar. So when it was separately suggested to me by both Andrew Mackay and John Russell Storey from Cofi-Com Trading (two Aussie coffee men I seriously respect) that I should write an Australian-"flavoured" how-to book on coffee roasting, I initially baulked at the idea. "Me? No-one knows who the hell I am!" I exclaimed. I also needed some time after selling the business to clear my head and to do things I'd let go over the years (like playing rock music) before I was ready to even think about doing anything coffee related again. Call it a coffee industry detox, if you like.

About 15 months later I met with John again. After several coffees he brought up the subject again. Once more I deflected the idea. Two weeks later though, I thought, "You know what, maybe he's right." So I started to think hard about the concept. There were several very good but quite technical books out there on coffee roasting and some lovely coffee table-style books about coffee (sounds like a Seinfeld episode). But these books don't really teach you anything about coffee or about how to start and run your roastery. So I thought, if I'm going to do this I'm going to give you, dear readers, the whole warts-and-all story from beginning to end. Not only am I going to give you a very practical resource on how to roast coffee, but I'm also going to give you an overview on how to run your business day to day. We'll cover the entire process, from the extensive planning required before you even open your doors for your first day of trade, to when you hand over the keys to the new owner and wish them the best of luck.

To write everything in infinite detail would require a 1,000+ page tome. So what I'll give you in this book is practical, no-bullshit information and I will highlight tips and tricks that I picked up over the years. You'll learn from my successes and, more importantly, my mistakes, and hopefully not repeat these yourselves – because if you do after I've warned you, then do so at your own peril!

Our first day's trade was $150 (a sum I'll never forget). I was 28 years old, my wife was expecting our first child and I had left my well-paid job as a Marketing Manager. WTF had I done?

There are many good books out there on each area I cover in this book if you want more detail, and I sincerely encourage you to further educate yourselves, for you never stop learning. I will give you what I consider to be the important information you need to know and then you can go off and explore the topics in greater detail in the other resources.

Lastly, the focus of this book is on the specialty coffee area of the industry rather than the commodity area, on artisan roasting (15kg roasters or less), and on setting up a retail-based coffee roastery/café (I won't cover industrial coffee roasting setups). I hope this book will be equally as useful to home enthusiasts as to those considering starting up their own specialty coffee roastery and brand, as well as established roasters who might be keen to hear what I've got to say. Finally, while this book has an undeniably Australian flavour to it, I have done my best to keep the topics and references as international as possible for coffee enthusiasts everywhere.

THE BOOK ITSELF IS SPLIT INTO THREE KEY PARTS:
➤ **PART A: GETTING STARTED**
➤ **PART B: ROASTING COFFEE**
➤ **PART C: RUNNING AND EXITING YOUR BUSINESS**

Each part is further broken up into the key topic areas and phases of the business. Along the way, I invite industry experts who I respect in their fields to offer their advice and expert tips on topics such as selecting your coffee roasting equipment, green bean sourcing and quality assurance (QA), design and branding, and sales and marketing.

Unlike beer brewing, coffee roasting is always marketed as one of the most serious things in the world. Why is that? Both brews give us equally great pleasure, but it just seems wrong to have a sense of humour in the coffee industry! You may have noticed by now that I write in a direct style and sometimes use mildly offensive language. Rest assured, however, that while I will occasionally joke around and mess with your heads a bit, I do approach the topics covered in this book very seriously. Seriously ...

Having said that though, one of the more interesting bonuses of running a specialty coffee roastery is the people who walk through your shop door over the years. I have struck up so many amazing friendships with awesome longtime customers. That said, you do encounter your fair dose of strange people too! So with that in mind, I may diverge from time to time, to share with you some stories from my time dealing with Joe Public in the specialty coffee industry.

Without fail the work Christmas parties of old would always end with drunken stories of some of the more interesting customers that came into the roastery, either as one-offs or regularly until they found another place to haunt. So stay tuned to read about "The legend of Hunchy", "The gentleman we fondly came to know as 50 Cent" and "The newspaper-snatching crazy woman we knew only as Blondie".

So let's get started! See you on the other side ...

DAVID ROSA

A BRIEF HISTORY OF COFFEE DRINKING

(THE CONDENSED VERSION)

Legend has it that an Arabian goatherd dude called Kaldi found that some of his goats got frisky around a dark green-leafed shrub with bright red cherries. Kaldi, being a lonely shepherd, liked the frisky goats as they were more outgoing and had a certain mischievous look in their eye. He soon determined that it was the bright red cherries on the shrub that were causing the peculiar euphoria and after trying the cherries himself he learned of their powerful effect. Kaldi shared his secret of the strangely attractive frisky goats and the stimulating effects of these magical red cherries with the local monks. The monks, to assist their brethren to stay awake during extended hours of prayer, then exploited this stimulating effect. Before long the secret spread to other monasteries around the world. Coffee was thus born, thanks be to God. The fate of the frisky goats remains unknown.

Of course, this story is complete bullshit, but as in the tradition of the great religions of the world, why let truth get in the way of a good story? More recent botanical evidence suggests a different coffee bean origin. This evidence indicates that the history of the coffee bean began on the plateaus of central Ethiopia around 850AD and that it somehow was brought to Yemen where it was cultivated from the 6th Century onwards.

> Legend has it that an Arabian goatherd dude called Kaldi found that some of his goats got frisky around a dark green-leafed shrub with bright red cherries. Kaldi, being a lonely shepherd, liked the frisky goats as they were more outgoing and had a certain mischievous look in their eye.

Kaldi with his somewhat stoned-looking frisky goats.

It wasn't until the 12th Century that Arabs brought coffee beans back home, roasted them over fire, ground them up, and stirred the grinds into animal fat. They called the drink "qahwa," reportedly meaning "that which prevents sleep". Incidentally qahwa, also written as "kahwah", was one of many Arabic words used for wine. You see, in the process of stripping the coffee bean's cherry-like husk, the pulp can be fermented to make a potent alcoholic beverage with quite a kick in the palate! While the Koran forbids wine or other such intoxicants, Muslims enamoured with coffee argued that the brew was actually a stimulant!

Photo courtesy of diavoletto2718.

Ottoman Empire Turkish coffeehouse.

Charles II rocking the Brian May hairdo.

Emilie du Châtelet.

As coffee roasting and brewing techniques evolved, the drink became so popular that, in Constantinople in 1453, the Turks in the Ottoman Empire amended divorce law to include a lack of daily coffee as grounds for a women to divorce her husband. Coffee had become a daily necessity.

By the 17th Century coffee appeared in Europe for the first time outside the Ottoman Empire. The first recorded coffeehouse in Europe was in Venice in 1647, although the Italians didn't really kick into gear with their coffee culture until the 18th Century, with the famous Caffè Florian (1720) being Italy's oldest continuously running café located in Venice's Piazza San Marco.

The history of Viennese coffeehouse culture is closely linked to the end of the Siege of Vienna in 1683. Legend has it that the Viennese citizen Georg Franz Kolschitzky (1640–1694) was the first to obtain a licence to serve coffee in the city following his heroic actions during the Siege of Vienna. The coffee beans left behind by the Turks were the basis of his success. However, the first coffeehouse in Vienna was actually opened by the Armenian spy Diodato. He served at the Viennese Imperial Court and was a man full of secrets. He knew about the dark beans and the art of preparing coffee from his home country.

Of all places, England was also an early coffeehouse adopter! The first coffeehouse in England was set up in Oxford in 1650. A building on the same site now houses a café/bar called The Grand Café. From 1670 to 1685 the number of coffeehouses began to multiply, and also began to gain political importance due to their popularity as places for debate.

Charles II later tried to suppress the London coffeehouses as "places where the disaffected meet, and spread scandalous reports concerning the conduct of His Majesty and His Ministers". The public, of course, flocked to them.

The rich atmosphere of early London coffeehouses was available to anyone who could pay the one penny entry fee, giving them the name Penny Universities.

Ah Paris, mon amour! Pasqua Rosée established the first coffeehouse in Paris in 1672 and was soon followed by the Sicilian chef Francesco Procopio dei Coltelli who opened Café Procope in 1686 in *rue de l'Ancienne Comédie*, 6th arrondissement. This coffeehouse still exists today and was a popular meeting place for enlightened dudes such as Voltaire, Rousseau and Denis Diderot. How cool is that?

Of course, as coffeehouses were fun places to be and debate the ills of the world, you had to ban women. The banning of women from coffeehouses was, however, not universal, although it does appear to have been common in Europe. In Germany, women frequented them, but (surprise, surprise) in England and France, they were banned. Rumour has it that Emilie du Châtelet, a French natural philosopher, mathematician, physicist and author cross-dressed to gain entrance to a coffeehouse in Paris in order to hang out with her Enlightenment mates, Voltaire and Diderot.

So there is a very condensed history of coffee drinking. What makes coffee so varied and delectable, however, isn't just the bean; it's also the roasting of that precious bean. When heat is applied to green beans, those beans produce and release oils, and their natural sugars caramelise, contributing to the bean's colour and flavour. Historically, roasting methods varied from one region to another, with roasting over open fires or baking inside ovens being the mainstays throughout the East and West.

A BRIEF HISTORY OF COFFEE ROASTING EQUIPMENT
(THE EXPURGATED VERSION)

In 1881 a gentleman by the name of Francis Thurber wrote one of the first extensive books on coffee called *Coffee: From Plantation to Cup*. He made a very important observation that: "The finest quality of coffee (bean) unskilfully roasted will give you a less satisfactory result in the cup than a poor quality (bean) roasted in the best manner". This is an important observation as it placed focus on technology and the skill of the master roaster in the quality of the final product in the cup.

So let me give you a very brief rundown from the 1700s.

From the 1700s until the mid-1800s various hand-held contraptions made of sheet metal, brass, copper or cast iron were used to roast coffee beans over a direct heat source (like wood fire, coal, coke). These various contraptions included:

Coffee: From Plantation to Cup by Francis Thurber, 1881.

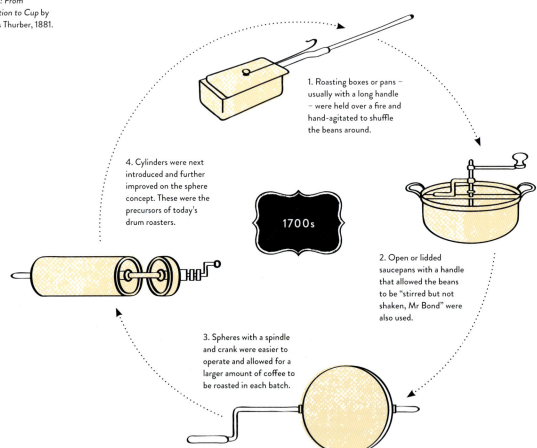

1. Roasting boxes or pans – usually with a long handle – were held over a fire and hand-agitated to shuffle the beans around.

2. Open or lidded saucepans with a handle that allowed the beans to be "stirred but not shaken, Mr Bond" were also used.

3. Spheres with a spindle and crank were easier to operate and allowed for a larger amount of coffee to be roasted in each batch.

4. Cylinders were next introduced and further improved on the sphere concept. These were the precursors of today's drum roasters.

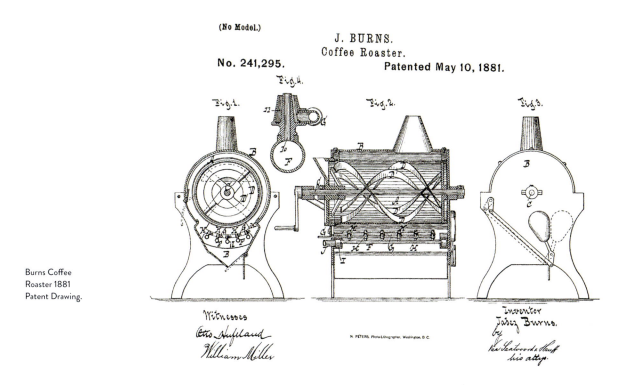

Burns Coffee
Roaster 1881
Patent Drawing.

A big breakthrough came in 1864 when a 20-year-old gentleman by the name of Jabez Burns of New York invented and then in 1881 patented in the USA what we now know today as an early version of the modern drum roaster.

The mid-1800s saw a rapid advance in coffee roasting technology. The industrial revolution changed everyone's focus to inventing machines that would produce a better quality product and in larger amounts – that is, the idea of economies of scale was invented.

One of the first significant machines of note was by a very clever Bostonian gent called Mr James Carter. In 1846 he patented a cylindrical pull-out roaster. This advance brought roasting times down from 60 minutes on average to about 40 minutes for a 6–9kg roast batch. It was still an imprecise, messy and dangerous art for the poor master roaster of the day as, when the coffee was ready, the cylinder had to be pulled out by two men and the roasted coffee dumped on the floor, where it was then sprinkled with water to try to cool it down.

J. Burns Coffee Roaster.

Jabez Burns himself.

A big breakthrough came in 1864 when a 20-year-old gentleman by the name of Jabez Burns of New York invented and then in 1881 patented in the USA what we now know today as an early version of the modern drum roaster.

In 1864 Burns emerged from his workshop with a revolutionary roasting machine. Burns' masterstroke was using a turning drum with flanges inside, running in the opposite direction than in previous roasters, that acted like a corkscrew inside the drum, pushing the beans from the back to the front. Once the beans had been roasted, a door at the front was opened, allowing the beans to pour out of the drum. It was the first machine that did not have to be moved away from the fire for discharging roasted coffee. The drum could carry on turning and a new batch of beans could be loaded via a rear door. Moreover, the turning of the beans by this double screw meant that the beans moved uniformly throughout the drum and were therefore roasted more consistently.

In the mid-1800s Alexius van Gülpen and his business partner Johann Heinrich Lensing teamed up with Theodor von Gimborn, a young engineer almost straight out of university who had the idea of building a foundry and machine-building company and designed and engineered their first roasting machines. Together the three of them founded the Emmericher Maschinenfabrik und Eisengießerei in Emmerich in Germany's Lower Rhine region. The first coffee roaster Theodor designed was the ball or sphere roaster in 1870.

Marketed as the Globe Roaster it quickly entered mass production and sold tens of thousands of units over the following decades.

Technology had continued to rapidly develop and roast batch times dropped to as little as 20 minutes through innovations such as perforated drum cylinders, the move from coal and coke heat sources to gas, and special lids that allowed for more temperature control. The advent of natural gas allowed for the burners to be placed directly under the roasting bin and, with a fan, the hot air was ducted through the roasting cylinder to provide convective heat transfer.

In 1884 Probat released their patented coke-powered Schnell or Rapid Roaster model, quickly followed by a gas version in 1889. This roaster featured cased worm-wheel gearing and an external belt drive. In the later 1890s the Rapid Roaster became known as the Probat Rapid Roaster.

PROBAT Coke heated Rapid Roaster

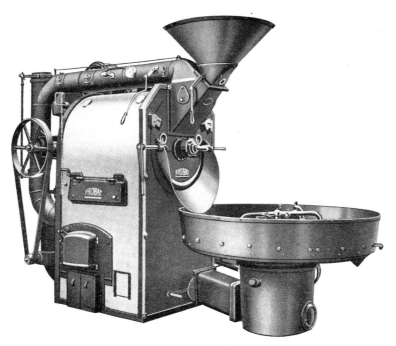

PROBAT with stationary self-emptying cooling sieve. (Attendance at the left).

PROBAT the first Hot Air Operated Rapid Roaster

is well introduced in the market since many years. Since propagation of the **rapid roasting** process this machine marked a new epoch for rapid roasting in thousands of enterprises throughout the world. The actual style of the machine also has been kept abreast of the present state of technics.

Furnace and roasting drum have logically been placed in a common well insulated casing; under double utilization of heat the hot air enters the **unperforated drum** which has been provided for that purpose with an admission at the rear. By that means the heat is transferred direct to the coffee being steadily shaked up. **A special roasting exhauster** evacuates the roasting fumes together with coffee membranes and any other impurities. After having crossed the **membrane catch** the roasting fumes are conducted to the chimney. The agitator arranged in the interior of the drum exposes the material to be roasted continuously and uniformly to the current of hot air and obtains a thorough satisfactory and homogeneous finish.

The operation of the hot air upon the material to be roasted is fully adjustable at any time. Cooling air can be supplied to the cooling drum in whatever volume.

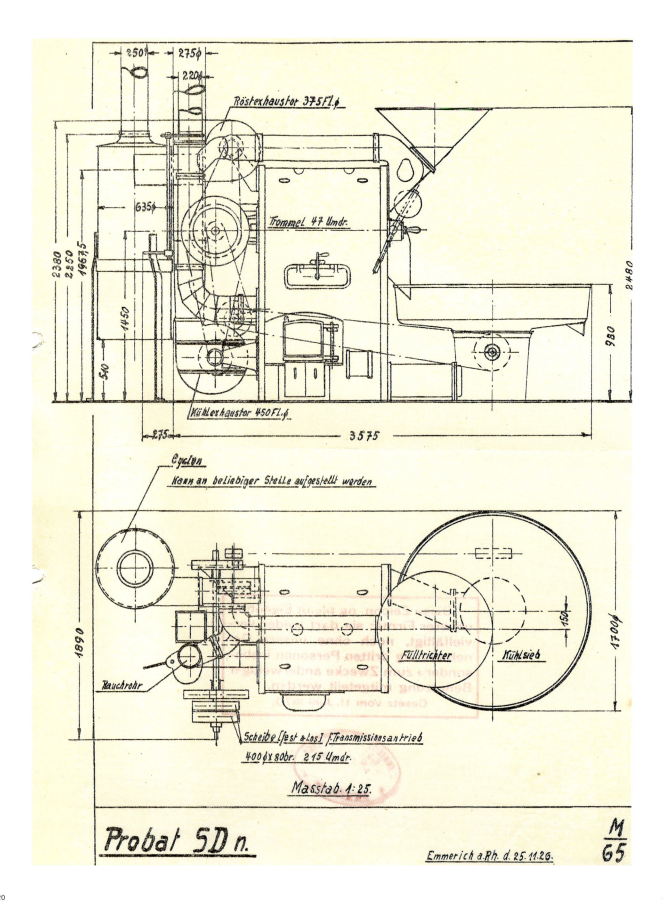

While researching this book I contacted Tina von Gimborn-Abbing, who runs the Probat Museum of Coffee Technology in Emmerich. Tina is the great-granddaughter of Probat's founder Theodor and has generously provided me with incredible archive material and pictures for this book. Tina also related the following story for me about her father trying to convince her grandfather to change the company name back in the 1950s:

Tina von Gimborn-Abbing.

"When my dad started in sales in the 1950s he would introduce himself with 'Hello, my name is Hans, I am from the Emmericher Maschinenfabrik und Eisengießerei in Emmerich'. The secretaries at those former or new customers would look at him as if he came straight from the moon and ask 'Who are you and how can I help you?' 'I would like to sell you a Probat coffee roaster ...' 'Ah you are Probat, come in, we have been waiting for you!' That really happened! Back home he began a discussion with his father Carl on the name change of the company; it took several years to convince Carl to change the company name to Probat-Werke. In 1959 my dad won the battle and since then we have been called Probat - the word Probat deriving from Latin as "tested and proven". Well, the testing and the proving still goes on and I hope for much longer."

TINA VON GIMBORN-ABBING
MUSEUM FÜR KAFFEETECHNIK

Opposite: Technical drawing of the Probat Rapid Drum Roaster from 1925.

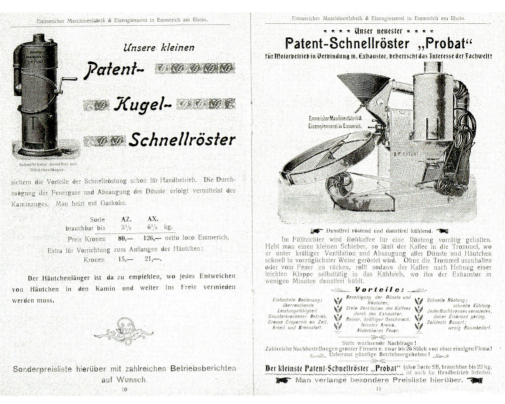

Probat Rapid Roaster catalogue from the late 1920s.

Recent advances in technology have moved us towards computer-controlled roast profiling automation. This has undoubtedly improved the quality, consistency and safety around the art of coffee roasting for modern roasters.

PROBAT COFFEE ROASTERS THROUGH THE AGES

1879
Ball or spheric roaster first-generation AZ 3kg per batch.

1900
25kg Rapid Roaster operated until 1981.

1930
45kg G45 Probat Roaster.

In the early 1900s both Probat and Burns continued to bring roast times on their roaster models down to as low as 16 minutes. From an economy-of-scale point of view, this allowed master roasters to now produce around three batches of coffee per hour. The Burns Jubilee Roaster had a 2–4 bag batch size (120–240kg). These roasters by now looked and operated pretty much like the modern drum roasters of today.

Importantly, other technologies improved, such as cooling trays which went from the aforementioned floor-based dumping, to troughs using rake-like wooden implements to move and cool the coffee, to the cooling sieves and trays with paddle rotation equipment powered by motors and fans that we still see today.

Recent advances in technology have moved us towards computer-controlled roast profiling automation. This has undoubtedly improved quality, consistency and safety around the art of coffee roasting for modern roasters. Oxidiser technologies and hot air recycling are also helping us save money by reducing fuel use, while also helping the environment by reducing emissions levels into the atmosphere.

Finally, I will also briefly mention some other non-drum roasting technologies that were developed during the 20th Century. My focus in this book is on drum roasters because that's what I know, but these inventions have been important breakthroughs in coffee roasting machinery history:

1. In 1957 Antonio Scolari developed a roaster that used infra-red lamps. However, it didn't really take off in a big way.

2. In 1926 the Cassen fluid-bed (hot air) roaster was released and further developed by other companies such as Gothot.

3. In the 1970s Michael Sivetz furthered this idea and patented his fluid-bed roaster on which German manufacturer Neuhaus Neotec still base their designs today.

I will go into more detail in Part A-3 on different modern roasting technologies in the current market. So there you go, a brief history of coffee roasting equipment in 1,500 words or less!

LIVING THE DREAM!

What's the Ongoing Attraction of Roasting Coffee?

Roasted coffee is a sexy beast. That satin-brown bean colour, the incredible aroma … and the flavour is undeniable. Chocolate admittedly runs a close second, but you need half a tonne of sugar added to it to make it palatable. The analogy between sex and coffee is not a coincidence. Both are very popular because they make you feel good and both are, because of this very fact, big business.

What initially attracted me to roasting coffee was how natural a process it was. Simply add heat at the correct rate and time, and around 15 minutes later – voila, it's done! No added ingredients, artificial colours or flavourings! The green side of coffee production was also still a very natural process, although granted, the washed-coffee process can be rather water intensive. Decaffeinated coffee is another story, but more on that in Part B.

I also liked the blend of art and science in coffee roasting. You need to be in tune with both sides of this equation. The trend of late has been to focus on the science side, with the onset of data-logging software and profile roasting semi/fully automated roasting machines. I sincerely believe that this technology has helped with consistency and quality. I do, however, feel that good master roasters also need to have a feel for the roasting process itself. This is the art side, and one that I believe is crucial to acquire, especially as an artisan roaster.

Younger master roasters appear obsessed with the science, and I guess it's a natural side effect of the geek culture/connected society of today. However, all the science in the world won't get around the natural variation in the green beans that you will encounter on a day-to-day basis. For this you need feel. This can't be taught with a textbook. It only comes with experience, mentoring and time. This is what I grew to love about becoming a master roaster.

If you love cooking and its various techniques (like applying the correct heat at the right times) and you love describing flavours, you will become a good master roaster. To me, when you post-blend different origins, you are creating a new dish, a new flavour for your customers to enjoy. Their positive feedback makes you feel good. This is the reward and the reason for taking up coffee roasting for a living. Financial reward will come if you consistently offer the best product you can for your customers. Without a good product you have no business. Marketing alone won't help you.

The coffee industry is a tough and competitive business, but it's also very rewarding. The culture bred by the third wave of roasters in recent years is one of collaboration and sharing, unlike the closed industry I encountered 20 years ago. This is a good thing and another reason why I am sharing my knowledge with you in this book.

My last tip here is to say this. Become an artisan coffee roaster only if you think you will love it and are willing to put in the time and effort. This will help you get through the highs and the lows, making it all worthwhile in the end – and then you too can live the dream!

PART

A

GETTING STARTED

TRUE
FICTIONS

The Legend of Hunchy

It's 4.55pm and we're five minutes away from closing our shop doors after another day that had started for us at 6.00am. Hunchy, as we had come to affectionately know him, is lurking just around the corner, ready to pounce at his usual time of minutes, if not milliseconds, before we physically close the doors.

"Hi guys! Sorry but I'm not too late to buy some beans am I?" Hunchy would say with a knowing grin as, with keys in hand, I approach the front door of the shop.

We then commence our dance to the same fortnightly routine. I say, "Oh no sir, of course we'll stay open for you to sell you some coffee," while actually thinking: "You do this every time you knob, you're not really sorry." This sounds harsh I know, but let me explain ...

"So tell me now, in infinite detail, about every single one of the eight varieties of coffee beans you have on offer today!" he would say EVERY SINGLE TIME HE CAME![1] "Oh, and what's the difference between a Brazilian and Guatemalan coffee flavour-wise?" Hunchy would further ask, the sense of power written all over his face as the clock now ticked over to 5:15pm, with the floor mopping still to be done and the cash register closed before I'd get out of there for the day ...

After playing this game for what seemed an eternity and having had several new coffee options presented to him in great detail, old Hunchy would finally declare, "Oh no, I think I'll just get the same one I got last time", and proceed to order the usual 100 grams of the same coffee he'd ordered every fortnight like clockwork for the past five years.

It's now close to 5.30pm and I'm closing the door as he toddles off into the sunset yet again, a full half-hour after closing time, and I've just made an extra $5.50 for the day's takings. Ah good old Hunchy, God love him!

A1

SETTING UP YOUR COFFEE ROASTERY/CAFÉ

First, a point of clarification before we start. The word roaster is very interchangeable in this business. It can interchangeably mean the machine you roast the coffee in, or it can mean the operator or the person who is roasting the coffee in the machine. So, for the sake of clarity, I will use the term *roaster* for the machine you roast the coffee in and, as much as I hate the term, *master roaster* for the operator – ie: you.

Also *Microsoft Word* doesn't seem to like the word *roastery*. It does, however, show up in the Oxford Dictionary as:

NOUN A place where coffee beans are roasted and processed. 'A café with an on-site roastery'.

So there. Get with the program, Word! And now you know what I mean when I use the word *roastery* throughout this book[2].

IN PART A-1 WE WILL COVER:

1. WHERE DO I ACTUALLY START?
2. DO YOUR RESEARCH
3. WRITE YOUR BUSINESS PLAN
4. SELECT YOUR SITE
5. NEGOTIATE YOUR LEASE

FOOTNOTE

[1] In retrospect it reminds me of the legendary Monty Python Bookshop Sketch: www.montypython.net/scripts/bookshop.php

[2] Note to self: Press 'Ignore All' in Spell Check.

1

SO NOW WE'VE CLARIFIED THAT, WHERE DO I ACTUALLY START?

So you've reached this stage! *"Good on you!"* as Big Malcolm[3] would say. I had the coffee roastery idea brewing (pun intended) in my head for a few years before I actually started the process of planning to open the coffee roastery. In your case you may have been roasting coffee beans at home in your garage or, even better, done some work at an established coffee roastery first.

Knowing where to start can be daunting; it's not for the faint-hearted. There is a lot of research involved and you will have to obtain a basic working knowledge of things you never knew existed. The key is to know who to ask for help and who to contract to do the work. Setting up a coffee roastery involves specialised trades and contractors. In Part A of this book I will attempt to break down each step of the process to help you. Of course, everyone's journey and situation will be different, so one size does not fit all comers. For example, state and local council[4] legislation and rules can differ from state to state, especially with the roaster's installation and pollution control requirements. Take the following advice as a starting point and go from there.

2
DO YOUR RESEARCH AND FIND YOUR PATCH/NICHE

I came from a corporate marketing background. At University it was literally beaten into me not to invest in anything without doing thorough research into the market and test marketing your product or idea first. Your research results will be the front-end and the scaffold of your business plan. So what do you need to research? The following list is indicative, but by no means exhaustive:

1. What is the market size and potential? Is it growing? Is there room for another player? What are the market niches you can identify?
2. Who are your direct and indirect competitors?
3. What are the entry cost/barriers of entry to this market?
4. What practical knowledge do you need to acquire to be successful?
5. What are the demographic statistics (socio/economic/cultural) and behaviours of the customers you wish to target?
6. Where do they live and, more importantly, WHERE and WHEN do they shop? What are their likes/dislikes?
7. And with all this considered, where are the geographic opportunities to open your business? Places where your target customers already shop and there is a lack of established competitors in your niche.

This list comes from the angle of opening a retail front artisan coffee roastery, as that is the focus of this book. If you were looking to open an industrial site your research questions would, of course, differ to some extent.

I'd like to expand further on a few of these bullet points as they are important.

POINT 3 LOOKS AT ENTRY COSTS AND BARRIERS TO MARKET ENTRY. IN SETTING UP A RETAIL COFFEE ROASTERY THESE CAN INCLUDE:

- Availability of appropriate retail sites that can accommodate coffee roasting (space required, ability to flue the roaster externally, friendly neighbours).
- Ability to get your local council/authority's approval to roast coffee in the area (residential/other objections).
- Does the proposed site have town gas or will it have to be brought on site?
- The financial cost of the coffee roasting equipment, its installation and the time it takes to order, manufacture and arrive on site.
- Acquiring the knowledge to roast coffee to an appropriate commercial standard.

None of these entry barriers need to be deal breakers if you plan well and do your research, especially with regards to your site selection, which we will examine in more detail soon.

FOOTNOTE
[3] www.facebook.com/BigMalTurnbull

[4] In Australia we have a very annoying level of local government called local government councils. The state of NSW alone had 128 local government councils at the time of writing.

3
WRITE YOUR BUSINESS PLAN

As painful as it may seem, actually writing a Business Plan document is vital. The research plan is essentially your feasibility study[5] and gives you a lot of the information you need to complete your Business Plan. Your research gives you the informed answers to your unique plans that you will explore in your Business Plan. If you are seeking finance as a start-up banks will want to see some evidence that you know what you're doing. They will not take your word for it unless you have some bricks and mortar collateral to put up as a mortgage on your word.

The main benefit of a Business Plan is that it helps you think things through critically and will often foresee potential issues you may encounter down the track. How much better is it to approach something with a plan and contingencies rather than dealing with unforeseen headaches (which I promise you WILL arise) and having to confront them without a Plan B. It may be something as simple as allowing an extra $10K in reserve start-up capital for unseen equipment installation problems. So many people just dive right in and get caught out badly, and run out of cash before they even open their doors!

There are numerous templates for writing a Business Plan. Not all of them will be 100% relevant or suitable, but you can adapt them to your needs. There are pretty good templates available at business.gov.au[6] that you can have for free! So no excuses – get writing and get planning.

THE KEY SECTIONS OF YOUR BUSINESS PLAN WILL BE:
- **BUSINESS SUMMARY**: A one-page written overview of your business plan.
- **ABOUT YOUR BUSINESS**: This is typically called the management plan or operations plan. It covers details about your business including structure, registrations, location and premises, staff and products/services.
- **SWOT ANALYSIS**: Strengths, Weaknesses, Opportunities, Threats.
- **ABOUT YOUR MARKET**: This is the marketing plan. It should outline your marketing analysis of the industry you are entering, your customers and your competitors. This section should also cover your key marketing targets and your strategies for delivering on these targets. Here you will explore your USB, or Unique Selling Benefit, that will make you a success in your market.
- **ABOUT YOUR FUTURE**: This section covers your plans for the future and can include a vision statement, business goals and key business milestones.
- **ABOUT YOUR FINANCES**: The financial plan includes how you'll finance your business, costing and financial projections. Here you will project sales, expenses and profit. You will calculate capital required for setting up and working capital to keep you going until those sales and profits start rolling in. This is CRITICAL! Be very conservative; allow way more start-up working capital (cash) than you think you'll need. Entrepreneurs tend to be optimistic by nature so halve your projected sales figures for the first six months' trade. Will you survive or not? If not, then have the cash there ready to cover it if you won't. If you don't use it, well and good. You'll thank me later for this tip …

Remember that business planning is an ongoing business activity. As your business changes many of the strategies in your plan will need to evolve to ensure your business is still heading in the right direction.

FOOTNOTE
[5] A study designed to determine the practicability of a system or plan.

[6] http://bit.ly/2V4Aknc

4
SELECT YOUR RETAIL SITE

All righty! You've written your Business Plan and it's a cracker! The banks have fallen over themselves to give you money and you're ready to rock!

Now comes the hard bit – finding the perfect and/or suitable retail site that will become your new home for the next however many years ahead. Believe me, you'll spend so much time there over the next few years that it will feel like your second home. Here are some important factors I would recommend when selecting an appropriate artisan roastery retail site.

1. Choose a location that already has people around looking for what you offer. My focus was selling freshly roasted coffee beans for home as well as locals enjoying our espresso bar. So I wanted to be near shoppers who were already out in numbers buying high-end complementary goods after their supermarket shop. So what other established retailers were already next to the shop I spied in Neutral Bay back in 1997? A high-end meat supplier and deli ☑; a high-end bottle shop ☑; a high-end fruit/veg shop ☑; a high-end fishmonger ☑; a natural food market ☑. To top this off we were all located opposite the busiest (per square metre sales) Woolworths supermarket in Australia ☑☑☑☑☑☑☑.

2. Choose a location that's close to the hub but just off the high street. Getting this right is critical. It will reduce your starting rent dramatically, being a little off the beaten track – but get it slightly wrong and you're stuffed. You are not a destination store. You need passing traffic.

3. Find a site that can have approved outdoor seating.

4. Don't get a site that's on a busy main road with thousands of cars and trucks streaming past all day. Noise and pollution will drive customers away.

5. Find a site that has town gas available or close by. If town gas is not available please ensure your site is able to comply with the safe storage of portable gas bottle regulations as stipulated by your local authority.

6. Find a site that has ducted air-conditioning already installed and lots of power. You may have to add three-phase power to the site. Make sure this is possible without too much trouble – ask a commercial electrician, not a domestic one!

7. Find a site that has high ceilings or where the ceiling can be removed. I will explain why later.

8. Find a site with a friendly human landlord and not a nasty multinational inhuman beast. Not as easy as it might sound these days.

9. Find a site with level access and enough space for a good, dry storage area for your 60–70kg green bean sacks.

10. Find a site that has a loading zone access close by where you can receive and dispatch goods.

11. Most importantly, find a site that fits your rental budget.

5
NEGOTIATE
YOUR
LEASE[7]

Here's the fun bit. Landlords see newbies like you as sweet bait to try on a new level of rent for their property. Remember, once it's set up moving a roastery to a new site is not easy, either logistically or financially. So you ideally need to find a site for the long haul. Your starting rental rate can only go one way as the years pass – up. So do try to negotiate the lowest possible base rental you can right from the start.

Coffee roasteries have a great tradition of opening just off the high street – usually for the trade-off in rent, but also for the cool cred factor. Before long that side of the high street won't be so shabby, but your rent will be locked in nice and low if you negotiated your initial rental terms right. It's critical though, as already mentioned, that you're not so tucked away that you're invisible. There is a fine line.

Your ability to negotiate with a landlord without having a track record in retail will be somewhat hampered though. They will be concerned about your ability to succeed as a start-up and, therefore, pay their rent long term. Coffee roasteries also scare the crap out of landlords due to the fire risk, and the potential to bother other tenants with the roasting odour and smoke and so on. So you need to have something up your sleeve to counter their arguments and concerns.

Do your research. What has been in that shop before? Why is it for rent again? Have the last several businesses in there failed? Why? In my case the shop I chose was tucked away in a corner and had previously traded fashion and, before us, terracotta pots. Nothing had lasted longer there than a couple of years. The landlord wasn't keen on us and was very wary of our roasting plans. We persisted though, and won him over. At the time of writing, the business has been operating there now for over 21 years and never missed a rental payment. My argument to the landlord at the time was that the shop was positioned perfectly for food/café production (not fashion/terracotta pots) and I was proven right.

If you have trouble finding a site that is perfect and up for lease just when you want it, another approach is to offer the current tenant "key money" to vacate the site for you. This will work if you suspect their business is already in trouble and they want to get out of their lease. You may not have to fork out too much as escaping a long lease when you're bleeding cash is like a gift from heaven.

Your lease isn't all about the monthly rental amount. You can negotiate extras. Some extras can be very useful at the start. Negotiating a rent-free fit-out period is very important. Often your coffee roasting equipment will be delayed from the manufacturer and other obstacles will arise. Your opening date will inevitably be delayed. Try for a three-month rent-free period (if you can get more, even better), because it's hard to be paying rent while you are not trading yet. You could also try for two-to-three months rent-free and then another two-to-three months at half-rent. No harm in asking, is there?

Some landlords will contribute a sum of money or rent in lieu towards your fit-out cost. The types who do this are normally those sitting on new sites that are still shells and have been empty since construction, often for months on end. They are paying a mortgage on this site with no rental returns as yet, so they're keen to talk and lock someone in. Be wary of new sites though. If other empty shops surround you it can make life very tough for you to get passing trade.

Let's talk about lease terms. Normally you will have the main lease term and options to renew. You will hear of 3 + 3 years or even up to 5 + 5 + 5-year leases.

FOOTNOTE
[7] Please note that while I am trying to keep this section as generic and international as possible my perspective and experience comes from the retail leasing market in Australia.

Your opening date will inevitably be delayed. Try for a three-month rent-free period (if you can get more, even better), because it's hard to be paying rent while you are not trading yet. You could also try for two-to-three months rent-free and then another two-to-three months at half-rent. No harm in asking, is there?

What does this mean? OK, so in the first case you have a three-year lease then an option to renew for another three years. This is your option as the tenant and not the landlord's. There will normally be a clause in the lease contract that says you need to give notice in writing about whether you wish to renew or not – usually about three-to-six months in advance of the expiry date.

THE ADVANTAGES OF HAVING LEASE RENEWAL OPTIONS ARE:
➤ You lock in the agreed method of any rent reviews/increases, giving you some assurance that the rent won't skyrocket in the near future.
➤ Drafting new contracts for new leases is costly each time.
➤ If you decide to sell, having a long lease with options is an asset.
➤ It's your option, not the landlord's, so he can't refuse or use it as an excuse to raise the rent.

Negotiating the lease the first time as a start-up can be tricky. You don't know how things will go or if you will get past the first year. I always tried to have a relatively short first term for this reason, with longer options. So say, 3 years + 4 year option + 4 year option. Technically the landlord can come after you for the remaining rent of the term even if you pull up stumps[8] within the first six months. This rarely happens though, and I'll explain why next.

To avoid trouble, I strongly suggest offering a Bank Guarantee as part of your lease agreement. This is where you deposit, say, two months' rent in cash into a locked bank account and the bank issues a certificate to the landlord. The idea is that this will limit your exposure to that fixed amount if you can't see the lease through for any reason. Most reasonable landlords will agree to this as it's guaranteed and gives them a few months to find a new tenant. If you sell your business or move to a new property, you have to get the original certificate back from the landlord. You then give it to the bank in order to have that money released back to you. So make sure: a) you keep a copy of it on file; and b) you tell your landlord he needs to keep the original in a safe place and remember where it is, as it could be many years before he needs to retrieve it again. You can't get your money back from the bank without the original copy!

Please avoid giving a Director's Guarantee, especially if your name is on your own home or other assets, because then you are fair game for them to pursue you in the courts for the remaining rent, however long that may be.

Once you are established and business is humming, make sure you have long terms and options in future leases, as this will be a major asset for you when it comes time to sell up. It will give the buyer a level of comfort that they are secure in that space for years to come and they will get a return on their investment.

On that point some landlords (like mine) never wanted to give me long terms. Why? Because I was a good tenant who never made trouble and always paid the rent on time. He probably knew that short leases would make it hard for me to sell my business to someone else (who may not be such a reliable rent payer). My final lease was 4 + 4 years, but initially it was three years with no options. So you can be punished for being too nice. Be wary that they don't have you by the goolies[9] with short lease and renewal terms.

In most Australian states retail leases are a standard contract, but you have to watch out for the special clauses added at the end. This is where things like outgoings (who pays for certain services, like water and waste) are listed. This is also where certain restrictions may also be noted. We had a clause in our lease, for example, that always scared me. It specified that if other tenants complained about the smell of our roasting we could be restricted to roasting only at certain times of the day. Thankfully we only ever received compliments and not complaints about the smell. So be wary that those deal-breaking special clauses aren't slipped through by the landlord.

Be clear on who pays for what in terms of maintenance. Our air-conditioning unit regularly broke down each summer, for example, but thankfully it was the landlord's problem and not ours. Landlords are notorious tight-arses and you will have to hassle them to get anything done.

FOOTNOTE

[8] Cricket (the game, not the creature) term for ending the day's play.

[9] Another Aussie slang term. Look it up …!

Setting up a roastery requires changes to the premises (tenant improvements), like putting a flue through and up the side of the building, bringing in town gas if required, adding three-phase power and so on. Sometimes a landlord may insist on a special clause where certain things you do to the property are returned back to original (called "make-good"). In some cases this is fair enough, in others not, and very costly, so be careful what you agree to. If it's a genuine improvement that others following can use, you shouldn't have to make good – and, in fact, the landlord should contribute something towards the cost in my opinion!

You also need to have an approval pending get-out clause for permitted use from council in case you get knocked back by council to use these premises as a coffee roastery or café.

Please do your Due Diligence and hire an experienced lawyer to review the lease contract for you. Remember that this is a legal contract, so please be aware of this before you sign. Lastly, please do not consider what I've written here as comprehensive or legal advice. It's simply a bunch of tips for you from my specific retail leasing experiences in Australia.

A2

DESIGNING AND BUILDING YOUR PERFECT RETAIL FIT-OUT AND ROASTERY/CAFÉ WORKSPACE

By 2012 our roastery was in desperate need of a facelift. Much had changed since 1997 and our 15th anniversary was looming, so I took the plunge to give the roastery the mother of all facelifts – and no Botox was spared!

I engaged some young and upcoming designers to help out. My brief was purely functional, and I left all the design aspects for them. Designers love freedom. One of these young designers was Margo Reed. Margo took the brief and totally ran with it. Along with her then business partner Vanessa they managed the whole project from go to whoa. Not only did they design the new store, they managed the council submissions and project-managed all the builders and tradesmen. The amazing part was that it was all completed in eleven days from strip-out to reopening.

Our customers were truly amazed at the transformation (and it was dramatic). It was often described as contemporary but timeless. Exactly what I had wanted. We built up the anticipation of the reopening with some clever marketing and our store sales rocketed by 50% and stayed there until I sold the business.

I asked Margo for some of her expert tips regarding the unique challenges of designing a coffee roastery/café:

Margo (right) and Vanessa (left) pretending to be customers at our photoshoot in 2012.

MARGO'S EXPERT TIPS

How do you want to engage with your customers? Do you want customers to be in and out or to spend time in your space? My motto is that every space needs to have "soul" as this is what customers respond to. Tell your story in the interiors and branding to touch customers' hearts. If you only want them to stay for a short time, set this off with hard seating, brighter lighting and louder music. For spaces where you want customers to spend time in, opt for comfortable seating, natural lighting and softer music.

With all design, the focus is always around function and aesthetics

FUNCTIONALITY: When designing Bay Coffee in 2012 there were a few different areas that needed to be addressed, as it wasn't just a café but also a coffee roastery. So it had to include point of sale, a roasting area, dining/seating options, coffee making and product display placement.

Before any kind of spatial planning, it's key to know how you intend to use the space. What are the actions of a sale from the retailer's perspective? What are the actions from the customer's perspective for a sale to be made? The functionality of a space is key for both staff and customer experience and nutting this out first makes designing the space much easier. Get creative and map out the floor plan in the space to make sure it works!

Functionality also meant we had to take into consideration the clientele, as this was quite varied, ranging from a mid-week older clientele who enjoyed their coffee and cake sitting at tables in the sun, remote workers on laptops who preferred the indoors with power points, to weekend families popping in for coffee, and also the morning rush of worker takeaways.

AESTHETIC: The overall aesthetic of your store or café is on par with the functionality as it's how you capture and connect with your customers' interest and recurring business. This needs to work on a few different levels, which can include:

BRAND/BRANDING: Reflecting your brand is a must in designing your fit-out. We worked alongside Todd from Creative Order, the graphic designer who was also rebranding Bay Coffee at the time. It's important to follow through on the branding with logo, menus, interiors and so on to really complete the overall look and feel, as it creates a defined and complete package.

WHAT ARE YOU SELLING? While you don't have to spell it out with flashing lights, there should be some kind of reflection of what you're selling weaved within the space. Whether it's the colour, the language, a feeling or images, it will help create that connection. At Bay Coffee we used darker tones to create a warmth and reflection of how our coffee made you feel, as well as telling a story through art of the bean-to-cup coffee roasting process, which created a connection between the brand and product.

IN PART A-2 WE WILL COVER:

1. FUNCTIONAL WORK ZONE DESIGN AND PLANNING
2. APPROVALS AND PERMITTED USE
3. SOME SHOP EQUIPMENT YOU WILL NEED – AND SOME YOU WON'T
4. FINANCING THE SETUP OF YOUR ROASTERY/CAFÉ
5. THE IMPORTANCE OF INSURANCE COVER

1

FUNCTIONAL WORK ZONE DESIGN AND PLANNING

If a project is to present a meaningful image to its marketplace, and deliver maximum value to your brand and the business, then all elements of the business must be aligned to reflect the brand vision.

This requires a multi-disciplinary and integrated response combining architecture, interiors, graphics, lighting, colours, textures, merchandising, promotions and service. All must work together seamlessly to reflect the brand vision of the business.

Workflow is a critical element that must be integrated into your design. Designers will often get caught up on beauty and visual effect without consideration for practicalities. A coffee roastery is unique as it is both a manufacturing/production facility and coffeehouse at the same time. A working roastery has to deal with heat, dust (oh, lots of dust!), noise and the ability to move heavy things like green and roasted beans around the place without getting impeded or causing a danger to staff or customers alike.

Betsy the Probat L12 Roaster and her "Mini-Me".

YOUR SHOP LAYOUT AND SUBSEQUENT FIT-OUT DESIGN NEEDS TO CONSIDER ITS FUNCTIONAL AREAS. A TYPICAL BREAKDOWN OF THE STORE AREAS ARE:

➤ Your Coffee Roasting Area.
➤ Bean Sales Service Area.
➤ Espresso Sales Service Area.
➤ Brew Bar/Cupping Area.
➤ Customer Seating Area and Facilities.

So let's now look at each of these functional centres separately:

YOUR COFFEE ROASTING AREA: Try to find a place with high ceilings. The obvious reason for this is that hot air rises. A shop will quickly heat up if you are roasting all morning. The radiant heat from your roaster and afterburner will make light work of your air-conditioning unit, especially in the summer months in Australia. The high ceilings make a huge difference.

I recommend making your coffee roasting area a feature of your shop. I had mine right up front in the shop window. This presented its own challenges, however. Everyone who walked in and out wanted to chat, once with potentially devastating consequences (think roaster fire). See Part B-5.

Importantly, leave more room for this important area than you think you'll need. Clear external access is important for many reasons. Think access for deliveries and dispatch of green and roasted coffee, access for fire fighters should you (God forbid) experience a roaster fire, and space for future add-ons (de-stoner, lab equipment etc.). Think about your comfort and safety as well. You need to be in a well-ventilated and cool workspace.

You will need a working bench and machine maintenance area near your roaster. Here you will have your laptop computer, your file notes and, if you can fit it in, a small lab testing area to compare your roast batches.

Close to your roaster you need to have your green bean storage and blending area. Don't flop 60kg coffee sacks on the floor around the coffee roaster. Not only is this a tripping hazard, it's not good green bean storage practice. You need to store them on pallets elevated off the ground for air-flow and to prevent potential flood damage (think malfunctioning espresso machine that goes off in the middle of the night).

You will need good lighting to be able to colour-match your roasts. If you do not have natural ambient light then use task-specific lighting above your roaster.

BEAN SALES SERVICE AREA: I explore the functionality side of this area in practical detail in Part C-1. Running Your Retail Artisan Roastery of this book, so I won't elaborate on this in great detail here as yet. The important thing to note here, however, is that it should function as a stand-alone area and one that allows the customer to feel they are an interactive part of the process of the sale. It is an area away from the noise and the buzz of the roastery and the espresso sections of the business.

Pre-opening day photoshoot of our roastery after our 2012 fit-out was completed. The hand-painted signage, drinking fountain and the new coffee bean display were my favourite features.

ESPRESSO SALES SERVICE AREA: This area should have a good vibe, be busy and be an area where your baristas can interact with customers – a little noisy and fun with a great positive energy. This is where the final product is made. It is an exciting and vibrant spot in the roastery. In terms of layout I like long benches with obvious ordering and pick-up points. On busy mornings it's important that the people flow through the shop much like the coffee service, quickly and efficiently.

BREW BAR/CUPPING AREA: If you have the space this is a great opportunity to use a separate area that can double up as an eye-catching brew bar and a public cupping table as required. It's also perfect for product demonstrations and events such as brewing competitions if that's your bent.

CUSTOMER SEATING AREA AND FACILITIES: This is where you can get really funky and creative. Give your designer some leeway here to think outside the square. The important thing is that customers should feel comfortable in the space and it should be easy to clean and service.

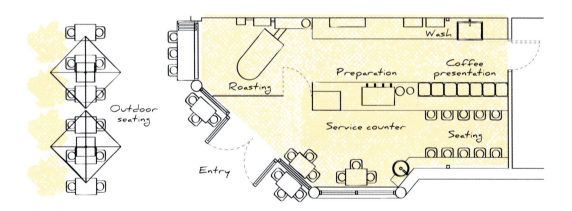

EXPERT TIPS

1. Have good lighting near your roaster and testing area.
2. Have a high quality commercial ducted vacuum cleaning system installed during the fit-out.
3. Aim for a theme or story in your fit-out design. It will give you something to photograph and promote. Be careful, however, that it doesn't date quickly.
4. Give your designers a clear design brief that covers both style and functionality aspects of your business. It's important to be as clear as possible here to avoid too many redesigns or design flaws.
5. Think about future growth and expansion if that's your plan and integrate that into your design brief.
6. Be mindful of the unique problems of a coffee roastery – that is, dust, heat, cleaning requirements and so on. Be mindful of customer comfort.

2

APPROVALS AND PERMITTED USE

In Australia, any changes you make to your site regarding usage need to be approved by your local council prior to commencement of works. You will need to make your lease agreement conditional pending this approval. The authorities are a lot tougher these days regarding emissions from your flue, so this also needs to be approved. It's not as easy to set up a coffee roastery in non-industrial areas as it used to be.

Your application will normally outline your intended use and trade on the premises. You need to be very clear on what you want to do there – that is, roast coffee in small batches, sell and serve coffee beans and operate as a café. Permits for outdoor seating will also be considered and granted at this stage. Seating numbers are linked to toilet facilities (abled and disabled) so be aware of this as well when you choose your site. Other things such as operating hours, signage and lighting will also be examined prior to a construction certificate being issued to commence works.

An experienced designer and shop fitter will understand and help you with the submission process and in dealing with the council.

3

SOME SHOP EQUIPMENT YOU WILL NEED (BESIDES YOUR COFFEE ROASTER) – AND SOME YOU WON'T

I will go into some detail in Part A-3 on coffee roasting equipment. For now, let's look at what equipment you'll need for the rest of the store. I won't go into the obvious such as tables and chairs, crockery and so on. I will highlight key equipment you will need to get trading … and it's surprisingly little.

For Bean Sales

CALIBRATED RETAIL BENCH-TOP SCALES

Get a model with an appropriately shaped weighing vessel that can transfer the coffee into the bag (I had mine custom-made by a stainless steel manufacturer). The scales have to be NMI approved for trade use in Australia. A 15kg model with 5g sensitivity will suffice. Remember to get them calibrated regularly.

DITTING KR1403 COFFEE GRINDER

This thing is a beast. It will be the grinder you use to grind the beans for your customers to take home. I have specified the 3-phase model as it's fast and can churn through 500g and 1kg of coffee in no time. It won't overheat and will go all day if you transfer it to a factory environment later on (you can add a 10kg hopper onto it later). Get the model with the bag shaker and the bag holder – you'll thank me later for this advice. It's not pretty and it weighs almost 40kg but it's designed to work hard, fast and last. In my 20 years it only needed to be serviced and have the blades sharpened twice!

MAHLKOENIG EK43 COFFEE GRINDER

Try pronouncing that after a few beers … This guy is a good backup for your Ditting KR1403 should it (however unlikely) conk out. Nowadays seen more on the espresso bench, this grinder has great grinding accuracy and operates on standard single-phase power. So maybe keep it on the espresso bench for your cold brews and pour overs and then transfer it to the bean bench in the (highly unlikely) event that the Ditting grinder dies.

BAG SEALER

I recommend a foot-operated constant heat sealer with a wide crimp seal. Don't get the Teflon-based ones – they're rubbish. Your coffee bag supplier should sell these.

SCOOPS

Buy various-sized stainless steel scoops for transferring your beans about the place.

For Espresso Coffee Sales

This is an area that will open up the proverbial can of worms when it comes to differing opinions and expertise, so I won't go into it in great detail. It's an area where technology is forever evolving, and there is a wealth of knowledge and information available online, so I encourage you to do your research. I will simply present here the equipment that I preferred to use in my store.

LA MARZOCCO LINEA PB 3-GROUP AV ESPRESSO MACHINE

A great workhorse with enough bells and whistles to keep your baristas happy. Never gave up when under the pump. Just keep her regularly maintained and she'll deliver day in and day out.

VICTORIA ARDUINO MYTHOS ONE GRINDER – MAIN ESPRESSO BLEND GRINDER

We switched to the Mythos One grinder after many years with the Mazzer Robur as we found that the grinding temperature was cooler and that it was more accurate with its programmed doses. The grinding temperature has a great impact on the constancy of the dose. The Clima Pro technology manages the temperature in the milling chamber, using a cooling system that starts automatically as soon as the sensor detects the need. It is a simple solution, but one that brings great advantages for quality extraction.

MAZZER ROBUR S AUTOMATIC GRINDER – SECOND BLEND AND BACKUP GRINDER

The industry standard until a few of the newer players came on board with various improvements. Conical blades (never use flat blade grinders if you are selling more than 20kg of coffee per week in espresso sales), fast grinding and dosing and a fan to cool the motor. A good workhorse. Limitations are overheating and high grinding temperature (when under stress), and inconsistent dosing at times. Blades need replacing quite often.

MAZZER MINI (FOR DECAF)

A basic simple flat blade grinder for those pesky decaf coffees.

> Purchase the best quality espresso equipment you can afford. You will be rewarded with the best representation of your coffee and years of reliable service.

For Brewed Coffee Sales

Things have certainly changed since I started back in 1997. Espresso was the go (still is really) but now you really do have to offer alternative brewing methods to stand out from the crowd. None of these methods are really new, but recycled and renamed brewing methods that existed a long time ago – mostly from Japan. We will explore the various fads in the following section but we seem to have settled on:

POUR OVER

What we used to call the single cup drip filter is now reimagined as the Pour Over. However, the technique has been been greatly refined and turned into a precise science, so now it's essential you have a set of Acaia scales (or the equivalent) that can measure both time and volume very accurately. Coffee for this technique is generally roasted much lighter to take advantage of the delicate brew it can produce. In short, you should taste the true characteristics of the bean and of the origin itself instead of experiencing the influence of the darker roast level on the bean. For this reason single origins tend to be used over blends for Pour Overs.

COLD BREW

Another Japanese brewing technique, aka Kyoto-style coffee, named for its popularity in Kyoto, Japan, is the earliest record of cold brew coffee. It's recorded that the Japanese were brewing coffee this way in the 1600s, although the record prior to that is unclear. Instead of submerging grounds for hours, the coffee is brewed drop by drop. A single bead of water is let down through the coffee grounds at a time, creating a process that takes time but is much more beautiful to watch. It wasn't long until tall, elegant cold-drip towers were being used in Kyoto to make cold brews[10].

AEROPRESS

A relative newcomer, some roasteries offer AeroPress coffee. An ugly brown plastic contraption, it makes a surprisingly good coffee. A gentleman called Alan Adler invented it in 2005. Basically an improvement on the French Press idea, the coffee is steeped for 10–50 seconds (depending on grind and preferred strength) and then forced through a filter by pressing the plunger through the tube. The filters used are either the AeroPress paper filters or disc-shaped thin metal filters. The maker describes the result as an espresso-strength concentration of coffee, but its most frequent use is more in the filter brew strength. It's become so popular, in fact, amongst the coffee nerds that there are now AeroPress brewing competitions in 50 different countries around the world! It's practical as a serving method as it is fast and clean.

FOOTNOTE

[10] A few years ago almost every café in Australia purchased a cold-drip brewing tower (the crappier the café, the taller the tower seemed to be) on the back of the trend. By my observations it normally took about a month before the cold-drip brewer was relegated to a lonely corner of the café to sit as an ornament. Like pour over you need the right bean, delicately lightly roasted, and at the correct water temperature/grind/dose/rate of drip to get the best quality brew. Get it right and serve it either neat, over ice and/or with sparkling mineral water and the flavours can be exquisite. Get it wrong though, and you'll have an expensive ornament in the corner of your café in about a month's time.

Beware The Brewing Fads! The Tale of The Clover and The Syphon

It's all too easy to get caught up in brewing fads in the specialty coffee industry. Quite often you feel damned if you do and damned if you don't hop on the bandwagon. Why? Because all of a sudden a new coffeehouse (usually in Melbourne) is offering an amazing new way of drinking coffee and EVERYONE is queuing out the door to try it. Fuelled by the hipster press, this new place goes off for a couple of months until everyone worth their salt in the hipster world has tried this fabled new brew method.

Of course, the coffee world has the fastest word-of-mouth transmission system outside of the fibre optic cable, and within nanoseconds everyone is ordering one of these new brewing systems and (trying to) offer it to their customers. And much like most fashion trends, they burn brightly for a short while, and then everyone loses interest almost simultaneously. Think tie-dye T-shirts, Tamagotchis ... and who'll ever forget in more recent times Pokemon Go!

The Clover Brewing System explained (sort of) …

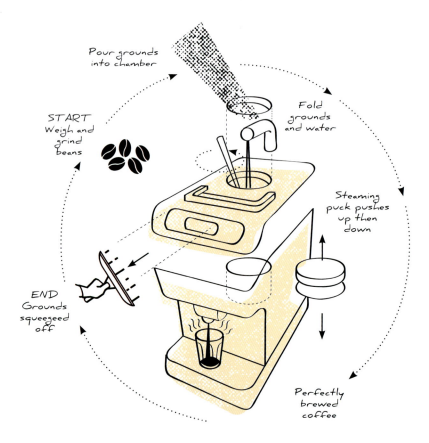

"THE CLOVER" WAS AN ABSOLUTE CLASSIC FROM THE MID-LATE 2000s. It was a convoluted brewing system that was purchased by Starbucks from the original company that invented it. This unusual brewer became the "must have" brewing system for upmarket coffee roasters. A few models of the Clover 1 were snapped up around the world and I visited a couple of roasteries in Australia (that I thought should have known better) that had them. Essentially an automated French Press system that cost almost A$20,000 once installed, it was fun to watch and the coffee tasted like something in between a French Press and a drip filter coffee. There are videos of them in action on YouTube[11]. Seriously, watch them and be tutored on probably one of the most pointless and ridiculously expensive coffee brewing fads ever to hit Australia or the world.

Not ridiculous by any means, but totally impractical for a busy coffee roastery, was another Japanese staple – "The Syphon" brewer. Also known as a Vacuum Pot in some countries, it makes a totally wonderful coffee ... but with the Japanese it's part ritual/part show and not easy to pull off in a busy café situation. Imagine this coffee being meticulously made at a Syphon bar after an incredible meal at an expensive Japanese restaurant. This is where it belongs.

The Syphon may look like a mad scientist's experiment, but it brews coffee that's velvety smooth in mouthfeel and richly vibrant in aromatics. The final coffee is so delicious that many around the world have dubbed it the finest filter coffee you can make.

HERE ARE THE BASIC STEPS:

1 Fill the bottom chamber with 335ml of hot water and light the alcohol burner below it.

2 Insert the cloth filter in the upper chamber and pour in 20g of medium-coarse coffee grounds.

3 Attach the upper chamber to the lower bulb and start a timer when the water rises.

4 After 30 seconds of water/coffee contact, stir the grounds slightly.

5 After 2 total minutes of brewing, remove the syphon from the burner.

6 Once the brewed coffee drains, remove upper chamber and enjoy.

FOOTNOTE
[11] The Clover – Be Amazed: youtube/ntbVGGMu_Ac

4
FINANCING THE SETUP OF YOUR ROASTERY/CAFÉ

There are many ways to finance your start-up business. The availability and cost of finance is, of course, driven by the risk to the lender. Depending on how much of your own cash you have to start up you may need to borrow the remaining amount to fund various things such as:

- Your retail shop refurbishment and fit-out.
- Marketing and other legal/administrative start-up costs.
- Purchasing your capital equipment such as your coffee roaster, espresso equipment, furniture and so on.
- Setting up your lease bank guarantee.
- Having start-up cash in the bank to purchase stock, pay staff, pay insurances and so on.
- Setting up a bank overdraft for rainy days (and Sundays …).

If you do not have a track record in business or, worse, have a poor track record in business or your personal finances, you will find it tougher to get finance than a few years ago, when it was a free-for-all with no-document loans etc. Those days are gone, and rightly so, with banks tightening up their lending criteria. Bank managers are, however, a lot friendlier than they were in 1996 when I started to seek finance as a 27-year-old for my first (and only) small business. They did not care to see my impressive business plan. The deal was simply put up your house as a guarantee against the loan or bugger off.

The banks are a lot more consumer-focused now and friendly to small business, as we now account for the vast majority (over nine in ten) of Australian businesses. In fact, a 2016 report by the Australian Small Business and Family Enterprise Ombudsman stated that small business accounted for 33% of Australia's GDP, employed over 40% of Australia's workforce, and paid around 12% of total company tax revenue[12].

So there are several finance products that I will outline below. This is purely a summary of available products, however, and should not be taken as advice. Please seek financial advice from your financial accountant and bank manager.

Business Bank Loans

Banks can offer secured or unsecured business bank loans. If you are a start-up it's highly unlikely you'll get approved for an unsecured loan. Secured loans (usually against your own home or other major asset) are significantly cheaper to fund in terms of interest rates offered by the bank. Loan terms tend to be flexible (with a usual maximum term of 15 years) and can be on fixed or variable interest rates. Some banks offer interest-only terms with a five-year maximum term. As with home mortgage loans you have the option to pay out your loan ahead of time without penalty in most cases.

You can use bank loans to fund just about anything to do with your business, such as capital equipment purchases, funding your shop fit-out, or cash reserves to fund day-to-day expenses until the profits start rolling in.

FOOTNOTE
[12] http://bit.ly/2ODgcGh

Asset Finance

For larger assets for capital equipment such as your coffee roaster and manufacturing equipment, espresso equipment and delivery vehicle, it may make sense to lease your asset and spread the repayments over the life of the asset. There are several advantages and disadvantages to this approach.

- Interest rates can be locked in at a fixed rate to make budgeting and forecasting easier, or you can choose to have a floating rate if you prefer.
- Approved customers won't have to pay a deposit, meaning valuable capital can be kept for other business needs.
- Depending on your circumstances, potential tax advantages may be available when using one of your asset finance products. You should speak to your tax adviser for independent advice and further information.
- You can choose the length of your financing as well as the payment dates to suit your cash-flow needs.
- Interest rates and repayment costs tend to be higher over the long term.

Common types of asset financing are Chattel Mortgage, Hire Purchase or Finance Lease. Each one differs slightly in what they offer and their terms. Please seek advice from your accountant as to which type is best for your needs and circumstances.

Overdrafts

A bank overdraft lets you withdraw money up to your approved overdraft limit when you need to, and make deposits when your business receives payments. The overdraft can be unsecured, or secured by residential, commercial or rural property, business assets or a combination of these.

Overdrafts should only be used as a last line of defence when cash reserves are low. The interest rates charged tend to be high and the limits low.

Bank Guarantees

An Indemnity Guarantee (or Bank Guarantee) is an alternative to providing a deposit or bond directly to a supplier, vendor or landlord. It gives them certainty that your bank will pay them, and you the flexibility to extend your payment terms. Most banks have flexible security options, depending on your business needs and circumstances. Security can include cash, residential, commercial or rural property, or a combination of these. Personally, I would recommend a Cash Cover Indemnity Guarantee Facility, which is 100% secured by cash. Then your cash is held in a dedicated bank account, earning you interest and not risking your other personal assets.

5

THE IMPORTANCE OF INSURANCE COVER

Yes, it's a boring topic but you can't open a coffee roastery without being properly insured. Especially one that is open and trading to the public. The requirement of some types of insurance is law, so let's break down the different types you'll need and why.

MANY OF THE LARGER INSURERS NOW OFFER PACKAGES FOR CAFÉS THAT WILL COVER ALL YOUR NEEDS FOR A ROASTERY/CAFÉ SET-UP. THE ESSENTIAL ELEMENTS OF COVER YOU WILL NEED ARE:

- Fire and Peril.
- Business Interruption.
- Theft and Stock Cover.
- Money Cover (on premises and on way to the bank).
- Glass Damage.
- Product Liability.
- Public Liability.
- Workers Compensation Insurance.

Fire is, of course, a no-brainer. While with modern roaster technology roaster fires are less common, they do unfortunately still happen and I am yet to meet a master roaster who hasn't experienced a fire, especially early on in their career. So you must have cover for fire, especially if you share a building with other tenants[13].

Business Interruption Insurance will keep you afloat financially should you have to close your business temporarily due to a fire or other catastrophic event. I was insured for the equivalent of 12 months' gross profit. Thankfully, I never had to call on this cover.

Theft of stock or equipment is what it is. If you have a separate warehouse remember to note that location (called a "situation") in your policy as well. The insurance should also cover stock or equipment in transport.

Cover for cash on premises or on the way to the bank is normally bundled into a set amount (say $8,000) and will cover in-store theft or an unfortunate mugging on the way to the bank.

Glass doors and windows do get broken, be it by break-ins, vandalism or general idiocy (special shout-out to my former staff member who twice smacked a steel umbrella base into the glass door!)

You will require Public Liability cover for your lease and outdoor seating. Generally it's in the order of $10m or $20m cover. This is in case anyone from the general public gets injured on your property. Product Liability cover is generally for a similar amount and covers anyone from the general public who gets injured, sick or dies using or consuming your product.

Workers Compensation Insurance is designed to cover the wages of your workers if they suffer a work-related injury. Workers Compensation Insurance is compulsory in Australia and it is vital in keeping your business and employees secure in the event of a claim.

The premium is calculated on a percentage of your annual estimated gross payroll plus superannuation costs. The percentage charged as your premium is generally based on the risk level of your declared industry and the duties that your staff carry out.

FOOTNOTE
[13] Your landlord should, of course, also have additional fire insurance cover for his building.

Me posing awkwardly in 2009 with Betsy – the Probat L12 Roaster – a complicated love affair spanning 20 years.

A3

PURCHASING YOUR COFFEE ROASTER

Purchasing your first coffee roaster is both an exciting and daunting prospect. Financially and practically making the right informed decisions up front will save you considerable heartache in the future. Having a reliable production machine is worth its weight in gold. Your coffee roaster, especially your first one, will become your lifelong friend and companion over the years. Many master roasters, in fact, give their roaster a pet name. My original Probat L12 Roaster was affectionately known as Betsy. I'll share my experiences (both good and bad) of my relationship with her as we continue through the book.

IN PART A-3 WE WILL COVER:

1. COFFEE ROASTER DESIGNS AND HOW THEY WORK
2. IMPORTANT FEATURES TO CONSIDER WHEN PURCHASING A COFFEE ROASTER
3. THE PURCHASE PROTOCOL – AVOIDING COMMON MISTAKES
4. BUYING USED OR REBUILT COFFEE ROASTERS
5. INSTALLING AND COMMISSIONING YOUR COFFEE ROASTER

1
COFFEE ROASTER DESIGNS AND HOW THEY WORK

Heat Transfer

Before we talk about the coffee roasters themselves it's important to understand the concept of heat transfer in coffee at a basic level at this stage of the book. I'll go into more detailed explanations about this as the book goes on. Most roasters use a combination of three types of heat transfer: convection, conduction and radiation.

Convective heat is transferred to the beans via a continuous flow of pre-heated air by the use of a fan that moves the air across the burners and through the coffee. Airflow speed can significantly increase or decrease roast times.

Conductive heat comes from the hot drum wall and, less so, from the other surrounding beans.

Radiant heat (aka IR)[14] comes from the heavy hot parts of the machine like the faceplate. Radiant heat should contribute little to the heat transfer to the beans in modern roaster designs.

Airflow, as you can see, is critical in roaster designs and other variables such as drum speed can also impact, although not to the same degree.

So with the concept of heat transfer firmly in our minds, let's now start exploring the different kinds of roasters currently on the market and how they work. We'll start with the classic single pass drum roaster.

Some roaster manufacturers have introduced a static heat shield plate positioned between the burner and the single drum in order to reduce the bean surface burning issue and avoid the much higher cost of producing a double-barrel drum. Don't go there, it's fraught with problems as the heat shield plate gets extremely hot and radiates a huge amount of heat onto the barrel even when the burners are turned down.

SINGLE PASS DIRECTLY HEATED DRUM ROASTERS

Also known as the "classic" drum roaster this guy has remained fairly unchanged in its basic design for the last 50 years or more. It's still by far the most popular machine design preferred by master roasters around the world.

A directly heated drum roaster will have burners that project an open flame directly onto the bottom of the spinning drum. The drum itself will normally be made from low carbon mild steel[15] and will have internal spokes/paddles that keep the beans agitated and moving to avoid prolonged surface contact with the hot drum surface, which can cause tipping or surface burning of the beans.

The diagram opposite shows the product and airflow direction through a single pass drum roaster. Why do we call it a single pass roaster? Well, as you can see the heated air flows, with the aid of a drawing fan, through the drum rotating the coffee beans and then exhausts out the flue with the aid of a cyclone, which also separates and collects the chaff in a separate vessel underneath. The hot air passes through the coffee once in a continual stream. Hence the term single pass.

It is estimated that this type of roaster will transfer heat to the coffee beans by approximately 70% convection (heated air flow) and 30% conduction (from the directly heated drum barrel).

FOOTNOTE

[14] Radiant Heat is also known as IR – Infra-red Radiation.

[15] It's generally misunderstood that classic drum barrels are made of cast iron. They are actually usually made of low carbon mild steel as it has much better heat transfer properties. The internal spokes and face plates are normally made of cast iron.

Drum roasters can come with a single wall drum or a double wall drum (some people also call this a single drum or double drum). A double drum features two concentric layers of metal with a gap of several millimetres in between. The air in this gap acts as an insulator and distributes a more even heat to the inner drum, thus stopping it from getting too hot (a problem when you have a long roasting day) and therefore reducing the chances of bean surface burning.

The roaster I purchased in 1996 was a classic Probat L12 shop roaster. It is a classic single pass directly heated single-walled drum roaster. Considering its lack of controls and modern day features that no modern roaster would accept, it proved itself to be a remarkably consistent coffee roaster. It certainly had its cons though, and I had to modify it considerably over the years to gain some semblance of consistency and control over my roasts. I will go over this in more detail as I progress through the following chapters.

Popular brands: Probat, Joper, Deidrich, Giesen, Roastmax, Toper

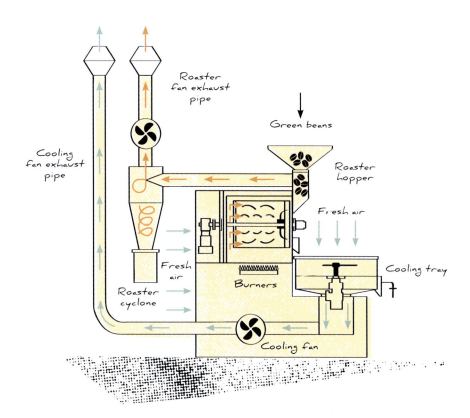

Single Pass Directly Heated Drum Roaster.

SINGLE PASS INDIRECTLY HEATED DRUM ROASTERS

One way of avoiding the need for a double drum (which is more expensive) is to use a different type of heating system that protects the drum from direct flame contact. This is achieved by using a different type of burner that heats a combustion chamber (or oven) and the hot air produced is once again drawn over the beans in the drum via a fan system. This allows for higher roast temperatures to be used without the risk of bean surface burning and the need for a double barrel. Like the direct flame option this type of roasting system will provide a clean roasting environment and permit fast roasting at higher temperatures. The downside is that it will use more fuel than a direct flame burner system.

Popular Brands: Probat, Joper

> My personal choice if I was setting up a coffee roastery in 2019 would be a recirculation drum roaster. The energy savings and the elimination of the need for an afterburner (and all the associated emissions issues with the local authorities) are a huge plus for the modern artisan coffee roaster.

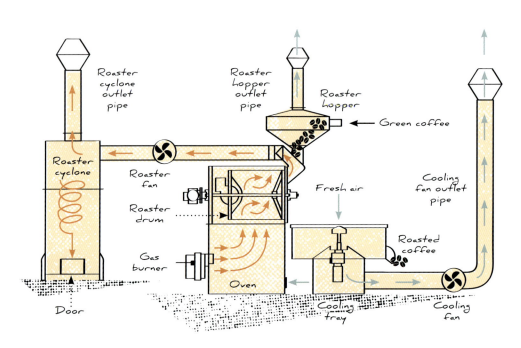

Single Pass Indirectly Heated Drum Roaster.

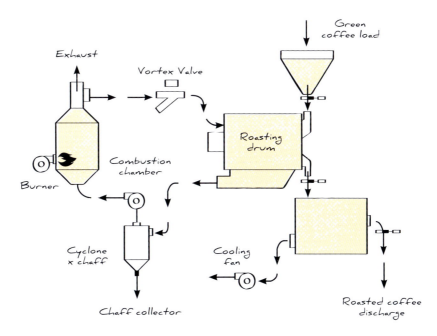

IMF Recirculation Drum Roaster.

RECIRCULATING HEAT ROASTERS

With energy prices skyrocketing and a generally more environmentally aware customer base, emerging roaster manufacturers have started to develop more energy-efficient roasters in response to these concerns. Companies such as IMF from Italy and Loring from the USA are leading the way with recirculation technology.

The IMF roaster uses a perforated drum and performs like a traditional rotating drum roaster. The Loring does not have a turning drum, but a chamber where the beans are kept in constant motion with agitating paddles. So it's not a rotating drum roast or an air roaster, but something in between – sort of...

IMF Roasters' Australian representative is Will Notaras. Will has been supplying the Australian coffee industry with his roasters for close to 12 years and has installed hundreds of roasters over that time. I have personally known Will for almost as long, and his knowledge of coffee roasters is second to none.

Will explains that a big advantage of recirculation roasters is that they eliminate the need for a gas-hungry afterburner to eliminate emissions. Unlike conventional roasters that use a burner for the roaster and a separate burner (afterburner) to treat the emissions, these roasters use a specially designed combustion chamber that simultaneously heats the roaster and treats the emissions. As the coffee is roasted, the emissions leave the roaster via a steel duct into the burner chamber to incinerate the emissions. Some of the heat in the burner chamber, which would otherwise be released into the atmosphere, is instead recirculated via a duct back into the roaster. Ambient air is mixed into the duct electronically to reduce the heat to the required temperature to heat the beans for roasting, and the cycle starts again. A minimum 30% reduction in gas consumption is claimed.

Recirculation roasters have been praised for their fuel efficiency and fast roasting times with limited risk of bean surface damage. They have also been praised for their accurate data-logging and profiling ability due to the stable internal environment of the roaster.

Popular Brands: IMF, Loring

FLUID BED (HOT AIR) ROASTERS

Fluid bed coffee roasters rely on high controlled airflow to keep the beans moving in the roasting chamber. Computer-controlled convective heat is transferred from a burner box using a fan system. There is no cooling tray as the beans are progressively cooled at the end of the batch by sending room temperature air through the roasting chamber at the end of the roast.

They feature very fast roast times and the ability to roast large batch sizes with a relatively small footprint. Not generally used in a retail coffee roasting environment these tend to be more popular with large-scale industrial coffee roasters. Coffee companies that use them swear by them. They are, however, criticised within the industry for the impact the high airflow has on the overall flavour of the finished coffee itself.

Popular Brands: Neuhaus Neotec

My personal choice if I was setting up a coffee roastery in 2019 would be to have a recirculation drum roaster. The energy savings and the elimination of the need for an afterburner (and all the associated emissions issues with the local authorities) are a huge plus for the modern artisan coffee roaster.

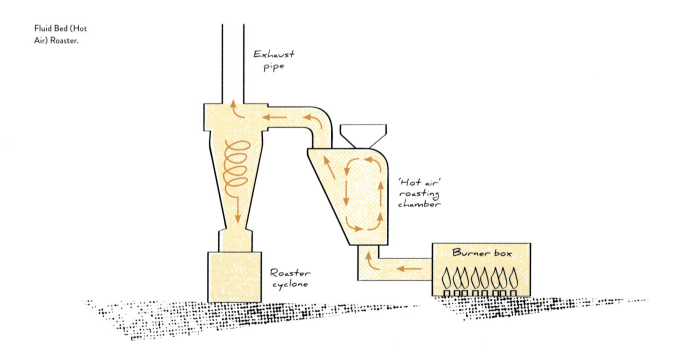

Fluid Bed (Hot Air) Roaster.

2
IMPORTANT FEATURES TO CONSIDER WHEN PURCHASING A ROASTER

So now you've decided what type of roasting system you want to purchase and you've identified several brands to investigate more deeply and get quotes. Now you can start to look at all the specific features, bells and whistles that these machines offer and begin to compare apples with apples. What are some of the key features of modern retail shop roasters you should look for? Let's take a look, shall we?

Size/Capacity

As we all know size does matter. As a retail roaster generally your choices are 3/5/10/15/25kg. If you're serious you have to go with either a 5kg or 15kg to start. The price difference between these sizes is often negligible (I'm talking about €2,000) so unless you're seriously restricted by space why would you not buy the 15kg capacity machine? Why is a 15kg a better investment than a 5kg capacity coffee roaster?

- The 15kg roaster's footprint will only be about 30% larger than a 5kg roaster.
- You should and will quickly outgrow a 5kg roaster. The cost of purchasing a new larger capacity model and replacing it within a few years is uneconomical.
- You have to do three times the amount of work on a 5kg roaster.
- You can roast down to 4kg safely in a 15kg capacity roaster if the 15kg batch size is too large to start.
- A 15kg roaster will give you the capacity to grow and easily roast 600+kg of coffee per week so you can start your wholesale business in-house down the track. Your next roaster investment should be for your factory setup with a 30 or 60kg semi-automatic roasting system (and not a 25kg retail coffee roaster).

So, as you can see, I believe the 15kg model is the best size to start off with for economic and practical scale reasons. I started with a 12kg Probat L12, which was the old-fashioned size of retail roasters past, but as close to the modern 15kg capacity as you could get. And it looked the business too – a 5kg machine still has a bit of an amateurish look about it in my opinion.

Renzo from Di Bartoli Coffee working hard on his 15kg Roastmax Shop Roaster.

Roaster controller on a Joper BSR Shop Roaster.

Airflow Control

This is very important. Make sure that your roaster has two separate fan motors and controls for the roasting and for the cooling of your coffee. This not only allows for simultaneous roasting and cooling of the coffee, which improves efficiency, but a dedicated fan motor also provides better airflow, which contributes greatly to the overall roast result. Make sure that your machine has variable speed RPM controls for your fans. This is especially important for the control of your roast (as we will find out later), as it allows for more subtle airflow changes and a better-controlled roast profile.

My L12 had a single fan motor and you had to use a fairly crude manual lever to switch the airflow between the roasting chamber/exhaust and the cooling tray at the start and end of each roast. The result was that the cooling of the coffee in the tray was not ideal, especially on hot summer days. Your coffee should cool in less than four minutes to room temperature. A dedicated fan motor will see to this.

I also had no fan speed control on the original L12. I had to use a manual dampener that was too extreme in its incremental variability, so I just used the gas modulation control to manage the roast rather than managing airflow – not ideal, so I later added a separate roaster fan motor and chaff collector.

Gas burners on a Roastmax Shop Roaster.

Gas Burners and Control

Should you go with a direct flame type burner or an indirect oven type burner? As discussed earlier in Heat Transfer both have their pros and cons. The direct flame can lead to bean surface burning unless you have a double wall drum and an indirect flame oven uses a tad more fuel. You can choose based on the information I've given you so far. Here I want to talk about control of the flame.

Once again, I'll go back to my original L12 for the sake of example. In its original state, it had a round knob control you would see on a domestic BBQ. Seriously. I put up with that for several years until I read a great article by coffee industry legend Willem J. Boot on how to modify your L12 to be able to do basic profile roasting[16]. Without going into detail we inserted new digital probes for the bean and environment temperature and hooked that up to a digital monitor that operated a gas modulator.

A gas train is a series of components that controls the gas flow and pressure to the burners. Make sure that these devices are designed and fitted to comply with Australian standards. Your roaster should offer a valve that will give you minute controllable adjustment to fine-tune the flame. A pressure gauge is essential to show the gas pressure applied to the burner. This will give you an accurate reading of the gas flow and flame strength to your roaster.

FOOTNOTE
[16] Ready to Roast – From Old-School Artist to Modern Artisan (*Roast Magazine*, Sept/Oct 2008, pg. 47).

Top: Over Temperature Sensor. **Bottom:** Pressure Switch.

Important Safety Devices

Modern coffee roasters come fitted with essential safety devices required to pass the AGA[17] AS3814 Standard for Industrial and Commercial Gas Fired Appliances[18]. Some of these safety devices are:

A Pressure Switch that is used to prove that the exhaust fan is running to remove smoke from the drum. The pressure switch is hooked up to a Solenoid Valve, which allows the gas to flow through to the roaster. A Purge Timer of typically 30 seconds will delay the opening of the solenoid valve until all residual gases in the coffee roaster have been purged.

An Over Temperature Sensor is connected to a temperature probe in the chaff collector (where a majority of roaster fires start). The sensor will automatically cut off the gas flow to the roaster once it is triggered as being over temperature in the chaff collector.

Many modern coffee roasters of all sizes now have an ability to connect a Water System to put fires out internally. Industrial roasters have featured these as standard for quite a while, but they are now appearing in smaller retail roasters.

These safety devices are there for a reason – to protect you and those around your roasting facility. For example, one danger is that of carbon monoxide build-up, which can occur if your roaster is not venting properly. Carbon monoxide is odourless, colourless and poisonous. A sobering thought.

EXPERT TIP
Who you purchase your roaster from will determine if these safety devices are fitted or not. This can add considerable extra expense if not fitted at manufacture.

Drum Speed Control

Not something I ever fussed too much about. Having control over the airflow and gas burners was enough for me. After all, how many balls can you juggle at once – two or three? The theory behind it, however, is valid, and that is that small, incremental increases in drum RPM will maintain ideal rotation for uniform roasting as the beans expand, through the increased control of conduction and convection heat transferred to the coffee beans in the drum. Adjustable drum speed control can also be useful if you are roasting a variety of batch sizes.

FOOTNOTE
[17] Australian Gas Association: www.aga.asn.au

[18] A copy of Standard AS3814 can be purchased online here: http://bit.ly/2Y5UZbQ

Data-Logging and Automated Profile Roasting Software

Often confused as being the same thing, but they are not. Data-logging software simply lets you log a temperature profile as you control the coffee roaster manually. It will track the bean temperature and the environmental temperature of the roaster in real time as long as you have the two digital probes properly positioned. The idea is that you can track your roast profiles in order to replicate them manually each time (that's the theory, anyhow). Modern roasters are set up to hook into third party logging software, or may even supply their own. The roaster itself may have a USB output that you can plug straight into your laptop.

Data-logging software does not, however, control your coffee roaster. Specially built automated coffee roasters will communicate with profile roasting software (usually supplied by the manufacturer) and control the airflow fan speed and the flame through the gas modulator in minute adjustments to try to maintain the current roast profile to a model profile. I say try, because it's not perfect. A bit similar to the issue with driverless cars really.

Whenever the roast does not track the model curve exactly, the software makes tiny adjustments, as often as multiple times per second, to stay on the curve. The problem is that the software can sometimes overreact by drastically changing the gas setting or exhaust fan RPM to stay on profile. So while the software may successfully track the profile, the result in the cup may differ from what you were expecting from the model profile. Probably for the same reason that driverless cars are not a reality as yet.

Below (from top to bottom): Artisan data-logging software is a free industry-sponsored roast profile data logger for roasters. BRIGAS is Joper's profiling roasting software especially developed for their BPR automated coffee roasters.

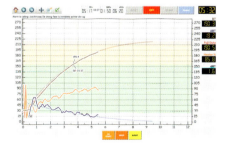

A FEW EXTRA THINGS TO NOTE HERE:

Most master roasters, even those in industrial settings where automation is more popular and economically beneficial, use the automated roasting system up until the first crack and then take over from there manually. Some just let it warm up the roaster and in between batches to free them up for a few minutes between roasts. You need to weigh up if the extra cost of the automated system is worth it.

Lastly, while data-logging software is easily adaptable to manual and vintage roasters, automatic profile control systems should not ideally be retro-fitted to manual roasters – either new or vintage models. It's cost prohibitive, it most likely won't work properly, and it will do your head in. Just buy a new machine that was made for that purpose.

Pollution Control

If you plan to run a coffee roastery in a retail situation, and unless you're in a really dodgy part of town, you will need to have a pollution control device attached to your roaster. Other retailers and shoppers do not like to see smoke and particulate matter pumping out of your flue every 15 minutes or so, and believe you me, even a small 5kg roaster will pump out an unbelievable amount of smoke in the last few minutes of your roast.

I have a friend with a 25kg drum roaster in an industrial suburb of Sydney. No names, no pack drill, but if you turn up there and get out of your car just as he drops his roast you'll get showered with fine coffee husk as it gently rains down from the sky! Fun times ...

But seriously, coffee roasting can emit some nasty stuff such as Volatile Organic Compounds (VOC), Sulfur Dioxide (SD), Particulate Matter (PM), Carbon Monoxide (CO) and Oxides of Nitrogen (NO). So you should do the right thing.

So what pollution controlling devices are available to you? The most common device is called an afterburner. There are two main types – a thermal oxidiser or a catalytic oxidiser.

A thermal oxidiser heats a roaster's exhaust gases to approximately 550°C–750°C (1022°F–1382°F) and retains the air for at least half-a-second. It does a great job of eliminating smoke and volatile organic compounds, but it does not eliminate the odours completely and it uses a lot of gas fuel, sometimes four times as much as the roaster itself.

Destruction of the VOCs takes place quicker at higher temperatures than at lower temperatures (75% at 750°C). This can be exploited, however, when deciding the size of the combustion chamber. A large combustion chamber with a low temperature has higher investment costs but lower fuel costs. A smaller combustion chamber at a high temperature will have the same yield, though lower investment costs and higher fuel costs.

Catalytic oxidiser afterburning works in a manner similar to thermal afterburning, with the difference being that the gas, after it has passed the flame, passes through a catalyst yet again. The catalyst ensures accelerated oxidation at lower temperatures. Therefore, afterburning can take place at lower temperatures. The gas is heated to approximately 300°C–500°C prior to the catalyst. The maximum gas temperature after the catalyst is typically 500°C–700°C. New low temperature catalysts are able to operate at 200°C–250°C.

Due to the lower temperature, the fuel required to achieve autothermicity is lower than that in thermal afterburning. This means that catalytic afterburning can be implemented at lower concentrations than thermal afterburning.

The used catalysts are typically precious metals (platinum, palladium, rhodium, etc.) on a ceramic or metal carrier, base metals on a ceramic carrier or metal oxides on a strong mechanical carrier. On the downside, the presence of catalyst poisons or masking products, such as chemical substances and dust particles, can considerably reduce the life span of the catalyst. Thus the catalyst requires periodic changing and frequent cleaning.

Most people will choose thermal oxidiser afterburning[19].

FOOTNOTE
[19] Electrostatic filters are not an advisable form of pollution control in commercial coffee roasting as they are very expensive to install and maintain.

Above from top:
Portable shop de-stoner.
Freshly de-stoned beans.

FOOTNOTE
[20] Nails are the worst, and are surprisingly common. De-stoners can't filter these out but I learned a neat hack from a fellow roaster and put a very strong magnet in my green bean hopper at the top of the roaster and it worked a treat. Each month I'd clean off nails and steel shavings.

De-stoners

If you sell your roasted coffee beans to the public or wholesale market you should consider purchasing a de-stoner. These are locally available and can be made to measure to fit your machine. Small de-stoners are usually on castor wheels so can be hidden somewhere until required.

Why do you need one? Well, sticks and stones may or may not break your bones, but they certainly can jam or break grinders. Coffee is a natural product mostly grown and processed in third-world countries. The term "Clean Coffee" is printed on the coffee sacks for a reason. Often it's not though, and I've had nails[20], stones, concrete, small furry animals (found that one before it went through the roaster, thankfully) appear. You don't really want pissed off retail customers and, worse still, cranky wholesale café customers coming after you to repair or replace their grinders now, do you?

How do they work? It's a surprisingly simple idea, similar in concept to a vacuum cleaner, only with adjustable suction. Roasted coffee beans display a comparatively high surface area and a lower density than foreign matter (like sticks and stones) does. A de-stoner's adjustable suction is designed to only lift out the roasted coffee beans. The foreign matter is left behind in the bottom tray to be disposed of. You do not de-stone green coffee beans.

There are afterburner suppliers who make generic afterburners locally and claim they will suit a variety of popular brand coffee roasters. You will save a lot of money buying the afterburner locally. Just make sure that the manufacturer/supplier certifies that the afterburner's control box and valve train are compliant to Australian Type B gas standards. All documentation supplied with the equipment should also be suitable for the appropriate submissions to the local gas authority.

Other Important Pre-Purchase Considerations

Other considerations, while not so critical, will also save you a lot of hassle later on if you can address them before you purchase.

1. Have you worked out the practical things like the floor space required, how you'll get it off the truck when it arrives? Will it fit through your shop door on a forklift? Don't laugh, our roaster just scraped in through the double doors at the front of our shop! I seriously had not given this fact one moment's thought up until then. Yes, I did hold my breath.

2. How will the ergonomics of the roaster work for you once it's in place? What side are the controls on? Will they be easily accessible? These things may seem a bit trivial right now, but they will annoy the hell out of you later on, I assure you.

3. Who will install the roaster for you? You need to have these tradesmen booked and ready to go when the roaster lands. They should be experienced with your type and brand of roaster. If you purchased the roaster from a local agent they should be able to organise this all for you. Make sure they are suitably qualified Level B gas plumbers and commercial electricians. Do not use domestic tradesmen, as it is a completely different field. See more regarding this topic in Installation/Commissioning in Section 5.

4. What is the availability of parts like for the roaster you have in mind? Often the electronic components will be easily available off the shelf locally. Companies like Allen-Bradley who manufacture commonly used PLCs will often have a local office in major cities. The same goes for gas train related parts – usually found fairly easily locally. Mechanical parts, however, are not so easy to find. Foreign-based coffee roaster manufacturers are notorious for charging exorbitant rates for parts to be shipped from their warehouses. Add shipping to our remote little island, and the price can skyrocket! I was once quoted AU$500 for a screw-on bolt for the back cover of my L12 roaster by Probat – I used a 5c cable-tie instead. Another example was when I had to have the main drive shaft replaced. It was going to take weeks to arrive and cost thousands of dollars. I contacted a local engineering firm who machined a new part within 24 hours and installed it the next working day at a fraction of the cost! So there are ways and means around this issue, especially when it comes to mechanical parts, which can be machined to order.

5. Another very important question is, how easy is it to service and do regular maintenance? How easy is it to clean – does it disassemble easily or are there annoying corners where you need a professional to come in to dismantle it over several costly hours? Cleaning is a big issue as you will do it almost every day to varying degrees. Are the bearings easy to grease? How much of the overall maintenance can you do yourself?

6. An additional issue to consider with automated profiling coffee roasting systems is software support. How easy is it to get the software up and running, does the manufacturer need to send a select hand-picked crack team from Europe for a couple of weeks at your expense[21]?

FOOTNOTE
[21] Some manufacturers like IMF fit a modem to your roaster for remote support and diagnostic software updates.

3

THE PURCHASE PROTOCOL – AVOIDING COMMON MISTAKES

Here are some tips to make your coffee roaster purchase less stressful:

1 Allow at least 50% more time in your schedule than they say it will take to build and deliver your roaster. Most roasters are made to order. They normally quote 18 weeks to build and four weeks to ship (to Australia). Allow up to 30 weeks. I've known some manufacturers to take up to a year to deliver. This is especially true if you are purchasing a retail coffee roaster[22].

2 Having said that, agree to a delivery date and consider financial penalties if it arrives later than one month over the agreed delivery date.

3 Put everything (specifications, add-ons/modifications, colour, agreed delivery date, etc.) in a written purchase order/agreement signed by both parties where everything you want and expect is listed on this document. Things can quite innocently simply get lost in translation and it can lead to unnecessary headaches.

4 If you can, inspect the unit before it's shipped. If this isn't practically possible, ask for a signed-off checklist and detailed photos to be sent[23].

5 Be aware that in Australia you will have to pay GST (VAT) upon arrival. On a $30,000 machine that's $3,000. Factor that into your budget. Currently, at the time of writing, there are no import duties on coffee roasters into Australia. Other costs you need to allow for will include local port, storage and local transportation charges. If you have an Australian agent they will work this all out for you in the initial quotation stage. If they don't, ask them to do it for you so you have the complete financial picture before you commit.

FOOTNOTE

[22] My experience as a short-lived sales agent for a European coffee roaster manufacturer (who I will not name here) was that the larger industrial roasters, especially if they were for a big customer (like the USA), would always get bumped up the queue in the manufacturing schedule – but you didn't hear that from me.

[23] I recall sitting in the aforementioned manufacturer's office in Europe one day and discussing our recent sale of a massive 120kg roasting system (which had already shipped) to one of my clients in Australia. I said to them, "Isn't it odd that they wanted it painted white?" Their faces collectively turned white. They checked the purchase order again – White. What colour was sent? Standard Black. Oh the joy …

4
BUYING USED OR REBUILT COFFEE ROASTERS

There is a certain charm in purchasing reconditioned vintage coffee roasters. Yes, they were extremely well built and ooze old-world charm but, like a vintage car, they need a lot of TLC.

The other thing to consider is that in original condition these roasters do not offer any of the modern features expected and required for modern profile roasting techniques. It all has to be retro fitted. I have already touched on several things I had to do to my Probat L12 over the years to keep it somewhat up to date – by rough estimations I would have spent at least $10,000 on these modifications.

JUST LIKE IN AN OLD CAR, THINGS BREAK DOWN OVER TIME WITH WEAR AND TEAR. YOU WILL END UP REBUILDING THESE THINGS. MY ROASTER OVER 20 YEARS SERVICE WITH ME HAD:

- A new drum barrel drive shaft and motor.
- 2 x new fan motors.
- New gas burners.
- Several new chains and drive belts.
- New gear box.
- New on/off switches for cooling tray mechanism.
- New insulation.
- Several paint jobs (after fires).

With the modifications made that I have already outlined in this chapter to bring it up to speed technologically, Betsy had morphed into Frankensteina over the years. So if you do still want to go down the vintage route, then make sure you at least ask the following questions:

1. Just as you would ask when buying a used car, ask who the seller is. Was it their machine? Can they tell you its history? What year was it manufactured?
2. Look for signs of roaster fires – check for warping.
3. Can they give you a service history (like a car's service log book) for the roaster and advise on what parts are original and replaced?
4. What is the condition of the bearings and of the motors? You can do a test yourself as you can hear these faults when it's running. I would, however, recommend that you get an experienced roaster technician to check it out for you and give you a comprehensive report.
5. Get the electrical wiring checked. If you are buying from overseas, does it comply with local voltage?
6. Get the gas train inspected by a commercial gas plumber. Are all the current safety requirements met?
7. Can you road-test the coffee roaster yourself?

So, as you can see, the process is not much different to buying an older car. Do your homework, get an expert inspection done, and test-drive it.

5

INSTALLING AND COMMISSIONING YOUR COFFEE ROASTER

Shop coffee roasters are not difficult to set up in comparison to industrial roasting setups, which are multi-part machines requiring expert assembly. Shop roasters are fairly plug-and-play these days. This does not mean you can just plug it in to your power point and gas bayonet and start roasting though.

In Australia, myriad gas appliance regulations need to be satisfied for your own safety and for that of the general public around you. Gas-fired coffee roasters and afterburners are considered to be Type B appliances and all states have regulations for their installation (including for second-hand appliances). A Type B appliance is a manned appliance with gas consumption in excess of 10MJ/h, including any components and fittings downstream of and including the appliance manual shut-off valve.

As discussed in Section 2 – Important Safety Devices – your coffee roasting setup must comply with the AGA AS3814 Standard for Industrial and Commercial Gas Fired Appliances. In Australia, the gas certifier who must approve your roaster before it can be used varies from state to state and region to region within each state. In Australia, to find out who your gas distributor is visit: www.aer.gov.au.

If I can offer you another tip to make your life a little easier with this (sometimes painful) process, I suggest that you send your coffee roaster manufacturer a copy of the AGA AS3814 Standard and ask them to make sure that the roaster is compliant prior to shipping. If you do this, it may arrive 80% compliant rather than 0% compliant.

Interpretation of the Gas Standard can also vary from state to state in Australia. I am told that Energy Safe Victoria[24] (ESV) has the toughest interpretation of the Standard, so comply with that interpretation to be on the safe side.

You must use a Level B gas fitter for your installation and certification work. These guys are a level above your ordinary gas plumbers and are licensed for this kind of Type B gas appliance work. They also have to have qualifications in electrical work so are worth their weight in gold when it comes to coffee roaster installations.

All the safety devices used on the roaster must comply with AGA standards, and the gas pipe size needs to be matched with the megajoule rating of your roaster (and afterburner if fitted). The gas meter also needs to be the correct size for the pressure required (2.75kpa meter, 5kpa meter etc.). So, as you can see it can get quite complicated, so always use a qualified commercial gas fitter.

Some coffee roasters of 15kg capacity and above may require 415v 50hz frequency three-phase electrical power to run. You will need to have this professionally installed by a commercial electrician. It is quite rare for retail shops to have this type of power, found more in industrial warehouse/factory situations.

EXPERT TIP
If three-phase power is required for your coffee roaster install an extra outlet for your Ditting KR1403 coffee grinder.

FOOTNOTE
[24] http://bit.ly/2JViu5b

The installation of your ducted flue is critical to the safe and efficient working of your coffee roaster. It's important that your coffee roaster flue has a good natural draw to vent the smoke and gas residues out. You should avoid too many bends in your flue prior to it exiting the building. Ensure that a tradesman experienced in building and installing flues for coffee roasters professionally installs your flue. I recommend spending a little extra in using stainless steel rather than galvanised steel. It looks better and will last longer before requiring replacing.

Another thing you may not initially consider but which may affect your approval is having adequate ventilation in your workspace. If you are in an enclosed room without adequate ventilation, you may run into trouble. Make sure you are situated in a well-ventilated area and that you have an accessible emergency exit.

In summary, there is a lot to consider when planning the purchase of your coffee roaster, its installation and commissioning. Seek expert advice and recommendations and use qualified tradesmen who have experience with coffee roasting setups. Doing it right the first time will save you a lot of headaches and money in the future. Remember that your coffee roaster will be your single biggest capital investment outside of your shop fit-out. It will produce the product that you sell and build your reputation on. So put in the time and effort this process deserves.

EXPERT TIP FROM WILL NOTARAS
Your roaster only performs as well as the flue installation. A poorly installed flue will produce excessive back-pressure and result in premature flue blockage, thus causing your roaster to perform poorly. The coffee taste will ultimately be inconsistent and of poor quality.

PART B

ROASTING COFFEE

TRUE
FICTIONS

The Garden Gnome – a.k.a. 50 Cent

The Garden Gnome was a gentle man who would come in almost daily and preferred the quieter times of day when he could get his specific table. I highlight the words 'specific table' because if this specific table happened to be occupied by another customer, panic would immediately set in. Firstly, he would hover uncomfortably around the table in question, invariably making the person sitting there, trying to relax with their coffee and paper, equally uncomfortable. If the table occupier didn't shift or look at him, he would go to the water fountain, then look at the magazine rack, and then head back and hover around the specific table once again. If there was still no reaction from the poor table occupier he would then do a strange turning-in-circles action, much like a dog getting ready to lie down in bed, and then hurriedly exit the store.

Half-an-hour later he would come back as if nothing had happened and either sit down at the now unoccupied magic table and proceed to order his coffee, or he would start the same dance routine again. From memory I think his dance routine record was three times in one afternoon.

He would never complain, was a lovely chap, a man of few words and, as you would expect, always ordered the same coffee.

Why did we lovingly call him The Garden Gnome? Well, he was quite short, had a long beard and was quiet and a little odd. Seemed appropriate at the time. He did, however, have the distinct honour of acquiring a second nickname a few years later, for he developed a strange obsession with collecting 50-cent coins.

Whenever we gave him his change he wanted us to search through the cash register for a particular collectible commemorative 1997 vintage 50c coin. Of course, there could be up to thirty 50c coins in the cash register, so we started to plan ahead and if we found any special commemorative coins we'd have them put aside for him for when he invariably came in each afternoon.

He, of course, never knew that his numismatic predilection would lead him to acquiring the unique status of being re-nicknamed after a notorious American rapper, but to us it raised him to the exalted "special customer" level. A great honour, indeed, for a very special and gentle man.

B1

LET'S TALK ABOUT GREEN COFFEE

Well, here we are! Your roastery/café is set up and your shiny new roaster is installed. Before we actually start roasting, however, I would like to talk with you about green coffee, because as you will see, having an intimate knowledge of the raw ingredient will really help you to become a better master roaster in the long run.

IN PART B-1 WE WILL COVER:

1. COFFEE GENEALOGY
2. WHAT IS A COFFEE BEAN?
3. GREEN COFFEE CHEMISTRY
4. COFFEE ORIGINS AND THEIR TYPICAL CHARACTERISTICS
5. GREEN COFFEE PROCESSING METHODS
6. COFFEE GRADING AND IDENTIFYING DEFECTS
7. IMPACT OF PROCESSING METHODS ON FLAVOUR
8. SEASONALITY, STORAGE, SHIPPING AND PACKAGING
9. COFFEE CERTIFICATIONS
10. PROS AND CONS OF DIRECT TRADE

1
COFFEE
GENEALOGY

Who do you think you are? Where did I come from? Is there a God?

Ancestry hunting has become a popular pastime for humans in recent times, with mail order DNA kits telling you if you're part hot-Scandinavian (come on, admit you'd hoped so) or part tight-fisted Scot (maybe keep that link quiet).

Coffee cultivation and breeding has an interesting history too and more information is coming to light as scientists piece together the coffea genus family tree to get to the coffee varieties we drink and love today. Thinking of this idea as a family tree will help you understand, if maybe not where you came from, where at least the coffee you're drinking right now may have. So let's start at the bottom rung of the family tree – the roots if you like.

Coffea is a genus that belongs to a large family of plants called Rubiaceae. There are hundreds of species within this genus, of which the two best known for their commercial production are Arabica (approximately 60% of world production) and Canephora (aka Robusta – approximately 40% of world production). In specialty coffee we focus mostly on Arabica coffee. The Robusta is a much sturdier, higher yielding plant but general consensus is that even the highest graded Robusta coffee does not compete flavour-wise with Arabica coffees and is, therefore, relegated to the soluble coffee backblocks or used as a low percentage blending option to bulk-fill cheaper premium blends.

In an odd *Days of Our Lives* kinda twist it's been relatively recently discovered that the Robusta species is actually a parent of the famed Arabica species. In gene sequencing it became apparent that the Arabica plant was the offspring of the Canephora and the Eugenioides species. The new species, known as Arabica, spread and began to flourish in Ethiopia.

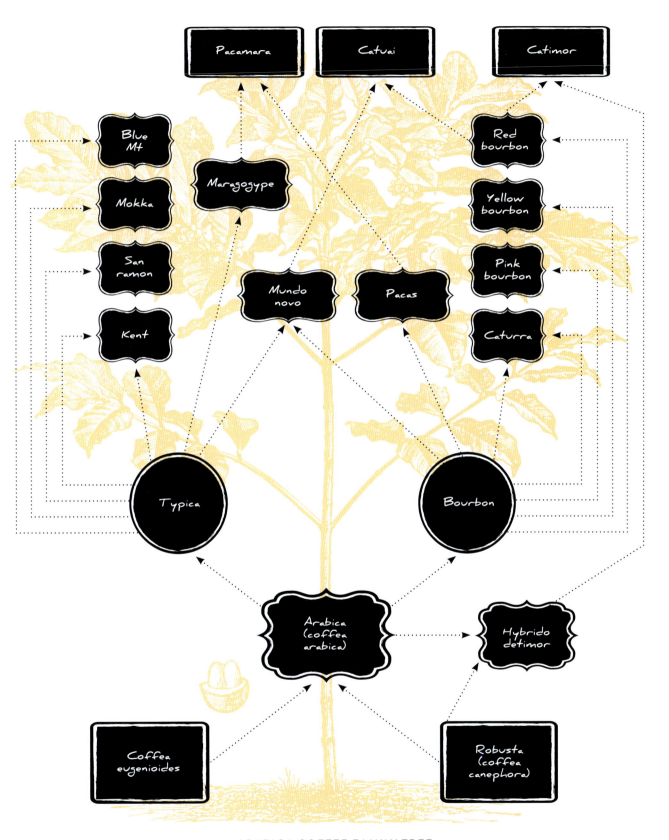

ARABICA COFFEE FAMILY TREE

There are two botanical varieties of the Arabica species and these are the Bourbon and Typica varieties.

A cultivar (a cultivated variety)[1] is a cultivated plant that has been selected for its naturally occurring desirable characteristics that distinguish it from other plants of the same species. They can occur as natural hybrids (see below) or as mutations (such as Maragogype).

Hybrids occur when a cross occurs either naturally (for example, Kent, Mundo Novo) or through selective breeding programs across members of the same species or genus. Pacamara, Catuai and Catimor are examples of breeding program hybrids.

As in most agricultural industries coffee plants are cultivated in order to make them more disease resistant (such as to coffee leaf rust)[2], drought resistant, produce larger quantities of fruit, cope better at different altitudes, improve flavour characteristics and so on.

COFFEE CHERRY VARIETIES

FOOTNOTE

[1] I prefer to use the term 'cultivar' to the word 'varietal', which causes confusion in the coffee world. It also sounds more pretentious.

[2] A nasty coffee tree fungal disease, it impairs photosynthesis, which causes the leaves to drop. It can eventually kill the whole tree. The disease itself has kept evolving and is getting around the hybrid plant DNA specially bred to resist it.

A very brief summary of the varieties and popular cultivars follows:

TYPICA: Where it all started. Originating from Yemen plants taken to India and from there to Indonesia. The fruit when mature is red. It is still grown extensively in different conditions around the world and can produce an excellent cup. Its fruit yield is low compared to the Bourbon variety and other Typica or Bourbon cultivars.

BOURBON: Named after the island we now know as Reunion. Bourbon was first discovered and grown there by the French and then planted in Brazil. It is now grown throughout South and Central America. It has a higher yield than the Typica variety and has a distinctive sweetness. The fruit itself can come in various colours such as red, yellow or orange, the latter two of which can make it difficult for pickers to know when they're ripe (as opposed to the red ones). Bourbon also has numerous hybrids, which have mostly replaced the base level variety in many producing countries due to their higher yields.

CATURRA: A natural mutation of Bourbon, the tree is a low-growing, high-yield variety popular for hand pickers. It is popular in Brazil, Colombia and Central America. As it is a small tree it can be prone to overbearing fruit and succumbing to dieback.

MUNDO NOVO: Translated as "New World" in Portuguese this guy is a natural hybrid of the two main varieties Typica and Bourbon. Call it a pure breed if you like, or the least 'mongrel' of the hybrids. It has good disease resistance and gives high yields at relatively high altitude growing. As you would expect by its name it's popular in Brazil.

CATUAI: The illegitimate love child of Caturra and Mundo Novo, developed in Brazil in the 1940s. Catuai was bred to have the dwarf characteristics of Caturra and the high-yield characteristics of Mundo Novo.

MARAGOGYPE/MARAGOGIPE: A mutation of Typica, the Maragogype cultivar produces a huge coffee bean. Also known colloquially as the Elephant Bean it was initially prized for this quality, but recently has become less popular as it is not considered particularly flavoursome. Many add it to their blends for effect rather than flavour contribution.

SL-28 AND SL-34: As you can tell by its name this coffee was bred in a laboratory in the 1930s. It produces a larger bean and has a well received fruit flavour. Performs best at higher altitudes in Africa. 'SL' stands for Selection.

HARRAR, SIDAMO, YIRGACHEFFE: Three Ethiopian hybrids named after their respective growing regions (allô Champagne!) and trademarked by the Ethiopian government.

BLUE MOUNTAIN: A Typica hybrid, it is grown in Jamaica, Papua New Guinea, Hawaii, Kenya and Haiti. It was internationally famed for its high quality and low yields, until this next guy came along …

GEISHA: Ah Geisha! If you want to get a coffee hipster salivating like Pavlov's dog, just say the word "Gei-shaaa". Named after the Ethiopian village of Gesha, this coffee has been smashing farm lot auction prices since 2004 when a Panamanian farm called Hacienda La Esmeralda won the Best of Panama competition with their entry. Since then it's gone nuts. Last year (2018) saw the record yet again smashed when someone paid US$803/pound for a natural process Geisha hailing from Boquette in Panama. Recently there has been a trend in the high-end specialty coffee market in which buyers from Asia, Australia, Europe and the U.S.A. are spending unprecedented amounts of money to secure what they believe is the best of the best. To put some of these numbers in perspective, the New York commodities exchange price[3] – or "C" price – for Arabica coffee recently traded at US$1.11 per pound, which by all accounts would not match the per-pound cost of production in much of the growing world. Anyhow it is a beautiful coffee. Believed to be originally from Ethiopia (see below) it came to prominence in Panama via Costa Rica. It displays an exceptional floral and aromatic cup. At a whopping US$800/pound (AU$2,360/kg) you'd want to be switched on when you actually roast it!

WILD ARABICA CULTIVARS: The newly famed Geisha is, in fact, a wild type Arabica coffee originally from Ethiopia. There are many other indigenous heirloom coffees in countries like Ethiopia and Papua New Guinea that can produce some interesting coffees. A result of cross-breeding amongst various varieties and species, they are a bit of a lucky dip. So you never know when you might discover the next Geisha!

FOOTNOTE

[3] Consumers and producers of coffee can manage coffee price risk by purchasing and selling coffee futures. Coffee producers can employ a short hedge to lock in a selling price for the coffee they produce, while businesses that require coffee can utilise a long hedge to secure a purchase price for the commodity they need. Coffee futures are also traded by speculators who assume the price risk that hedgers try to avoid in return for a chance to profit from favourable coffee price movement. Speculators buy coffee futures when they believe that coffee prices will go up. Conversely, they will sell coffee futures when they think that coffee prices will fall.

2
WHAT IS A COFFEE BEAN?

You know, most people don't know where coffee comes from! Simply put, three to four years after the coffee seedling is planted, sweetly smelling jasmine-like flowers grow in clusters in the axils of the coffee leaves.

Fruit is produced only in the new tissue. The Coffea Arabica coffee plant is self-pollinating, whereas the Robusta coffee plant depends on cross-pollination. It takes about nine months until the fruits are ready to harvest.

The cherry contains two seeds – the coffee beans we know and love. Most of the volume of the cherry is made up of these two seeds. There is a thin layer of fruit skin and pulp and the two seeds with the flattened sides facing each other. The seed itself has a protective layer known as parchment and a thinner layer over that known as the silverskin. (We will discuss processing and milling techniques in more detail shortly.) Sometimes the seed will be malformed and not have a flat side but a rounded curvature and be quite small in size. These coffee beans are known as peaberries and are separated from the flattened beans and processed and sold separately.

Picking the cherry at optimal ripeness is important for the flavour development of the coffee bean. The cherries start out green and evolve until they are a deep red colour.

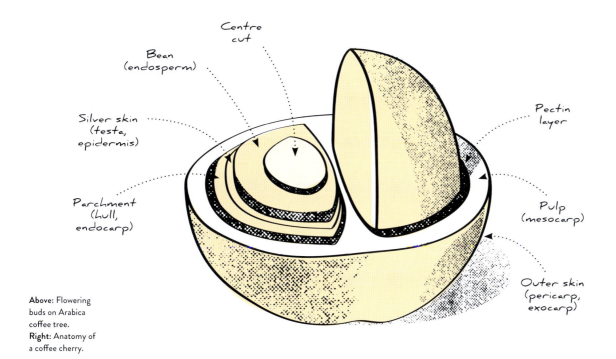

Above: Flowering buds on Arabica coffee tree.
Right: Anatomy of a coffee cherry.

Mature Kenyan Ruiru 11 cherries ready to harvest.

3
GREEN COFFEE CHEMISTRY

I'm not going to get overly technical here. You can read a multitude of books on this single topic if it interests you. A basic knowledge of green coffee chemistry, however, is useful for when we get to the roasting coffee part of this book. So here is a fundamental green coffee chemistry lesson.

Structure

The chemical composition of coffee varies from the Arabica and Robusta species and varies again in their various natural hybrids and mutations. In addition to these intrinsic factors, extrinsic factors such as soil composition, climate and agricultural practices will, to a lesser extent, affect the coffee bean's chemical composition.

Most of the chemical constituents are shared by both the Arabica and Robusta varieties, but their relative proportions can vary significantly. This is what gives them their unique characteristics. For example, Robusta varieties' resistance to pests and diseases due to their higher chlorogenic acid content is also the same feature that marks them as the inferior cousins of the Arabica plant flavour-wise. This is because high amounts of chlorogenic acid are thought to lead to poor cup quality during roasting.

Half of the bean's weight is made up of a cellulose (polysaccharide) structure. It contributes little to flavour but contains volatile compounds responsible for roasted coffee aroma. About 100 volatile compounds such as alcohols, esters and hydrocarbons have been identified in green coffee seeds. The maturation stage of the coffee fruits is important for the volatile composition of green coffee. Overripe coffee berries, which produce dark defective seeds, exhibit high concentrations of volatile compounds. Roasting the coffee, however, creates most of the coffee's aromatics, with hundreds of compounds identified in research studies.

CHEMICAL COMPOUND BREAKDOWN FOR ARABICA AND ROBUSTA GREEN BEANS

Concentration (g/100g)

COMPONENT	ARABICA	ROBUSTA
Carbohydrates/fibre	45–53	56–59
Nitrogenous compounds	12–14	14–19
Lipids	18–23	12–15
Minerals	3–4	4.5
Acids and esters	5–8	7–11

Non-volatile Compounds

Green coffee beans are made up of numerous non-volatile chemical compounds such as water, carbohydrates (sugars), proteins and amino acids, lipids, minerals, chlorogenic acids, trigonelline and caffeine.

The bioactive compounds most likely to contribute to the beverage flavour after roasting are as follows:

Caffeine is an alkaloid with a bitter characteristic, although it only contributes about 10% to brewed coffee's perceived bitterness. Robusta green beans have about a 50–70% higher caffeine level than their Arabica cousins. Another alkaloid, and one that contributes significantly to a brewed coffee's bitter flavour, is *Trigonelline*. Its demethylation during roasting produces nicotinic acid, a B-complex vitamin known as niacin B3.

The previously mentioned *Chlorogenic Acids* confer astringency, bitterness and acidity to the coffee brew. The content of chlorogenic acids is generally twice as high in Robusta green beans than in Arabica green beans. As mentioned already the higher levels of this compound are what give the Robusta plant its superior pest resistance properties over the Arabica plant.

Carbohydrates (the dreaded carbs!!!) account for more than 50% of the green bean's dry weight. 44% of this is made up of polysaccharides, which contribute little to the roasted coffee's flavour, but do give body to the brew. Sucrose, however, which makes up 9% of the green bean dry weight certainly does contribute significantly to the roasted coffee's flavour and aroma. Carbs, very importantly, are precursors to the Maillard Reaction[4] and caramelisation, important for colour, aroma development and acidity during and after roasting. The higher sucrose content is the reason for the superior aroma and overall flavour of Arabica coffee.

Proteins, *peptides* and *free amino acids* are vital for coffee flavour since they are needed for the Maillard Reaction. Coffee is not, however, a good nutritional source of protein because it lacks essential amino acids (sorry, gym junkies ...).

In fact, gym junkies look away now! *Lipids* account for about 14% of a green bean's dry weight – but relax gymbos, most fatty acids in coffee are unsaturated. Lipids contribute to brewed coffee's aroma and how it feels in your mouth. Arabica green beans generally have a 50% higher lipid content than Robusta green beans. Fatty acids are not only important to our health, but their integrity is important to keep coffee fresh and avoid staleness caused by hydrolysis and oxidation.

Lastly, the water or moisture content of green beans is critical to the roasting process. Producers dry their beans using various methods, which we will explore in the following section of this chapter, and aim for a moisture content level of about 10–12%. Water or moisture content impacts on heat transfer during the coffee roasting process. High water content can make the green beans prone to mould development and taste grassy in the roasted coffee cup. Equally, when moisture content is too low the roasted coffee can taste hay-like in the cup.

FOOTNOTE
[4] A very important reaction I will explain more fully in Part B-2.

4
COFFEE ORIGINS AND THEIR TYPICAL CHARACTERISTICS

You can't simply pick a continent such as Africa or Asia and describe its typical overall flavour profile. Differences in climate, cultivars used and processing methods will significantly affect the flavour characteristics of the coffees produced in the different countries within these vast continents. So here I will pick out a few popular origins from within the greater coffee growing continents and highlight their typical key characteristics[5].

Why is this important? Well, as with wine grapes we blend different coffees to come up with a balance of flavours that we can then proudly call our own roasted coffee blends. We will focus on blending in Part B-4, but this is the immediate connection I'd like to make in this chapter. Also please note that some of these countries have a wide array of coffee processing methods and quality levels. Here we just describe the flavour profiles of their specialty-grade Arabica coffees.

FOOTNOTE
[5] For a more comprehensive overview of coffee origins I highly recommend reading James Hoffmann's book *The World Atlas of Coffee* and having it on your reference bookshelf at the roastery.

NORTH AMERICA

1. HAWAII
- Fruity, cocoa, creamy
- Clean and well-structured body
- Delicate with low acidity

2. MEXICO
- Caramel and toffee
- Dark chocolate
- Smooth finish

CENTRAL AMERICA

3. GUATEMALA
- Chocolate, nutty, spice
- Sweet and fruity
- Complex flavours and balanced acidity

4. COSTA RICA
- Chocolate and honey
- Fruit and citrus
- Light bodied
- Clean and sweet

5. PANAMA
- Floral and citrus flavours
- Light bodied and delicate
- Complex flavours
- Recently famous for Geisha coffees

SOUTH AMERICA

6. COLOMBIA
- Flavours can vary greatly by region
- Chocolate and spice. Full bodied (eg: Sierra Nevada)
- Fruit sweetness and complex (eg: Huila region)

7. BRAZIL
- Heavy body and buttery sweet
- Chocolate/cocoa and nutty flavours
- Low in acidity

AFRICA

8. RWANDA
- Mixed fruits and floral flavours dominate
- Berries, aniseed, fine chocolate
- Bright pleasant acidity

9. TANZANIA
- Stone fruit, chocolate, sweet
- Berries, citrus overtones
- Bright and clean acidity

OCEANIA

15. AUSTRALIA
- Clean and sweet
- Light to medium bodied
- Nutty finish

14. PNG
- Lemon acidity
- Full mouthfeel
- Sweet and complex fruit
- Cocoa, chocolate

ASIA

10. KENYA
- Complex bright blackcurrant berry and fruit qualities
- Dark chocolate overtones
- Intense acidity

11. ETHIOPIA
- Citrus, candied fruit and tropical fruit flavours
- Dark chocolate overtones
- Elegantly complex and diverse washed coffees
- Wild fruit-driven natural process coffees

12. INDIA
- Raisins, plum, cocoa
- Low acidity
- Heavy body

13. INDONESIA
- Intense heavy body
- Berry flavours
- Spice and earthiness
- Low acidity

The unique challenges of harvesting coffee on the terraced Colombian coffee plantations.

5
GREEN COFFEE PROCESSING

Harvesting

Ripe cherries are either harvested by hand (selective picking), stripped from the tree with both unripe and overripe beans (stripping), or all the coffee beans are collected using a harvesting machine (mechanical harvesting).

Coffee cherries do not, however, ripen uniformly on the tree. This presents an inherent problem at harvesting time. Hand picking is the best method (in theory) of picking ripe cherries and leaving the unripe cherries on the tree to mature further. This, however, presents a few issues in the real world.

In countries like Brazil, where the trees mature relatively uniformly, harvesting the same coffee tree several times is less cost effective than separating and discarding the unripe or overripe cherries. Therefore, Brazil typically harvests using the stripping method when 75% of the coffee crop is perfectly ripe. In stripping, the coffee beans are pulled from the tree and fall to the ground where they are caught by sheets.

In certain terrains, such as the steep terraced mountains of Colombia and Guatemala, hand picking is just about the only option available as the terrain makes it impossible for any type of mechanical harvesting to occur. In Colombia this is also presenting as an economic issue at the moment. The younger workers no longer want to do this type of manual work as the population has become more educated and white collared, and the existing pickers are starting to age.

Hand pickers are also usually paid by the weight of the baskets of cherries they pick. So picking a percentage of green cherries is perversely encouraged, as they weigh more than the ripe cherries[6] – and, of course, you can pick more in a day.

FOOTNOTE
[6] Just make sure the green ones are at the bottom of the basket.

Pulping coffee in PNG.

Coffee Processing Overview

PROCESS: WET MILL – SEPARATING FLOATERS AND SINKERS

Irrespective of the harvesting method, green coffee beans and overripe coffee cherries inevitably end up mixed with the perfectly ripe cherries and must be separated during coffee processing. As it turns out, overripe coffee cherries, undeveloped coffee cherries, as well as sticks and leaves, float in water. Ripe coffee beans and green coffee cherries are dense and sink. So step one consists of separating the "floaters" from the "sinkers".

The coffee floaters will either be discarded at this point or sent directly to a concrete patio to be dried and slated for internal consumption. All coffee cherries go through this stage. The ripe and green cherries can be sent to the patios to be dried using the natural process of preparing coffee or can be sent to the wet process coffee pulping machines. A more detailed explanation of these different processing methods and their impact on the coffee's flavour characteristics follows in Part B-7.

PROCESS: PULPING COFFEE

Washed process and pulped natural coffees are pulped using a pulping machine to release the coffee beans from the fruit. In the first stage of pulping you want to separate the green cherries from the ripe ones. By regulating the pressure of the pulping machinery only the ripe beans will break open and release the coffee beans through screens that are designed so only the beans can pass through them. The green cherries are hard and cannot be pulped. Instead of passing through the screen, the green coffee beans pass to the end of the barrel system and are separated from the ripe coffee beans. It is necessary to continuously monitor the pressure of the equipment so that about 3% of ripe cherries are not pulped and are removed with the green cherries. This margin of error ensures that no green cherries are mistakenly pulped. The pulp and coffee beans are then separated by centrifugal force and a barrel screen system.

PROCESS: COFFEE FERMENTATION

The coffee beans covered in the slippery mucilage can be sent to the patios to dry as pulped natural process coffees (a.k.a. honey process) or can be sent to coffee fermentation tanks (washed process). In the washed process the coffee fermentation tanks are used to remove the mucilage before drying. The pulped coffee beans are then put into cement tanks with water and are allowed to ferment for 16–36 hours. On the way to the fermentation tanks, another density separation can occur. The highest quality coffees are the densest and should be separated and fermented in a different tank. As previously mentioned, natural process coffees are patio sun-dried with their skin on (and are not pulped).

FOOTNOTE
[7] Moisture meters are typically used to measure the bean's moisture content.

[8] See one in action here: http://bit.ly/2IdwHrw

PROCESS: COFFEE DRYING

Coffee must be dried from approximately 60% moisture content to 11–12% moisture content[7]. Coffee is typically dried on large concrete patios and then transferred to mechanical dryers. The coffee on the drying patios is shifted every 30-40 minutes and is shaped into long rows of no more than 5cm in height. Next to each row is open ground, which is warmed and dried by the sun. The coffee is then shifted onto the dry portion of the patio, and the section where it was previously is now allowed to dry in the sun. This helps accelerate the coffee drying process and prevents fermentation and mouldy beans from developing.

Drying coffee solely by patio takes 6–7 days for washed coffees, 8–9 days for pulped naturals (semi-washed) and 12–14 days for natural (dry processed) coffees. Some countries dry their coffee on a patio until they reach a moisture content of 15% and then transfer it to mechanical dryers. At 25% moisture content the coffee can be piled at night and covered with cotton cloths to allow the coffee to breathe.

The best, but least utilised, method of drying coffee is by using raised-bed drying tables. In this method the pulped and fermented coffee is spread thinly on raised beds, allowing the air to pass on all sides of the coffee. The coffee is mixed by hand and the drying that takes place is more uniform, making fermentation less likely. Most coffee from Africa is dried in this manner and select coffee farms around the world are following their lead.

MECHANICAL DRYING EQUIPMENT

Drying coffee by using mechanical dryers accelerates the slowest part of the coffee drying process (from 15%–11%) and helps prevent fermentation. In some environments that have a high humidity level the entire drying process must take place in mechanical dryers.

PROCESS: COLOUR AND DENSITY SORTING

Colour sorting is frequently used to remove the defective coffee beans that were not removed during coffee processing or hulling. Many countries sort coffee beans by hand due to inexpensive labour, but for most countries investment in a colour sorting machine, or colour separator, is necessary.

Molecular density sorting is one of the best ways to separate broken, small, undeveloped and otherwise defective coffee beans. There are usually two to three stages of density sorting. In the first stage, the very dense rocks and stones are removed from the coffee. In the second stage, the coffee is hulled and the debris is removed. The third stage is most important and typically uses a densimetric table[8] to separate the coffee into three or more densities.

6

COFFEE GRADING AND IDENTIFYING DEFECTS

I have sourced coffee from and worked with the team at Cofi-Com Trading since I started in the coffee industry. I'm proud to call its founder Andrew Mackay a mentor and friend. In more recent years John Russell Storey (Marketing Manager) and Dariusz Lewandowski (Operations and Coffee Trading Manager) have proved to be invaluable fonts of knowledge for me and have provided a great deal of the information, photos and proofreading for this section of the book. Dariusz has first-hand coffee growing experience in Indonesia.

Green bean quality assurance and grading are critical parts of the bean-to-cup process and are often taken for granted when you start out. The bags of green coffee you order for your roastery have been through a strict QA and vetting process by the importer and trader. Companies like Cofi-Com are global concerns with people on the ground both at origin and here in Australia. Following, we will look at what screen sizes are all about, discuss how defects are sorted, and finally examine the various coffee grade definitions and what these really mean to you as the end user.

Sharing war stories with John and Dariusz from Cofi-Com.

Identifying coffee defects and understanding how to grade specialty coffee are important skills. Until you acquire these skills, I suggest you allow your specialist coffee merchants to handle these processes for you.

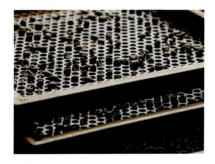

Coffee screens in action.

Screen Size

All green coffee is bought with a screen size reference. This is a process where a set amount (let's say 300g) of green coffee is passed through a series of interlocking trays placed one on top of the other. The largest screen size (19) is on the top, the smallest size (13) on the bottom. The screens are shaken vigorously by hand and the beans are either retained by the screens or fall through the various screens. Retained beans in each tray are counted and a percentage can be worked out of each different screen.

Defects

Most defined coffee standards allow a certain number of defects: broken beans, insect damage, quakers (underripe beans) brown beans and the infamous 'stinker' or black bean. Add to this tiny stones, sticks and dried cherries, all of which can affect taste or damage a grinder. Removal of defects happens at origin through sorting equipment or by hand. The best guide on defects is the *SCA Defect Handbook*[9], with its clear explanations and pictures. The SCA (Specialty Coffee Association of America) Green Arabica Coffee Classification System (GACCS) is a detailed universal system approach to identifying and grading green coffees.

A 350g sample of green coffee is tested for moisture content, bean size and imperfections. The imperfections are divided into two categories of defects. Category 1 defects are the most severe and one defect typically eliminates a sample from receiving specialty status (see Coffee Grades overleaf). A cumulative score of five Category 2 defects does the same. Defects are based on appearance and categorised according to how the defect affects the flavour. Once the sample coffee is roasted there is an additional step to count the number of quakers.

FOOTNOTE
[9] You can purchase a digital copy here: http://bit.ly/2YLs0et

---

A VARIETY OF COMMON GREEN COFFEE DEFECTS

Insect damage   Shells   Parchment

Blacks   Sours   Unripes   Broken/chipped/cut

THE FOLLOWING TABLE IS DERIVED FROM THE SCA DEFECT HANDBOOK AND GIVES A BRIEF DESCRIPTION OF THE MOST COMMON DEFECTS FOUND IN GREEN COFFEE:

Green coffee moisture meter.

Category 1

DEFECT NAME	# BEANS EQUAL TO FULL DEFECT	DESCRIPTION
Full Black	1	Opaque colour. Due to overfermentation.
Full Sour	1	Yellow/brown/reddish colour variants. Inside of bean typically black. Sour smell.
Dried Cherry	1	Dried pulp covers parchment, may show mould.
Fungus Damage	1	Fungal spores covering part or whole of bean. Reddish/brown colour.
Foreign Matter	1	Sticks, stones, nails.

Category 2

DEFECT NAME	# BEANS EQUAL TO FULL DEFECT	DESCRIPTION
Partial Black	3	Less than half the bean is opaque.
Partial Sour	3	Less than half the bean is sour.
Floater	5	Has a white, faded, mottled appearance. Floats when placed in water.
Unripe	5	Silverskin has yellow/green colour. Smaller than other beans and usually malformed.
Broken/Chipped/Cut	5	Dark reddish colour due to oxidation that took place during pulping.

EXPERT TIP

Another defect, interestingly not defined by this classification system but commonly heard in the coffee industry, is one charmingly known as a "stinker". It is, in fact, a fault caused by inconsistencies or delays in drying and it displays as a dull brown or graying colouring. Its flavour is delightfully described as "fermented rotting fruit, foul, rotten fish flavour".

Q-Grading Courses

There are many more defects within these two categories described in the table. If you'd like to learn more you can buy the printed or digital version of the *SCA Defect Handbook* or consider doing a Q-Grading course, which are now available worldwide since the first one was developed in 2003 by the Coffee Quality Institute (CQI). A Q-Grader certification program/course normally runs for several days and features hands-on tutorials and exams, which you must pass in order to gain the Q-Grader certification. The certification lasts three years and you need to then pass a "calibration" exam every three years to maintain your certification.

SKILLS AND EXAMS TYPICALLY COVERED IN THESE COURSES ARE:
- Sensory Skills
- Cupping Skills
- Olfactory Skills
- Organic Acids Identification
- Arabica Green Coffee Defect Identification (as per GACCS standards)
- Arabica Roasted Coffee Defect Identification
- Roasted Sample Flaws Identification.

> Buying from experienced green coffee traders like Cofi-Com and other established coffee importers can prove to be invaluable. These guys only buy grades of coffee that pass their own strict standards. It's a process that starts with personal knowledge of the origin and direct, longstanding relationships with growers built on trust. They don't buy coffee they don't cup multiple times from pre-shipment to arrival.

Coffee Grades Explained

SPECIALTY GRADE: By strict SCA definition, this is a coffee scoring 80+ using the Q-Grade protocols that include the SCA's GACCS (do you remember what that stands for?) grading protocol. It ensures that farmers get feedback from a universal system whether the cupper is in Singapore, Sydney or Nairobi. In reality though, Specialty Grade is a term that covers a multitude of meanings to different people.

John Russell Storey from Cofi-Com states that "Specialty Grade is one those terms open to so many variations and interpretations. For us to grade a coffee as Specialty it has to have a GACCS score of 84 or over and stand out flavour is the driver behind the score. Our recommendation is to use scores as a guide only, and to go by taste".

PREMIUM AND EXCHANGE GRADE: The SCA defines coffees that don't meet Specialty Grade standards as Premium Grade. Below Premium is Exchange Grade. Premium Grade coffees can taste great and Exchange Grade coffees can work well in certain blends where price point is critical.

ORIGIN GRADE: Explaining each country's grading system would require its own book, and that's one of the reasons the SCA established its universal grading classification system. As an example of an origin grade, the letters EP are often seen on Central American coffees and mean 'European Preparation'. This grade is defined as being: "Beans that are 100% above screen 15 and allow a maximum of 8 defects per 300g. Coffee should cup as clean".

7
IMPACT OF PROCESSING METHODS ON FLAVOUR

Dry/Natural Process

The dry process (also known as the natural method) produces coffee that is heavy in body, sweet, smooth and complex with fruit notes. Using this method the entire cherry is dried in the sun and the sugars and other properties from the fruit or mucilage are absorbed into the bean. The dry process is often used in countries where rainfall is scarce and long periods of sunshine are available to dry the coffee properly. Many coffees from Ethiopia, Brazil and Yemen are dry processed.

Wet/Washed Process

Wet processing coffees is a relatively new method of removing the four layers surrounding the coffee bean. This process results in a coffee that is cleaner, brighter and fruitier. Most countries with coffee valued for its perceived acidity will process their coffee using the wet process. The wet process is often used in countries with high rainfall that makes the longer natural process of drying more difficult to achieve. Countries with predominantly washed process coffees are PNG and Colombia.

PROCESSING METHODS

Washed

Natural

Pulped natural

Origin field visits are invaluable to learn and see the different coffee processing methods first-hand. Often in remote locations, half the fun is in the journey of getting there in the first place.

Pulped Natural/Semi-Washed

The pulped natural method consists of wet pulping a coffee, but emitting the fermentation stage to remove the silverskin. This results in a beverage that has characteristics of both a dry and wet processed coffee. It is often sweeter than wet processed coffees, has some of the body of a dry processed coffee, but also retains some of the acidity of a wet processed coffee. This type of processing can only occur in countries where humidity is low and the coffee covered in the sweet mucilage can be dried rapidly without fermenting. Brazil has made this method famous and produces some of the best pulped natural coffees in the world.

Honey Process

Much the same as semi-washed, cherries are pulped then sun-dried with as much mucilage or fruit remaining on the bean. As beans dry in the sun, the mucilage darkens. There are a number of variations such as Black Honey, Red Honey, Yellow Honey, 30% Honey and 40% Honey. Most depend on the time taken to dry and exposure to sun. A coffee processed this way will have a lovely, bright sweetness to it, created by the sugars being absorbed from the mucilage into the bean. Costa Rica and Nicaragua are well regarded for their honey processed coffee.

Other Flavour Contributors

The processing method used on a coffee is usually the single largest contributor to its flavour profile. Assuming the processing is carried out properly, the microclimate and soil are the next major contributors to a coffee's flavour profile.

PNG Amakai Honey process coffee.

8
SEASONALITY, STORAGE, SHIPPING AND PACKAGING

It can be useful to understand when the harvest times in the various origins are. This will help you work out how old the coffee you are buying may actually be, and assist you in your purchase decision. You should always ask which harvest the beans you are buying have come from. Older coffee beans will have a lower moisture content in general, and will be more challenging to roast to their optimal level.

Coffee is picked during the dry season, although in equatorial countries, it can technically be picked year-round depending on conditions. Generally speaking, however, the coffee you buy that was picked mid-season will be the best-tasting of the year. Cup quality will fade slightly towards the last of the season's production.

Opposite is a table with normal harvest times for coffee growing countries around the globe. Please note, however, that in some countries with different growing regions the harvest times can vary greatly.

COFFEE PRODUCING COUNTRY	COFFEE HARVESTING TIME
Australia	April–May & September–October (Far North)
Brazil	April–September
Colombia	September–December & April–June
Costa Rica	November–March, but can vary greatly from region to region
Dominican Republic	October–May
El Salvador	October–March
Ethiopia	October–January
Guatemala	December–March
Hawaii	August–January
Honduras	November–March
India	October–February
Indonesia	Java: June–October Sumatra: January–March
Jamaica	June–August
Kenya	October–December (main) & June–August
Mexico	High altitudes: November–January Low altitudes: August–November
Nicaragua	South: November–January & August–September North: December–March
Panama	December–March
Papua New Guinea	April–September
Rwanda	March–June
Tanzania	July–December
Uganda	October–January
Zimbabwe	July–October

Kenyan burlap bags.

GrainPro bag inside a Jamaican Blue Mountain coffee barrel.

Some coffee defects develop during the storage and shipping phase. While importers test pre-shipment samples, what actually arrives at the warehouse can differ markedly. The green coffee at some point in its pre-shipment storage or in transit could be exposed to unfavourable atmospheric conditions. This factor has started a relatively recent revolution in green bean packaging methods, especially in the specialty coffee sector.

Traditionally green coffee was packed and transported in 60kg burlap (also known as hessian here in Australia) bags made of jute. It's cheap and economical and allows the coffee to breathe. It doesn't, however, protect the coffee from excessive moisture of high humidity (or water contact damage), or odours.

In the last ten years a lot of the higher-end specialty coffee I used in my roastery started to arrive in 30kg vacuum packs and, increasingly more commonly, in 60kg GrainPro bags. The GrainPro bag will normally sit inside the traditional burlap bag. Both vacuum packing and GrainPro bags prevent the development of mould and micro-organisms during shipping and storage.

I swear that you could actually smell the difference when you opened the GrainPro bags. The aroma of fresh fruit smells was fantastic. I had never smelled such fresh green coffee before. Without fail, the visual quality of the coffee inside these bags was exceptional as well. The impact on the final roast cup was very noticeable in my opinion, especially with the naturals. It showed to me without a shadow of a doubt how important the packaging of the green beans was to the overall bean-to-cup equation. More and more specialty producers have turned to GrainPro bags in recent years as they are relatively economical and keep the green beans protected and fresh during the time it takes to arrive at your roastery from shipment at origin.

EXPERT TIP

When buying specialty green coffee from your coffee trader, ask if the coffee you are ordering comes in GrainPro bags and if it's current season.

Vacuum-packed coffee.

Post-shipment warehouse QA sampling.

A modern green bean storage warehouse.

Another factor that is becoming increasingly important in the specialty market is the time it takes for the green coffee to arrive from origin to roaster. Artisan roasters are more aware these days of the importance of fresh green coffee. Make sure you ask the age of the coffee you are buying. Avoid buying coffees that are previous season coffees.

A recent development in, and an unfortunate side effect of, this rapidly growing industry is medium-sized coffee roasters buying direct from origin, they end up stuck with aging coffee that they try to flog off to unsuspecting novice roasters for a "bargain bro!". Minimum quantities apply to get even remotely competitive pricing and to make shipping economical, so they'll bring in half-a-container load of coffee and get stuck with it, paying warehousing fees and the like. I lost count of the number of other medium-sized roasters calling me trying to flog off their dodgy old green beans. Don't go there …

This leads nicely into the last bit of this topic: atmospheric conditions at your trader's warehouse and your roastery storage. Follow these simple rules and you should be fine.

Green coffee likes similar conditions to what you and I like – around 20–22°C (68–72°F) and humidity under 65%, which allows the beans to maintain their 10–12% moisture content by weight prior to roasting. The warehouse should have stable temperatures (wildly fluctuating day/night temperatures in some regions is a huge problem for green coffee bean stability), good airflow – and the coffee should be stored off ground level on food grade pallets. It should also be kept away from other food items with strong odours and, of course, any pest activity.

With this in mind be wary of storing your green coffee in off-site third party general storage warehouses. For obvious reasons you won't know what they do with your pallets when you're not around. I've seen appalling things at these places. Pallets left outside in the burning sun all day, entire pallets "lost" and so on. You get the picture. Having said that, there are specialty climate-controlled warehouses now available, especially useful in very humid cities such as Brisbane in Australia and North Carolina in the USA.

My advice to you as an artisan roaster is to keep it simple and just buy what you will use within a two-week period. Even the larger green been traders have a one pallet (8 bag) minimum for delivery, and some smaller suppliers will let you buy by the single bag, so happy days!

9
MAKING SENSE OF COFFEE CERTIFICATIONS

Below: Some examples of international green coffee certification bodies.

There are certainly a lot of certification bodies out there these days. Many are region based. Some have an environmental focus and others are more economic/social in their focus, working within the coffee communities they support. Many cover both areas equally. A summary table is below[10].

I had first-hand experience with several of these certification bodies. Some were invasive (wanting you to pay a percentage of your roasted coffee sales – unworkable and impossible to audit). Others not so – it was basically just costed into the green bean price and your green coffee trader took care of the compliance side of things.

Recently, Third Wave coffee roasters have started to move away from the Fair Trade idea and more towards Direct Trade. This is, of course, not so easy for a small artisan roaster to do due to the volumes required. However, in recent years more and more producers have been sending their family members around the world to set up direct importing businesses and warehouses, meaning they can then sell direct to smaller roasters this way. It's a tough gig for them. Many have failed, but a few good operators have flourished and with hard work and dedication have grown into sizeable green bean traders themselves.

CERTIFICATION	FOCUS
Certified Organic – OCIA	Organic certification and minimising deforestation of coffee ecosystems by encouraging coffee tree biodiversity.
Bird Friendly	Conservation of migratory birds and their habitats through maintenance of forest and shade trees and waterways. Organic requirement.
Fairtrade International	Promotes small farm sustainability through minimum price levels, providing community support, organisation of cooperatives and financing. Long-term contracts with buyers.
Rainforest Alliance (RFA)	Protection and conservation of ecosystem using low-impact agriculture. Shade-grown encouraged. Minimum wages for employees and community contribution expected.
USDA Organic	Reduced use of pesticides and fertilisers. Improvement of soil and water quality. Land management and renewable resource advice. Traceability of organic and non-organic product.
UTZ Certified	Sustainable farming and production practices and social, labour and environmental traceability. Promotes good housing and education in communities as well as minimum wages for workers. At the time of writing the Netherlands-based UTZ Certified and New York-based Rainforest Alliance have announced their intention to merge under the Rainforest Alliance name.

10
PROS AND CONS OF BUYING FARM-DIRECT GREEN COFFEE

As just mentioned it's now much easier to buy coffee "direct from farm" through local representatives. The volume restrictions of buying and shipping from an overseas farm/producer have been overcome to some extent. There are, of course, some pros and cons to this exercise, which I point out below. Please note that some of these points apply more to the exercise of shipping direct from source, which will be a very unlikely scenario for a small artisan roaster. I will probably cop some criticism for some of these points. It's just my opinion, so it's up to you to make the commercial decision based on your own objective research:

PROS

1. In theory the producer should receive a much better price per kilo of coffee by cutting out middlemen.
2. You are part of a global movement to improve the livelihood of coffee producers and the community they live in.
3. You may have more say in how the coffee is processed, packed and stored.
4. You might be able to justify origin trips to exotic parts of the world to your life partner and your accountant.

CONS

1. You lose the accountability that you have with a larger green coffee trader for the farm to roastery QA processes and follow-up. I've heard of bags half-full of rocks turning up on the ship.
2. In reality you may end up paying a lot more for an inferior product if you don't know what you're doing. Especially if there is no local representation.
3. You may have to deal with complicated and costly Australian Quarantine inspections and paperwork.
4. You may get done on the exchange rate or other variable financial and logistical factors due to your inexperience.

EXPERT TIP
Don't get confused by a coffee's certification. For example, Fair Trade Certified does not necessarily mean that the coffee is certified organic.

FOOTNOTE
[10] Table correct at time of writing but is subject to change. This is a summary of major certifiers only.

B2

LET'S START ROASTING COFFEE!

OK then! I've only made you wait 100-odd pages to get to this bit, which is probably the main reason you purchased the book. If you've cheated and come straight here by skipping the previous bits – "BE GONE WITH YOU!" or, at the very least, please read through Parts A-3 and B-1 first, as some of what we will chat about in this section will flow on from what I discussed in those sections.

Of course, readers of this book will come from very different starting points – I totally understand that. Some of you may never have roasted a coffee bean in your life; others have done some sample roasting in all sorts of contraptions, from a popcorn maker to a proper sample roaster. Or you may already be a professional coffee roaster just looking to see if what you're doing already lines up with my techniques, or you may be looking to acquire a few new tips.

This overview is simply that – an overview. I will share what I think are the most important coffee roasting steps and rules to follow for a retail based artisan coffee roaster. Not all of you will agree with my ideas and processes, for others will have their own theories and methods they have developed and follow, and which you may have adopted as gospel truth.

Either way, you will most likely need to adapt the steps I offer here, even if ever so slightly, to fit in with your own coffee roaster's unique behaviour and your own roasting style and philosophy. This will come in time. You will develop your own unique style as you absorb and learn from others, and I fully encourage that.

So let's start by expanding on the basic chemistry of coffee by looking at what happens to the coffee bean when it's roasted.

IN PART B-2 WE WILL COVER:

1. COFFEE ROASTING CHEMISTRY 101
2. LET'S DO A ROAST TOGETHER
3. PLANNING YOUR BATCH ROAST BY ROASTER CAPACITY
4. AIRFLOW – WHAT DOES IT DO?
5. WARMING UP YOUR ROASTER AND CHARGE TEMPERATURES
6. STAGES OF THE ROAST
7. WHY DEVELOPMENT TIME IS EVERYTHING – AND WHY YOU NEED TO UNDERSTAND THIS
8. TWO ROAST PROFILES TO GET YOU STARTED
9. ROAST LEVELS AND AGTRON READINGS
10. ROASTING TECHNIQUES FOR ACHIEVING WELL-DEVELOPED LIGHT ROAST COFFEES
11. THE IMPORTANCE OF COOLING YOUR ROAST FAST
12. WHAT TO DO IN BETWEEN ROASTS – BEING PREPARED
13. SOME EXTRA TIPS ON ACHIEVING ROAST CONSISTENCY
14. DE-STONING YOUR COFFEE – THE LAST STEP
15. 'THE LAST ROAST OF THE DAY' PROCEDURE

1
COFFEE ROASTING CHEMISTRY
101

We have already talked about green coffee chemistry in the previous section. A coffee bean's chemistry continues to evolve during the roasting process and, in fact, the brewing process as well. I will give a simple overview here as to what happens chemically to the coffee bean during the roasting process, but I really do think it's important that you expand your knowledge about coffee chemistry in this area across all three processes: Green/Roasting/Brewing. It will really help you understand what you're doing right or wrong in your roasting and brewing processes and how to correct faults you learn to detect during cupping.

Now, I am no scientist but what I can do is recommend where you can go to learn in detail all about this important area of coffee knowledge.

Coffeechemistry.com was launched in 2004 as the coffee industry's leading information portal on all aspects of coffee science, chemistry and technology.

Using their extensive years of experience and vast network of international partners, they provide the industry with the most up-to-date information on coffee science.

Joseph A. Rivera, founder and creator of coffeechemistry.com, served as the former Director of Science and Technology for the Specialty Coffee Association of America (SCAA) and the Coffee Quality Institute (CQI) from 1999 to 2009. He's the co-creator of the internationally recognised Q-Certification program since its inception. In short, he is The Man – or to be more precise, The Coffee Chemistry Man. I highly recommend you read his published articles, freely available on his website, to expand your coffee chemistry knowledge. I have shamelessly sourced and summarised much of the following information from Joseph's writings on the topic[11].

The coffee bean is an incredibly complex little dude (chemically speaking). While coffee chemistry is still very much an evolving science, there are now thought to be over 1,000 compounds evident in roasted coffee. Compare this to chocolate (350 compounds) and wine (150 compounds) – what lightweights!

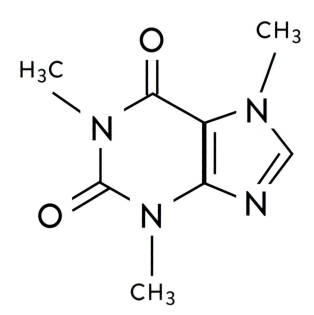

Caffeine molecule.

FOOTNOTE
[11] Please see the Bibliography for more details on articles used for source information for this section.

Caffeine

Caffeine is an alkaloid that acts as a natural defence mechanism to ward off pests, as they do not like its bitterness. Nature, being a wonderful thing, has ensured that the Arabica plant has 50% less caffeine present (1.2%), as the risk of insect attack is reduced by its higher growing altitudes. The Robusta plant, on the other hand, grows at lower altitudes and needs higher levels of caffeine to protect itself, so it displays a 2.2% level on average.

Caffeine has a very high melting point so it's quite resistant to the roasting process. So essentially, on a dry basis, these percentage levels do not change out of 100g of roasted coffee. However, remember that the longer you roast the coffee the more you lose mass – around 10% for a light roast and up to 20% in a dark roast. So while the caffeine levels remain unchanged during roasting, the proportion of caffeine by weight increases during roasting. So assuming all brewing ratios being equal, brewing darker coffees will result in a brewed coffee with a slightly higher caffeine content.

Lipids

Oils in coffee are important during the brewing process to impart mouthfeel and deliver aroma in brewed coffee. This is because most aromatic compounds are oil soluble. Arabica coffee has around 60% more lipid content than its Robusta buddy. These oils are very temperature-stable and, like caffeine, are not greatly troubled by the roasting process.

Most of the aromatic compounds in these oils are released during the brewing process. Roasted beans will lose these aroma compounds during prolonged storage and de-gassing, and darker roasts lose their aromatics more quickly than lighter roasts due to their less stable structure.

Carbohydrates, Proteins and Browning Reactions in Coffee Roasting

You can't really talk about carbohydrates and proteins in coffee roasting without talking about the science of Browning Reactions in coffee roasting, as they are intrinsically linked.

The browning reactions that occur during coffee roasting are known as Non-Enzymatic Browning[12]. These reactions are discussed a lot in the coffee roasting world as they're pretty important in the roasted coffee's flavour development. They are known individually as Caramelisation and the Maillard Reaction.

Caramelisation is fairly easy to understand as we've all seen what happens when we melt sugar in a pan over heat. Basically it's the thermal decomposition of sugars (mostly sucrose) into colour and flavours. At about 170°C sucrose starts to melt, becoming a viscous liquid as it loses water molecules. At about 200°C the compounds begin to rearrange, forming brown caramel compounds and releasing their burnt caramel aroma. It's not the sweet caramel you eat in candy though – in fact, quite the opposite. That has a tonne of things added to it to make it pleasantly sweet. It's a bitter sweetness[13].

FOOTNOTE

[12] Some fruits, like an apple, will release an enzyme designed to protect the apple when its surrounding tissue has been cut. As soon as it's exposed to air this enzyme turns the apple brown to ward off bacteria. This is known as Enzymatic Browning. Pretty cool, huh? This does not happen in coffee – but hey, now you've got another stimulating dinner party trivia fun fact to use! Thank me later …

[13] "Such as life itself" said some famous philosopher sometime, somewhere, maybe …

During coffee roasting, as the sugar decomposes it produces a carbon dioxide gas, which increases the cell pressure inside the bean causing it to rupture during the first crack, and creates that rapid popping sound you hear during the second crack. Hence, coffees that go deep into the second crack stage of roasting are described as being "caramelised".

Caramelisation causes up to 90% of sucrose to decompose during roasting and creates two byproducts in the form of formic and acetic acid. Acetic acid is a weak and volatile acid that affects perceived acidity and overall coffee quality in the brewed cup. So now you can make the correlation that because Arabica has almost twice the concentration of sucrose to Robusta, we therefore usually perceive a greater intensity of flavour and aroma in the brewed cup.

Caramelisation does not, of course, work on its own to generate those unique roasted coffee flavours we all know and love. The James Brown[14] of browning reactions in coffee is known as the Maillard Reaction.

So what do roasted meat and roasted coffee have in common? The Maillard Reaction, of course. The same act of roasting that imparts the complex depth of flavour and aromas in meat does so for coffee as well, and many other foods for that matter. How does it work?

Well, we have to trek back to 1900 to visit Dr Louis Camille Maillard who was busy in his lab researching if the human body actually created proteins. One day, mucking about in his lab, he decided to combine glucose and the amino acids and apply heat to the solution. He immediately got a woody[15] and knew he was onto something. As the clear liquid heated it turned brown and gave off some awesome nutty/bread-like aromas. A star of the manufactured food industry was born, as he had discovered the chemical process now named after him.

So the Maillard Reaction requires sugar and amino acid (protein) plus heat to occur. Aroma development starts in earnest from about mid-roast and at about 160°C the Maillard Reactions become self-sustaining.

So although caramelisation and the Maillard Reaction follow different paths, they end up at the same destination of creating colour and flavour in coffee.

FOOTNOTE
[14] James might be the Godfather of Soul, but the Maillard Reaction is the Godfather of Coffee Browning Reactions.

[15] Australian colloquial slang term.

2
LET'S DO A ROAST TOGETHER

You would have fired up your roaster a few times during the testing and commissioning phase. After certification, you are allowed to put some coffee through. Unfortunately (or fortunately, depending on which way you look at it) you won't be serving these beans to your customers. Drum barrels require "seasoning" to burn off any impurities that land on the surface during its manufacture. This is best done by roasting a couple of batches of coffee and discarding them. So when you buy your first batch of green beans from your supplier ask them for a small bag of "seasoning coffee" – they'll know what you're talking about. It will usually be some ultra-low grade or damaged Robusta beans that they can't sell and which you can have for free or very cheaply.

As you won't be serving these beans it will give you a couple of test runs of the roasting process that we're about to explore before you put some real and saleable coffee in (about $500 worth in retail sales value) – getting nervous yet?

So let's pretend that you're about to do your first roast in-store on your newly commissioned roaster. We will all go through these tentative first steps. I still remember our first roasting day, the day before we opened our doors on September 9, 1997. Of course, you may have done a bit of sample roasting at home, but this is the big time.

Let's assume for this exercise that you have purchased a new 15kg coffee roaster. You have decided to purchase a directly heated traditional drum roaster with four motors, giving you control over roasting and cooling airflows. You have a bean and an environmental (EV) temperature probe connected and you can monitor these temperatures digitally. Your roaster is set up with data-logging software but without roast profile automation. Fully installed and commissioned with all the relevant approvals, you are now ready to rock (and roast some coffee).

I will present this initial roasting guide using the scenario that you are roasting a batch of single origin Specialty Grade Arabica coffee to a classic espresso roast level. We are also roasting green bean batch sizes that are equivalent to 80% of your coffee roaster's stated capacity.

Lastly, rather than discussing coffee roasting theory and then moving onto the process of roasting a batch of coffee separately, I will integrate the theory into the process itself, as I think that will make more logical sense to you.

So let's now look at the step-by-step process of roasting your first commercial batch of coffee.

3

PLANNING YOUR BATCH ROAST BY ROASTER CAPACITY

Yes, size does matter as it turns out. You have a 15kg roaster in our example. This is the theoretical capacity of your roaster in green bean coffee weight.

Personally, I always felt that my roaster worked best at 80% of its stated capacity. One of the reasons for this, I believe, is that the drum is not as full, resulting in better airflow through the drum, which in turn provides a more conducive environment for more even roasting of the coffee bean – and, therefore, a better-tasting coffee as a result.

With single pass roasters a lot of the heat created does not transfer to the bean – a lot goes up the chimney flue or transfers onto you, the humble (and very hot and bothered) master roaster on a hot summer's day. So for that 15kg capacity roaster I'd be starting with a batch size of 12kg and experiment from there. Your roaster's optimal batch size may vary, of course, depending on your airflow range, actual burner output and your flue's drawing efficiency.

Minimum batch size is never stated, and I know of guys who do ridiculously low volumes in large barrels, but I personally never liked to roast at less than one-third of the roaster's stated capacity (in this case around 5kg green weight volume). Volumes lower than 25% of stated capacity really require great skill in managing your roaster's airflow and drum speed (assuming your roaster allows control of this variable). My advice here is to not drop below 5kg in a 15kg stated capacity roaster. If you need to roast very small batches for sampling/testing I suggest you use a dedicated sample roaster.

4
AIRFLOW – WHAT DOES IT DO?

What does airflow do during roasting? Well …

1 Remember that "good airflow is king". It is responsible for 70%+ of your actual roasting, especially during the roast development time.

2 It affects the speed at which your coffee roasts and will, therefore, have a major impact on the final result.

3 It draws out smoke and chaff from the roaster.

4 It evens out the air temperature inside the drum, avoiding hot and cold spots, thus ensuring more even roasting of the coffee beans.

Point 2 is obvious but Point 1 is critical. Very simply put, increasing airflow will slow down the coffee roasting process while decreasing airflow will speed up the coffee roasting process. You are basically drawing (sucking out) hot air through and out of the coffee roaster. The fan speed you choose will increase or decrease this draw. By managing airflow you manage the speed of your roast and directly impact your coffee's development time – and, by doing so, the coffee's roasted flavour profile.

What is the ideal starting airflow? Let's work out and set your roaster's ideal starting airflow draw.

At the early stage of a roast, pull out your sample tester (some people also call this tester a "trowel"). The open hole will expose the region where your beans are tumbling inside the barrel. Cut out a piece of paper just bigger than the hole and place it in front.

The draw of the fan should just hold the paper against the hole. It should not let it fall nor should it threaten to suck it in. If either occurs, simply adjust your fan speed higher to increase the draw or lower it to decrease the draw. Now you have a good starting airflow point and your roaster's draw of air through and out of the roaster is calibrated with the natural draw of your chimneystack.

Remember that "good airflow is king". It is responsible for 70%+ of your actual roasting, especially during the roast development time.

5
WARMING UP YOUR ROASTER AND CHARGE TEMPERATURES

You have a huge chunk of cold steel you need to heat up there. It will take time. Your machine's thermal energy is hard to calculate. Using a drum roaster the temperature of the drum itself will differ to what is showing on the bean or EV temperature probe. We base our charge temperature[16] on what the probes say the temperature is in an empty roaster heating up prior to our first roast. However, as no two roasters are the same in design and setup, you will have to work out the best charge temperature for your setup. For my directly heated Probat L12 drum roaster, I charged to 210°C, but indirectly heated drum roasters will be higher.

So light her up and put your burners on full bore. Your roaster should have an analogue pressure gauge between the gas throttle and the burners. This gauge will provide an accurate indication of the kPa[17] of the burners. Keep your exhaust fan speed slightly below what you would normally roast at, so she heats up faster and you're not piping too much hot air straight out of the roaster.

Prior to your first roast set your roaster to heat up to 15°C above your ideal charge temperature (for the sake of this exercise, let's say that's 210°C (410°F)). You'll notice that the EV probe will lag behind the bean probe temp at this point. Let your roaster cycle up and back to this temperature a few times until the bean and EV probes have the same reading. Let it idle for about 15 minutes once it reaches this temperature. Then lower the gas setting and drop to your ideal charge temperature and let it idle there for a further five minutes or so[18].

If you find that your first roast is slower than your usual later batch roast times then let it idle longer at the charge temperature, or for less time if it's too fast. You will work out what's best for your situation after a few goes.

VARIOUS FACTORS THAT WILL INFLUENCE YOUR CHOSEN CHARGE TEMPERATURE WILL NEED TO BE CONSIDERED AS YOU BECOME A MORE ADVANCED AND EXPERIENCED MASTER ROASTER. SOME OF THESE ARE:

- **BATCH SIZE:** If you are doing batch sizes less than your 80% stated capacity you will start at a lower charge temperature.
- **BEAN PROCESSING METHOD:** In general, washed coffees will tolerate a higher charge temperature, naturals slightly lower.
- **BEAN DENSITY:** You will really notice this quickly timewise. Denser beans will require a slightly higher charge temperature.
- **ROAST TIMES:** You may decide that a 13-minute roast is appropriate for a dense washed type of bean and a 15-minute roast for a lower density natural process bean. Batch sizes will also influence this decision. So for a faster and larger roast you will need a higher charge temperature.

Please remember, however, that we're not talking a massive difference in charge temperature here. In most cases I never varied more than 10°C either way myself, with the exception of very light roasts which we will discuss later.

Please note that for later roast batches directly heated drums can get very hot. So a good trick is to charge the green beans when the burners are turned down or the gas modulator is on the downward cycle. We're only talking 5°C–10°C though (so at about 205°C in this case).

Analogue gas pressure guage.

FOOTNOTE

[16] The Charge Temperature is the temperature reading of your bean probe at the moment you release your batch of green beans from the hopper into the drum or roasting chamber.

[17] kPa = Kilopascal is a unit of measurement, in this case of gas pressure. Simply put, the higher the pressure, the higher the gas flow, the stronger the heat. Simples.

[18] Of course this depends on your starting EV temperature. If your roastery is cold on a winter's morning and your EV temperature probe says 10°C before you fire her up, then it will take longer to warm up. Obvious I know, but ...

119

6
THE STAGES OF THE ROAST

OK, so this is where we are. Your 15kg capacity roaster has warmed up, and your bean probe and environmental temperature (EV) probe are both saying 210°C (or whatever your optimal charge temperature is). You have 12kg of green beans in the hopper. Your temperature has just cycled to the 210–215°C mark and it's either on its downward slope or you manually lower your burners to achieve this. As your bean probe temp hits 210°C let the green beans into the roasting chamber.

The first thing you'll notice is that the temperature readings will plummet. The bean temperature probe will drop faster and further than your EV probe does. At this point your roaster will recover to full burner strength if you have a gas modulator; if not, then manually adjust your burners back to maximum power now.

As this is your first roast of the day, the bean temperature should bottom out between 80–90°C and start to climb back up again. Any lower than this and your initial charge temperature may be too low or you did not get the burners back up to maximum power fast enough after letting the green beans into the roasting chamber. Later roasts will bottom out a few degrees higher as the roaster itself takes on more retained heat.

FUN FACT
I once had another master roaster ask why his roasts were taking 20+ mins in a new drum roaster. He had heard of this new technique of dropping his first roast in when the roaster temperature had dropped to below 160°C and was wondering why his roaster took so long to recover. This is not wise – especially with your first roast.

COFFEE BEAN DEVELOPMENT DURING ROAST STAGES

Raw coffee
10-12%
moisture content

Drying phase

Yellowing
(Stage 1)

WHEN I WAS TEACHING MY APPRENTICES HOW TO ROAST COFFEE I WOULD EXPLAIN THE STAGES OF THE ROAST AS SUCH:

➤ The First Boring Bit.
➤ The Middle Bit, maybe it's time to pay attention now …
➤ Getting Serious Stage: The First Crack to completion.
➤ Getting Really Serious Stage: The Second Crack to completion.

Yes, I know there are more technical terms for these stages but I have a weird sense of humour. My point is that as long as you navigate through these stages in the appropriate time then the serious end of business is really from just before the first crack starts.

Despite my humour, making sure that you don't reach the first crack stage too quickly or too slowly is critical to the coffee's development and the final roast/flavour profile you achieve (I will go into what the implications are of not managing this a little later on). You, of course, achieve this by managing the roaster's thermal energy level by adjusting your burners and fan controlled airflow during the roast – your two levers.

Think of it as a balancing act using time-based targets as your guide. Also, try to achieve a smooth roast curve and not a knee-jerky reaction type curve constantly overcompensating with dramatic heat and airflow changes. Think of a person who brakes last minute and then 'guns' (accelerates) his car all the time – don't do that.

Depending on your roaster, you will have to manage this thermal energy adjustment yourself throughout the roast. I cannot recommend one single step-by-step strategy to follow, as every machine is different in terms of power output. Remember you can use your burners or your airflow to speed up or slow down roasts. Traditionally, however, you reduce airflow until the first crack and increase it towards the end of the roast (partly to assist with the venting of the smoke that comes at this stage). Inversely, burners are on high early in the roast and come down later to slow things down.

Yellowing/ Cinnamon (stage II)

First crack

Developing coffee

Developed coffee

Let's quickly look at what's happening to the beans themselves during these early stages of the roast:

At the 3–4-minute mark the coffee will start its Stage 1, the drying phase, steadily dropping its moisture content from its 10–12% starting point. You will notice condensation on the sight glass of your roaster as this moisture is drawn out. This drying process requires a large amount of energy, hence your burners should be set at 100% kPa and your exhaust fan at our worked-out starting point. It is very important to apply maximum energy at this stage. You should see the biggest gap between your bean and EV temperatures at this point as your bean starts to take on heat energy and gain momentum to narrow the gap as we close out the roast.

From about the 6-minute mark the water has been driven out of the beans and the coffee can start to brown. The beans will still be very dense and have an aroma of bread and rice. The browning reaction will continue as the coffee moves towards a cinnamon colour. This Stage 2 yellowing/browning phase will continue in this vein up until about the 10–11-minute mark at which point the first crack phase will occur.

At this point let me reiterate why it's so important to manage these early stages time/temperature wise.

You need to ensure that your roaster has adequate energy to achieve Stages 1 and 2 in good time. You can't compensate by increasing energy at the latter stages of the roast, as what will happen is that you will have an undercooked inside and an overcooked outside of the coffee bean. This will result in a finished product with a burnt bitter outside of the bean and a sour and grassy flavour coming from the underdeveloped inside. Not ideal.

This brings us to Stage 3 – the first crack. This is where the real fun begins and the magic happens. During Stage 2 the production of steam and CO_2 increases pressure in the beans causing them to expand. A couple of minutes before the first crack occurs this expansion causes the silverskin to free from the centre of the bean. Once the pressure gets too great the bean starts to "crack", as fissures form and the familiar popping noise of the first crack occurs as vapour and gases are violently expelled. You will note that the first crack sound is different to that of the second crack – the first crack is louder in volume and slower in tempo.

Think of it as a balancing act using time-based targets as your guide. Also, try to achieve a smooth roast curve and not a knee-jerky reaction type curve constantly overcompensating with dramatic heat and airflow changes. Think of a person who brakes last minute and then 'guns' (accelerates) his car all the time – don't do that.

7

WHY DEVELOPMENT TIME IS EVERYTHING – AND WHY YOU NEED TO UNDERSTAND THIS

Technically we are still working through the stages of the roast but Stage 4, the Roast Development Time, is such an important topic I wanted to highlight it in its own section.

The first crack needs to keep its momentum and should sound vigorous to your ears – especially with harder beans. You do not want it to peter out or be half-hearted. This may happen if your roaster does not have enough energy to keep the momentum going. As you get towards the end of the first crack (it should last for about one minute or so) the bean will now have developed enough internal endothermic heat to carry on with its development until the end of the roast. Up until this point the heat has been externally applied/absorbed (known as exothermic heat).

At this stage you must slow things down. Remember though, that there is a time lag between turning down your burners and increasing the fan speed (remember that these are your two levers to speed up or slow things down) and the bean itself responding. At this point you just want to decelerate but not stop things altogether. So with that reaction time lag in mind, you need to work out when to apply the levers and by how much.

EXPERT TIP

If you are roasting for a classic medium espresso roast you want to have at least a three-minute (or four minutes for a darker roast) Roast Development Time from the start of the first crack to the end of your roast.

I cannot emphasise how important this rule is! If you take nothing else away from this book please just take in this point. As I would tell my guys, these 3–4 minutes of the roast is where the magic happens and you have to concentrate and be on the ball.

So what happens if you stuff it up? Well, go too fast, let's say from first crack to end in 90 seconds or less, your coffee will taste underdeveloped – cooked on the outside and undercooked on the inside – flat and grassy. If you slow things down too much – for example, you have dropped your burners way too early before the first crack – the beans lose their roasting momentum, and your roast curve flatlines or starts to decline. Your usual 13–14 minute roast will become an 18–20 minute roast and, although the outside of the bean may appear to be the correct colour, your inner bean will be overdeveloped (or 'baked' as we call it in the industry).

When the first crack ends, it's time to start using your sampler to check your roast. Each master roaster will have a different approach. I liked to have a sample of the previous roast of this coffee type in a scoop and use it as a colour match guide to help me approximate the moment to drop the coffee.

AS THE COFFEE DEVELOPS AFTER THE FIRST CRACK YOU WILL NOTICE THE FOLLOWING:
➤ The developing beans will initially look mottled and patchy. You are getting distinct coffee smells and the smoke level off the beans is increasing.
➤ A further minute in and the outer surface of the bean will start to become smooth and the aroma will become increasingly more pleasant.
➤ A developed coffee will have a beautiful satin sheen and this is traditionally where I would drop the coffee into the cooling tray.

It's up to you when to drop your coffee. It depends on how light or dark you want to go with your particular roast. Very light roasting needs a slightly different technique, which we will discuss in Part B-10. Firstly though, let's look at going darker with your roast and into the second crack.

Going into Stage 5 – the second crack – is not very fashionable these days. Assuming though, that the inner bean is well developed and that you don't go too far into the second crack, it's not all bad.

Once the second crack starts going it takes off rapidly and, assuming you still have some energy (say 25% kPa) being applied to your roaster, you will have probably about a minute to play with before you need to call the fire department. Don't f#*k around here. You need to sample your beans and make your mind up quickly when to drop them. The depth of the roast will accelerate very rapidly and you'll notice a change in colour every five seconds or so. The cracking will also be very rapid and vigorous – quite a different sound to the first crack. The smoke coming off the roast as you test it and when you drop it will also be spectacular – so be prepared. The beans will look very shiny/oily, although much of this will dissipate as the coffee cools in the tray.

If the bean is properly developed a darker roast can have nice caramelised cut-through in milk-based espresso. The disadvantage is that it will have a much shorter shelf life to sell and, subsequently, for the customer to use it up before the oils resurface and the flavours deteriorate markedly.

Sample testing.

To summarise, I suggest following these five basic roasting rules as a guideline to achieve the optimal development time and consistency:

1 Make sure your coffee roaster is properly heated prior to roasting your first batch and know your ideal charge temperatures for your batch sizes, bean type, etc.

2 Make sure that your roaster has adequate energy at the beginning of the roast to ensure that the drying stage and yellowing/browning stage are completed within an appropriate time (8–10 mins).

3 Ensure that your roaster has adequate energy to take you into the first crack and keep the roast momentum going until reaching the endothermic heat stage.

4 The Rate of Rise (ROR) in bean temperature should constantly rise, but at a decelerating rate as the roast progresses. Beware of the ROR flatlining or declining before the drop time.

5 The Roast Development Time from the start of the first crack to the end of the roast should be approximately 3 minutes. It's a false idea to extend this time longer to compensate for a slow stage.

8
TWO ROAST PROFILES TO GET YOU STARTED

Here are two suggested roasting profiles you can follow to get you started. You can play with these as you wish. These recommended profiles are simply a starting point that should work on most classic single pass drum roasters. Remember, however, that no two roasting machines are identical, for the reasons we have already outlined in this book, so experiment a little. I also want to keep the explanations and graphs simple for you to follow, so I have only plotted the Bean Temperature in Celsius against time elapsed, as these are the most important variables to track when you start roasting.

Profile 1 is better for a less dense bean like a Brazil natural process, roasted to a medium level (Agtron 60). I will explain roast levels and Agtron readings and what they mean shortly. Profile 2 is better for a high-altitude dense washed process bean like a Guatemala SHB or Kenya AA roasted to a full espresso roast level (Agtron 50).

Look now at the roast curve profiles below. The key difference between roast Profile 1 and Profile 2 is *when* we drop the burners and *by how much*. In Profile 1 we drop the burners to around 40–45% kPa about 30 seconds BEFORE the time we estimate that the first crack would occur. The less dense and natural process bean will dry yellow-brown with less energy than the denser/washed process bean, so we can pull it back a little earlier. So in this profile we drop the burners earlier but by a lesser amount, to keep the roast energy level sufficient for the first crack phase and to ensure our 3–4-minute Roast Development Time. We also do not want to rush the roast in either the pre- or post-first crack stages of the roast. We then drop the roast about 30–60 seconds BEFORE the second crack starts.

PROFILE 1: FOR SOFTER BEANS/ NATURAL PROCESS/ MEDIUM ROASTS

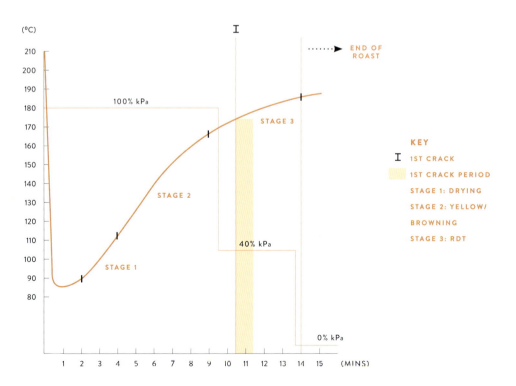

Profile 2 illustrates that after charging the roast we immediately turn up our burners to 100% kPa. We keep it there until about 20–30 seconds AFTER the start of the first crack when we drop the burners to 25–30% kPa. The idea behind this is that we want to build a strong momentum into the first crack, which we need to do to develop the coffee, as we have a denser bean and we want it to be developed both internally and externally. We then decelerate the energy being provided to slow down the roast to ensure an adequate roast development time. Lastly, we drop the burners to zero just before the second crack starts and drop the roast just as the second crack starts. Medium level in-tray cracking will continue after the drop for about another 10–15 seconds until the cooling tray fan does its work and the roasting quickly decelerates.

Remember, you can also speed up your roast or slow it down using your exhaust fan speed. For me, it was always my second lever of control. Remember though, that it can be a pretty blunt instrument prone to over-reaction. You do, however, have to increase your fan speed a tad after the first crack to ensure adequate draw to remove the smoke produced at the end of the roast. This will have the effect of decelerating your roast as well, so keep this in mind when you adjust your burners.

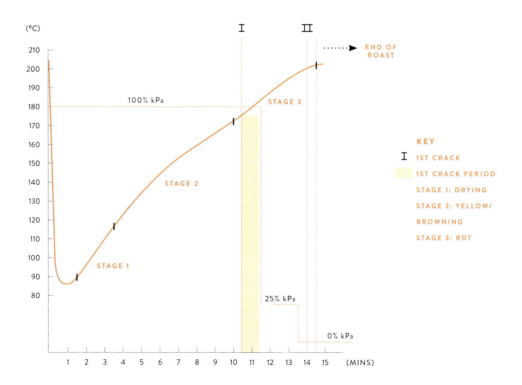

PROFILE 2: FOR HARDER BEANS/ WASHED PROCESS/ DARK ROASTS

9
ROAST LEVELS AND AGTRON READINGS

I'm not a big fan of those old-fashioned roast level terms like City, Full City, Viennese, Italian, French, blah, blah, blah ... Look them up if you like, it's useful to know what they mean. I prefer to use the terms Filter Light, Medium Espresso, Full Espresso and Dark Roast.

How would I describe them?

FILTER LIGHT: Dropped about 1 minute after the end of the first crack. This coffee is very light and is popular with Third Wave coffee roasters. It displays very light, acidic tea-like qualities in its flavour profile and is popular for pour over/filter and cold brewing methods. This roast level shows the bean's natural characteristics clearly, however, these coffees can display grassy flavours if underdeveloped. You can improve the inner bean's development by modifying your roast profile to compensate for this. We will cover this in the next section. **Agtron: 65**

MEDIUM ESPRESSO: Becoming the most common roast level favoured by modern master roasters. Profile 1 will realise this roast level. It is ideal for espresso and most other coffee brewing methods, with a nutty, medium full flavour where the natural characteristics of the bean still come through. **Agtron: 55**

FULL ESPRESSO: The favoured pre-millennium roast level, slightly darker and just into the second crack as per Profile 2. Rich caramelised flavours, good cut through with milk, with dark chocolate bitterness notes. The roast level is starting to influence flavour more here. Fruit turns chocolatey, hints of roasty bitter sweetness emerge. Muted acidity and (sometimes) heavier body. **Agtron: 50**

DARK ROAST: Pretty old-school roast levels – aka Italian or French Roast level in old days. Roast level dominates flavour over origin characteristics now. Bittersweet, scorched-wood roast notes are prominent. Acidity is muted. **Agtron: 40**

STEP 1
Roasted bean sample inserted for analysis.

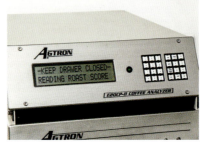

STEP 2
Agtron reader analysing the bean sample.

STEP 3
Result: Agtron 62.7 Gourmet Score.

So what do these Agtron levels actually mean?

Degree of roast can be measured with some precision through the use of a specially modified spectrophotometer popularly called an Agtron reader. The most common is the M-Basic or "Gourmet" Agtron scale, and for each coffee measured the readings are presented both of the whole beans before grinding (the number preceding the slash) and the same beans after grinding (the number after the slash).

For example, a reading of 55/68 would describe a coffee with an external, whole-bean M-Basic reading of 55, and a ground reading of 68. Agtron readings range from the lightest, around 70 whole-bean and 95 ground, to 25 whole-bean and 30 ground (very dark; essentially burned, although some coffee drinkers without taste buds actually like the style).

The table overleaf can be used as a general guide to describe different roast levels. The number used reflects an average of the two values indicated for each coffee, whole-bean and ground. Thus a coffee with a whole-bean reading of 50 and a ground reading of 60 would land at 55 ("Medium") in the table.

The Agtron reading is a great indicator of the inner and outer bean development of your coffee. A wide discrepancy between whole-bean and ground readings can indicate an issue with bean development. In general, the darker the roast, the narrower the gap in whole-bean and ground Agtron readings, while lighter roasts tend to show a wider range. You should not take roast colour measurements into consideration when undertaking sensory assessment of coffee. Take Agtron readings into consideration only after your sensory evaluation process of the coffee is complete. This added information often corroborates the characteristics you notice in the cup. For example, a narrow delta on a light roast may explain the limited aromatic range of the coffee you may identify in cupping.

EXPERT TIP

I roasted most of my coffees from a medium to full espresso range. This is the sweet spot in the overall consumer popularity stakes. Stick to that and you'll play it safe. Having said that though, there are times when you may want to delve into the light roast coffees when you want to showcase a special origin coffee as a filter or cold brew in your roastery/café.

The following table is adapted from various sources and from my own readings. Published Agtron roast level tables like this can vary wildly in range so don't place too much emphasis on them.

ROAST	AGTRON	CHARACTERISTICS
Light	> 70	Stage: Just as first crack completes Light brown to cinnamon colour Lightish body, sometimes muted aroma, tea-like flavour No oil on surface of bean
Medium–Light	61–70	Stage: Between 1–2 minutes after the end of the first crack Moderately light brown colour Bright, sweet acidity, green coffee distinctions clear Surface of bean remains dry
Medium	51–60	Stage: At least 30 seconds before the start of the second crack Medium brown colour Balanced acidity, fuller body, green coffee origin characteristics still apparent Generally dry bean surface
Full Espresso	41–50	Stage: Second crack just about to start Some gentle cracking in the cooling tray Rich brown colour Muted acidity, sometimes heavier body Fruit notes turn chocolatey, hints of roasted bitter sweetness emerge Droplets of oil may appear on the bean surface
Dark	35–40	Stage: Second crack is about 25% complete Deep brownish/black colour Bittersweet, scorched-wood roast notes are prominent Acidity muted Spots of oil to shiny surface
Very Dark	25–34	Stage: Second crack is at least 50% complete Bitter/bittersweet tones dominate Body thins, green coffee distinctions are fully muted Black surface covered brightly with oil Don't go there …

10 ROASTING TECHNIQUES FOR ACHIEVING WELL-DEVELOPED LIGHT ROAST COFFEES

When this fashion took off a few years back a lot of master roasters had to figure out how to roast so light without producing a horribly underdeveloped coffee for their customers. Many failed. Grassy, acidic espresso coffees were served up everywhere. The hipsters grimaced and smiled as the battery acid-like brew slid "effortlessly" down their throats. "Oh, this is amazing!" they exclaimed as their throats collectively burned.

Two points here. This is a coffee that's been roasted barely beyond the first crack – sometimes during. The acidity will invariably be high no matter what you do. The espresso brewing method highlights acidity. Slowly brewed filter and cold brew techniques will dampen this acidity, but also highlight the coffee's delicate tea-like flavours. Always consider what brewing technique you are roasting for.

The second point is that you can't roast these coffees using the same roast profiles as you would for medium or full espresso roast coffees and simply drop them way earlier. You need to modify your roast profile to give the inner bean sufficient time to adequately develop.

Although I do not claim by any means to be an expert on this type of roast profile, I found success in improving the development of very lightly roasted coffees by slowing down the rate of rise of the bean temperature during the Stage 2 yellowing/browning stage and then ramping up the rate of rise again about 10°C out from the first crack. This meant the beans still had good momentum during the first crack point and yet had a more advanced development of the inner bean as well. Allowing the inner bean to develop a little longer reduces the issues of the overtly acidic and grassy flavours associated with the underdeveloped inner bean.

PROFILE 3: A LIGHT ROAST COFFEE PROFILE

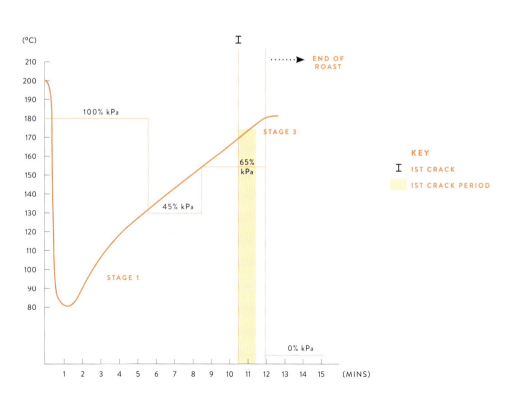

11
THE IMPORTANCE OF COOLING YOUR ROAST FAST

So now we are about to drop our roast and complete the process. In the last minutes of your roast the coffee beans have developed so much endothermic heat that the heat supplied by your roaster isn't really contributing a great deal to the process any longer. So it's important that you cool the coffee very rapidly once you end your roast and drop the beans into your cooling tray.

Modern roasters have dedicated powerful cooling tray fans that draw the heat out of the coffee beans very quickly. They tend to have deep trays with hundreds of precision cut holes, cut out of a heavy stainless steel base plate, designed to efficiently draw heat out rapidly of the smokin' hot coffee beans. Stirring arms with strategically placed brushes keep the coffee beans moving uniformly to prevent scorching while cooling. The arms and brushes are also designed to efficiently push the cooled beans out of the tray and into your storage container or de-stoner once the beans have sufficiently cooled.

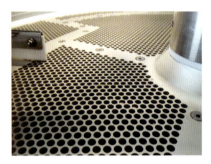

Precision-perforated stainless steel cooling tray for cooling roasted coffee.

So I'm going to give you a couple of important practical roasting tips here.

Firstly, be prepared. About 30 seconds before you expect to drop the roast, turn on the cooling tray mechanism (the fan and stirring arms will start) so that it's going BEFORE you drop your roast. Secondly, if you are sample batch testing your roasting coffee by colour as an indicator (of when to drop your roast), get into the habit of dropping the roast about 10 or so seconds prior to the shade you are actually after, as the beans will continue to cook for about another 10–20 seconds after you drop them into the cooling tray.

Remember that the fan draws ambient air from the room and through the beans (another reason to ensure your roasting room ambient temperature is not too hot) and sends the extracted hot air out through the flue. Once the initial heat is out (after about one minute) an old trick is to stop the turning arms (but keep the fan on) and let it draw air through the still beans before turning on your stirring arms again. It really helps the beans cool rapidly. Ideally your beans should be cool to touch within 2–3 minutes.

Some old-school master roasters back when I started would quench the beans with a spray mist of water. This was done to compensate for older style single fan motor shop roasters that did not cool efficiently and also some silly idea about putting some weight back into the beans on dark roasts. Don't do this, there is no need.

Just-roasted coffee being rapidly cooled.

12
WHAT TO DO IN BETWEEN ROASTS – BEING PREPARED

At the beginning of this section we spoke about the importance of warming up your coffee roaster prior to your first batch of the day and the challenges this presents. Equally you need to ensure that your roaster does not lose too much heat in between roasts or, conversely, overheat in between roasts.

Consistency of roast batches is the bane of inexperienced master roasters. Making sure your roaster maintains a good consistent charging temperature for each roast is critical in achieving a level of roast batch consistency.

Another factor is energy usage. If you can manage your in-between roast temperature within your coffee roaster, you will ultimately save energy by not having to heat up a cooling coffee roaster between batches.

It's important to be prepared. Try these pre- and during roast routines between coffee batches.

1 Ensure your coffee roaster is clean and ready to go before you fire her up for the day.

2 Weigh out your green coffee batches for the day's roasting and line them up near your roaster in order. Do the softer bean types first and the denser/harder ones later in the day's roast schedule. If you have to roast any smaller batches than your normal batch size, do them first.

3 Have clean roasted coffee pails ready to go near your roaster.

4 Just before you drop your finished batch, turn on your cooling tray fan motor and stirrer and drop your gas flow kPa to zero.

5 A minute into the cooling phase turn your gas burners back up (if you have just done a dark batch of coffee or your roaster is hotter than normal, wait a little longer) so that your coffee roaster is ready to cycle back up to your ideal charge temperature (about one minute) and idle there for another minute before charging your next batch of coffee.

6 Adapt these tips to fit your particular circumstances – your particular type of roaster, the roasting room environment, for the type of coffee you roast and so on.

It's all about being organised.

13
SOME EXTRA TIPS ON ACHIEVING ROAST CONSISTENCY

Many factors can impact roast consistency. A lot of it, as we have already touched on, comes down to being focused while you are roasting and being organised between batches. There are, however, some other factors you may not have considered. Let's briefly look at a few of these.

Let's start with your green beans. Especially with your blends, try to be consistent with the green coffee you purchase. If your blend relies on a specific coffee type – say it's a honey process natural from a particular region of Costa Rica – you can't keep changing that bean regularly. It will make your life difficult in achieving roast and blend consistency. Some green bean suppliers will hold stock back for bigger clients or try to offload older (yellowing) beans to you. You will soon work this out with experience. If they do try some of these old tricks on you, then maybe it's time to talk to another supplier. You can lock in volume contracts with your supplier to ensure consistent supply. So try to be consistent with your green bean inputs.

Green bean storage is another factor. As an artisan roaster, you should only really need to carry a maximum of two weeks' stock. In any case, make sure that your storage room is as temperature- and humidity-stable as possible, and try to buy as much product as you can in modern GrainPro bags or vacuum-sealed packs. You will recall from Part B-1 of this book that the old style hessian/burlap bags are not ideal. If you live in an area with either very high or very low humidity and extreme temperature ranges, then consider rigging up a climate-controlled room to store your green coffee in.

As already mentioned, the ambient temperature of your roasting room can impact how your coffee roaster heats/cools and recovers. Colder external temperatures can increase the natural draw of your flue. For your own personal comfort too, I strongly encourage that you work in a climate-controlled roasting room. The benefits will flow onto your roasting process and consistency as well.

The cleanliness of your roaster and flues/chimney will also impact your roaster's draw and airflow. It's important you keep your roaster and flues clean and avoid build-up over time as this will dramatically impact your batch roasting consistency and can also pose a serious fire hazard. We will cover this serious topic in detail in Part B-3 of this book.

14

DE-STONING YOUR COFFEE – THE LAST STEP

> "Sticks and stones ... will break your grinders, and really annoy your customers."
> AUTHOR UNKNOWN

Most retail-based artisan coffee roasters do not start out with a de-stoner. De-stoners take up room, make a lot of noise when they operate and are just another capital expense. Can I just dispel some of these objections?

Firstly, yes they do have a relatively large footprint but de-stoners designed for retail use are far more compact and are usually built with heavy-duty castor wheels, allowing you to wheel them in and out as you need. You also do not have to immediately de-stone your coffee straight from the cooling tray as larger industrial coffee roasters do. You can store your de-stoner out the back and do you de-stoning post-roasting.

This brings me to the noise. It's basically a glorified vacuum cleaner, and we know what they sound like, so simply do it out the back as just mentioned or do it after hours if you have to. Each 10kg batch will only take a few minutes to de-stone.

Lastly, in the scheme of things they are not that expensive. Compared to the cost of repairing your grinders and that of your customers/clients you will be back in the black before long, I promise you. A typical retail de-stoner will set you back about AU$5,000.

As you sell roasted coffee to home users remember that their grinders will be fairly basic and will break quite easily. Before we purchased our de-stoner we had a particularly messy batch of PNG that came through. Not only did the stones jam our commercial grinders, we also had a couple of angry retail customers come back complaining that their $200 grinder was rooted. Having sweet-talked my way out of that one, I quickly took measures to fix the source of the problem.

A de-stoner will not pick up iron nails or metal. So a great simple solution is to buy an industrial magnet and place it in your coffee roaster's green been hopper/shute. Every few weeks I guarantee that you'll be picking off nails, metal shavings, and paper clips – you name it!

So yeah, do yourself a favour and buy yourself a de-stoner (and a magnet).

15
'THE LAST ROAST OF THE DAY' PROCEDURE

After your last roast of the day, drop your roast, turn off your roaster's gas flow and your afterburner. Complete cooling your roast and remove it from the tray. Turn off your cooling tray but let your roasting fan continue to run to gradually cool down your coffee roaster. I had my roaster hooked up with a 20-minute automated cool-down cycle that would power the roaster down once the cool-down cycle was complete.

After the roaster has cooled, you may want to then clean out the chaff collector, clear the cooling tray vent holes and do your other cleaning routines. Generally though, I would do these chores the next morning once the roaster was cold to avoid accidental burns on the still-hot roaster's outer surfaces.

So there you have it. A basic rundown on roasting your first batches of coffee in-house. May the coffee lords watch over you!

WTF is this?
A 50:50 mix,
so I'm told ...

FUN FACT
Mierda Loca! Torrefacto Roasting: What NOT to do!

I've been roasting coffee for 20 years in Australia and I had never heard of the torrefacto method of coffee roasting – to say I was horrified when I read what it was is an understatement!

Torrefacto is the odd practice of adding sugar at the final stage of the roasting process (in fact these specially made coffee roasters have a unique compartment/shute for this very purpose). It's not a small amount of sugar, either – typically, it makes up 20% of the weight of the coffee. The late stages of roasting are typically the hottest and so, rather than adding sweetness, the sugar burns and coats the beans in a shiny, black film. This coating slows down oxidation, preserving the roasted coffee for longer. Torrefacto beans produce a thick, dark crema and a bitter taste. Some people claim the process creates a sweeter aroma or even a sweeter coffee, but really, it's just about preservation. Rather than enhancing the flavours, it masks them in a coating that's likely to go rancid.

Despite the startlingly adverse effects it has on flavour, torrefacto is still common in countries such as Spain, France, Argentina, Portugal, Costa Rica, Bolivia and some parts of Mexico. In Spain, supermarkets sell a 50/50 torrefacto and regular coffee bean mix. Hotels often serve it too, at a 70/30 ratio of normal/torrefacto. You'll get a slightly better cup, but it still tastes terrible.

To understand torrefacto's omnipresence, we need to go back to the Spanish Civil War. Spain suffered from a lack of basic goods and services – including coffee. Torrefacto seemed like the perfect solution: it would last longer, you could use fewer and lower-quality beans, and on top of that, the added sugar increased the roast's volume without really increasing the cost. As torrefacto became the standard, consumers came to expect its dark, oily appearance and flavour.

Mierda loca indeed! Please don't EVER try this at home or in your coffee roaster.

B3

QUALITY CONTROL AND IMPLEMENTATION

If you were to ask me for the number one reason coffee businesses fail, I'd say it's because of a lack of a consistently implemented and clearly defined quality control system. The following section gives an overview of a basic quality control system that everyone can implement and follow.

IN PART B-3 WE WILL COVER:

1. SAMPLE ROASTING – A DIFFERENT ROASTING TECHNIQUE/ART
2. CUPPING AND SENSORY EVALUATION OF YOUR ROAST BATCHES
3. FIXING COMMON ROAST FAULTS
4. PACKING AND STORAGE OF YOUR ROASTED COFFEE

1
SAMPLE ROASTING – A DIFFERENT ROASTING TECHNIQUE/ART

Sample roasting on a 2-barrel Probat BRZ.

Completing the sample roast.

Yang-Chia Mini500 sample roaster.

Now the first question you're probably going to ask me is, "Do I have to invest even more money in my new roastery and buy a sample roaster as well? Do I really need one to start off with?"

Hmmm, I'd say yes, for the following simple reason. Sample roasting, more so than production roasting, is a sensory art form. It will help you become a better production master roaster simply because it's still quite a manual process, and even the most modern sample roasting machines lack accuracy in their data readings. You will learn to roast coffee with your senses and then be able to make better use of the data-reading gadgets that will be at your disposal on your production roaster when you get there.

Another point is that you should probably purchase a sample roaster to learn how to roast coffee at home before you move on to production scale roasting. Using this logic you would then just bring the sample roaster with you when you open your roastery/café!

Besides learning your craft, why do we use sample roasters in our business? Firstly, they can be used to assess green coffee bean samples prior to purchase from our green bean suppliers. Secondly, we can use a sample roaster to develop our roast profiles prior to starting production batches.

Older sample roasters were extremely simple contraptions, usually just with a gas control knob and a very dodgy analogue environmental temperature probe. Old-school master roasters would pump out six-minute roasts in these multi-barrel babies. They could produce underdeveloped coffees that really did not do the green bean justice in roasted sample evaluation unless you knew what you were doing.

Newer sample roasters, such as the Yang-Chia 500g roaster (shown left at bottom), have airflow control as well as gas flow controls and some have digital environmental and bean probes. They can even be hooked up to modern data-logging software packages as well. Beware though, the small sample size can make it difficult for the bean probe to display an accurate temperature reading and will, therefore, affect your data-logged roast profile. So I recommend that you train yourself in the sensory method that I'm about to describe and use the modern sample roaster features to assist you to put it all together. Newer machines with more control can produce 11–13-minute roast times as well, thereby replicating production machines more closely.

So here is a simple sensory method sample roasting timeline for you to follow to get started. This assumes you are roasting to medium roast level of Agtron 60. Follow the same roasting protocols you learned in this section regarding heating your roaster, controlling your roast through gas burner and airflow controls and the cooling/in between batch protocols.

I encourage you to use paper-based sample roast logs to monitor and evaluate your sample roasts, especially when you are in your learning phase. You can download a free pdf sample roast log from my website, www.theartisanroaster.com. Plotting the roast stages you identify through sensory means and plotting it all manually on a time-based data-logging sheet will really help you understand the development of the roast. The sensory connection you make by handwriting the data is critical in making it all fit together in your mind.

This is the art of roasting. Remember that while the science is also critical, it's the combination and understanding of these two approaches and how they interact that will make you an excellent master roaster in time.

SENSORY METHOD SAMPLE ROASTING

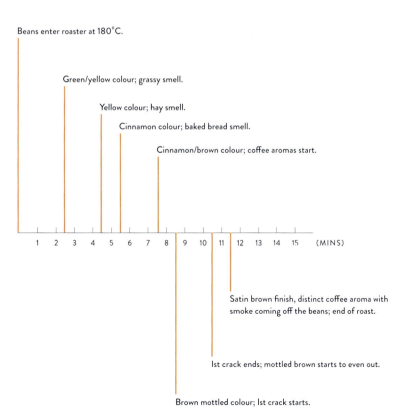

- Beans enter roaster at 180°C.
- Green/yellow colour; grassy smell.
- Yellow colour; hay smell.
- Cinnamon colour; baked bread smell.
- Cinnamon/brown colour; coffee aromas start.
- Brown mottled colour; 1st crack starts.
- 1st crack ends; mottled brown starts to even out.
- Satin brown finish, distinct coffee aroma with smoke coming off the beans; end of roast.

2
CUPPING AND SENSORY EVALUATION OF YOUR COFFEE ROAST BATCHES

So many artisan roasters do not cup their coffee batches regularly or even keep detailed notes to track variations. They may do it when they first start working in coffee, but a combination of time constraints, experience, and the day-to-day issues of running a business get in the way of making it a regular habit. However, just as regular exercise is important to your personal health, regular systematic cupping of your coffee batches is vital for your coffee business's health.

So what is cupping? Well, it's a wanky coffee term for taste-testing your coffee in a systematic way. Part ritual, it follows a brewing and tasting procedure that I will outline in a moment. It takes a while to get the hang of it and get it right but it's worthwhile learning and doing it properly.

Of course, it's also very important to test/drink your coffees brewed as your customers do (be it a plunger, espresso, filter or cold brew coffee) and do this regularly. If you are sampling single origin coffees or new green coffee batches available to you, traditional cupping is by far the best way to identify faults, certain characteristics and maybe find that next Geisha micro-lot!

First of all, you have to have a clear purpose for your cupping session. What is your objective, what are you trying to identify – are you testing roasted green bean samples for evaluation of a new purchase, are you testing for faults, are you comparing batches of the same coffee you roasted last week or month, or are you simply trying to learn more? For example, understanding the different origins (Kenya v. Brazil), different processing methods (washed v. naturals), understanding acidity, body, sweetness characteristics? Build your tasting table and methodology around your objectives. Then you can start cupping ...

So let's do this step-by-step with pictures!

STEP 1
Roast your single origin coffee ideally to a light-medium roast level (Agtron 60-65).

STEP 2
Set up your cupping table with a sample of the green bean, a sample of the roasted bean batch and 2 x 210–260ml wide-mouth coffee sampling cups side by side to test for sample variations.

STEP 3
Using a medium grind setting, grind 10g of the coffee into each tasting cup.

STEP 4
Boil clean filtered water in a kettle, and allow to cool to approximately 96°C before pouring into the cups.

STEP 7
Now the ritual starts. If you have a guest, they are normally offered the chance to "break the crust" in the same order as they were poured. You do this using two tasting spoons crossed over and pushing the crust to the edge of the cup. Make sure as you do this that you bend down low, with your nose almost in the cup, and take a long, slow sniff of the aroma as the crust is broken. Make a note of the aromatics you can identify. Remove the crust and foam into a dregs cup.

STEP 8
Try to now taste each cup in succession and at different temperatures. You will be amazed at the differences. Taste different cups of the same batch for variation and also compare between batches/coffees if that is your plan for this session. Taste the coffee by scooping up a spoon of the liquid and slurping so you cover your tongue and mouth, then spit out into your spittoon! The flavours slowly burst through your mouth and your senses activate.

STEP 9
Write down notes and identify everything you taste/sense. Using a cupping guide worksheet really helps when you are a novice taster. It will have a list of keywords under the different categories for you to circle and scale.

STEP 10
Clean your tasting spoon in fresh water between each tasting cup, especially if you taste a table with other germy people.

STEP 5
Pour 170ml into each cup in a slow swirling motion. You can use a gram scale to measure this accurately.

STEP 6
Pour the other cups in quick succession. Allow coffee to "crust" and sit for about 4–5 minutes.

STEP 11
Repeat every 5–10 minutes until coffees have cooled to room temperature. Take more notes and compare.

STEP 12
File your notes in a logical system to allow for future reference and comparison.

Some additional thoughts on cupping protocols:

1 Avoid sampling more than six coffee types in one session until you have more cupping/coffee tasting experience.

2 Try to cup blind occasionally, especially if you are trying to learn about origins, processes etc., or are evaluating new green beans.

3 Beware of taster fatigue. If everything is starting to taste the same, then have a break.

4 Be rigorous about creating a fair comparison. Be meticulous with your measurements, pours and methodology. Treat it like a serious science experiment and make sure all coffee samples are treated identically.

5 Make sure you take in coffee aroma, both wet and dry. If you have trouble identifying aroma, I highly recommend Le Nez Du Café – a system that trains you to identify common coffee aromas[19].

6 Use the results as a way to learn and grow. Identify faults in your roasts and how to repair them. For example, a baked flavour in the coffee tells you that your bean temperature rate of rise has declined too quickly towards the end of your roast and you need to apply more energy beforehand (or decrease less) to ensure a steadier rate of decline. This topic is explored next.

FOOTNOTE
[19] www.lenez.com/en/kits/coffee/revelation

3 FIXING COMMON ROAST FAULTS

Based on the cupping regime of your roasted batch samples, you may identify some problems with your roasts from time to time. Here are some common roasting faults and how you can fix them.

GRASSY FLAVOURS = UNDERDEVELOPED COFFEE. Steepen the early stages of the roast curve by using more gas in the early stages of the roast, or try charging your beans at a higher starting temperature.

BAKED POTATO, CEREAL FLAVOURS = OVERDEVELOPED OR BAKED COFFEE. Check when you decreased your gas kPa and by how much. If the rate of rise of the roasting coffee has fallen or flatlined you have probably decreased your energy levels too early or by too much. Maybe you increased your fan speed too early or by too much – check.

CHARRED COFFEE = OVERHEATED DRUM BARREL. Check your total roast times. If too fast (say 10 minutes) consider lowering your gas settings and let your roaster cool for longer between roasts.

SMOKY = AIRFLOW ISSUES. INCREASE FAN SPEED IN LAST THIRD OF THE ROAST. Check that your roaster/flues are clean of build-up. Check/test airflow using draw paper test.

BITTER/ACRID/CARBON = OVERROASTED. Roast to a lighter level. Avoid roasting beyond 20 seconds into the second crack.

4 PACKING AND STORAGE OF YOUR ROASTED COFFEE

The roasting process creates gas and pressure within the bean, causing the gas to be released slowly. This initial pressure from roasting also stops significant amounts of oxygen entering the bean, which causes oxidation and resultant flavour loss and staleness. The darker the roast the more bean pressure and gas is produced. Darker roasts also degas more quickly than lighter roasts, reducing their shelf lives.

So you have to be practical and get real here. A well-respected coffee book I read recently recommended that you use nitrogen-flushed, pressurised containers to store your beans as the nitrogen prevents oxidation and the pressurised container prevents degassing. Really? What small roaster could do that in reality? Heck, I've been to some pretty big roast facilities that don't do that! Yes, in theory and in the perfect world you could do that, but in reality, no.

Nothing beats turning over your roasted coffee stock quickly. Sell what you roast within seven days – especially in the retail, take-home situation. I elaborate more on this topic in Part C of the book.

After roasting I would store the 10kg batches of roasted coffee in airtight Rubbermaid Brute containers and let them air overnight to degas. I would then put small amounts of the coffee into our display bins for fast retail sale or pack them into 1kg one-way valve bags.

One-way valve bags have quickly become the standard in the specialty coffee industry. It is not the perfect solution, but it allows you to pack your coffee fresh from the roaster without having to flush the bags with nitrogen. The idea is that the one-way valve allows the CO_2 gas to escape while preventing oxidising O_2 from entering. That's the theory, but the one-way valve technology is not perfect – so still make sure the roasted coffee gets sold/used within a few weeks of packing.

Good storage and packaging practices will ensure your customers receive their coffee at peak freshness.

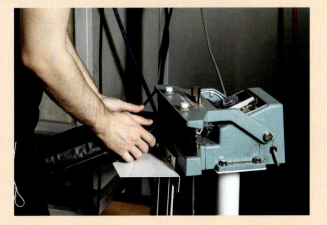

Clockwise from top: One-way valve coffee bags; Freshly roasted beans in a 10kg pail; Sealing your bags; Don't ask ...

B4

SINGLE ORIGIN ROASTS AND BLENDING COFFEE

Enjoying the beautiful characteristics that single origin coffees reveal is a joy. To be able to skillfully blend them and create something new is an art form.

IN PART B-4 WE WILL COVER:

1. SINGLE ORIGIN COFFEE V. BLENDED COFFEE
2. THE JOY AND ART OF COFFEE BLENDING – A DELICATE BALANCING ACT
3. PUTTING TOGETHER YOUR FIRST COFFEE BLENDS
4. SOME COFFEE BLEND RECIPES TO GET YOU STARTED
5. WHAT IS DECAFFEINATED COFFEE? THE PROCESS AND HOW TO ROAST IT

1
SINGLE ORIGIN COFFEE V. BLENDED COFFEE

In reality, there is no "versus" in this discussion. Both are beautiful things to appreciate and behold. After all, you can't have a blend without the single origins that make it up! As any chef or good cook will tell you, it's important to understand your ingredients and the flavours, textures and nuances and how they contribute to the final dish. It's simply a recipe at the end of the day. So getting to know your single origins and their flavour characteristics, what roast levels bring out their best features, and how they interact with other components, like milk in espresso coffee and so on, is essential.

Part B-1 covered coffee origins and gave you a broad overview of the typical flavour characteristics of the different origins. We also covered what impact farm processing has on a coffee bean's flavour and how you should roast it. A single origin coffee is strictly defined as coming from (surprise, surprise) a single known point of geographic origin.

A SINGLE ORIGIN COFFEE CAN BE DEFINED AS:
➤ Coffee entirely from one farm.
➤ Coffee from multiple farms in the same general area.
➤ Coffee from multiple farms in the same country.

Estate coffees are a specific type of single-origin coffee. They are generally grown on a single farm, which might range in size from a few acres to large plantations occupying many square kilometres, or a collection of farms which all process their coffee at the same mill. Micro-lot coffees are another type of specific single origin coffee from a single field on a farm, a small range of altitudes, or a specific time of harvest.

My point here is that you should continually taste/cup various single origin coffees, make notes and learn how they might contribute to any blend you create in terms of body, acidity, sweetness, cut-through and aftertaste. Roast your coffee samples to no more than a light/medium roast level so you can taste the characteristics of the origin itself and not be overwhelmed by the contribution of the roast level itself.

Once you understand your single origins you can start, like a chef, to create your own recipes or blends, and this is what we will explore next.

2
THE JOY AND ART OF COFFEE BLENDING – A DELICATE BALANCING ACT

Who remembers the Mocha Java blend? Probably you first heard the term in a Nescafé® television advertisement way back in the 1970s or 80s. Well, this coffee blend, made up of (usually very dark roasted) coffees from Yemen and the Indonesian island of Java, reportedly dates back to the 17th Century.

Very much in the way winemakers blend grapes to come up with a wine blend, we blend coffee beans from different origins, at varying roast levels, in different ratios, to create our own unique blends. Now this is where the fun begins, my dear fellow master roasters! This is where you can express yourself, and put your brand's signature coffee out there on the world (or suburban) stage!

You will learn a lot from experimentation and let me give you a tip straight up. TAKE NOTES! Take notes about how you roasted each coffee that became part of your blend. Take notes about the various ratio percentages you have tried of the various input coffees. It's easy to forget what went into that perfect blend if you haven't kept detailed notes, especially if it has been an evolutionary process.

In a retail roastery/café I believe you need at least three successful ongoing coffee blends in your business. It's important that these blends are good "all-rounders" suitable for espresso and other popular home brewing methods like filter, AeroPress and French Press (plunger).

So what are some of the advantages of creating coffee blends? You'll find that most high-volume espresso coffees on the market are blends. The main reason is for the quality and consistency of flavour throughout the harvest year. Customers get used to a particular coffee flavour and don't really care about seasonality.

Creating a blend where the ingredients and the ratios can be adjusted as needed during the year can allow you to keep the coffee stable and vibrant without diverting too far from its essential character, thus maintaining the consistency of your product. This is a REALLY important factor when you supply to the wholesale café market. That said though, you will find that your own customers in your roastery/café will fall in love with your "house blend" and be reluctant to let you change it too often. In my roastery/café the roasted coffee bean offering to "take home" was always a 50:50 split of single origin coffees to blended coffees.

The other reason we blend coffee is to create a coffee flavour profile you simply can't achieve from one single origin coffee itself. Some coffees complement each other really well (and some don't). Some coffees will provide the acidity for cut-through in milk-based coffees, others the body, others a fruity sweetness. It's a beautiful balancing act of flavours and mouthfeel. As you can see, I love the art of blending, even though it's somewhat less fashionable these days.

A signature blend will define your coffee company, its name and reputation, so choose your coffees wisely when creating it! To be honest though, it will probably happen by chance. You'll create a few blends and try them out in your café and the one that everyone loves will usually become your house blend by default. This happened with our Bay Roast signature house blend. It was never my personal favourite, but it was universally loved by our café customers, our take-home roasted coffee customers and, later on, by our wholesale café customers. The recipe itself evolved over the years, so much so that it was a completely different coffee blend from when it started. This happened to cater for changing coffees, changing tastes and the constant desire to improve on a good thing. If you do it in increments and avoid major changes your audience will come along with you,

THE ART OF BLENDING COFFEE

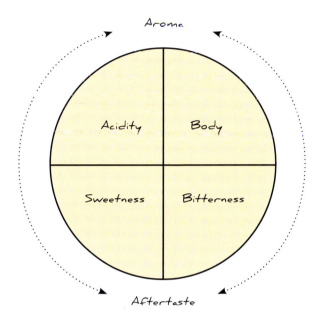

The idea of having proprietary signature blends[20] goes against the modern coffee trend, where punters want to know the origins and the ratios used in the coffee they are drinking. My advice is to share the origins but keep your ratios close to your chest – a happy compromise.

to use a musical analogy. Twenty-odd years later it's still going strong – and I'm very proud of that.

Blends can be long-term (like your signature or house blend) or seasonal. I had great fun each year coming out with seasonal blends – either based on coffees that were at peak season at the time or festival seasons such as Christmas – such as our annual favourite known as Bad Santa after the movie by the same name. People loved the limited run appeal of the concept!

Coffees can be "blended" at many stages and for many reasons. Farms may blend different varietals at origin for both flavour profile and economic reasons to hit a certain price point. Pretty much the same reasons we blend roasted coffees as well.

The blending of roasted coffees can also occur for price point economic reasons and it's certainly very relevant in the wholesale coffee market to target certain market segments. However, in the specialty trade the focus should always be on producing a high quality finished product over price point. One thing you must never do as a specialty roaster is to try to mask a cheap or deteriorating coffee with other coffees to "pep it up". It's a false economy that will catch up with you.

The next argument in the blending world is: do you pre-blend or post-blend? First of all let me explain the difference. With pre-blends we blend the various green beans PRIOR to roasting. Post-blending is where we roast the various blend input coffees individually and then blend them AFTER roasting. There are pros and cons to both styles. The most popular method is to post-blend.

FOOTNOTE
[20] Intellectual property (IP) is the property of your mind or proprietary knowledge. It is a productive new idea you create. This can be an invention, trademark, design, brand or even the application of your idea. https://bit.ly/2KOncNI

ADVANTAGES OF POST-BLENDING ARE:

1. You can roast each bean type to its optimal roast level considering its moisture content, density and processing method.
2. You can cup them individually at different roast profiles in order to assert what they will individually contribute flavour-wise to your overall blend.
3. You can more easily identify problems or variations in future batches of your blend by isolating problem origin inputs and you can keep better QA tracking notes.

DISADVANTAGES ARE:

1. It's a lot more manual work – about three 15-minute roasts on average, plus the blending time.
2. You will use more fuel (gas/power) and labour to produce the coffee.
3. You need to be able to sell the leftover input single origin coffees (as some may only contribute as low as 10% of your finished blend volume) to avoid wastage.

Pre-blending coffee tips:

Obviously the advantages and disadvantages of pre-blending coffee will be the inverse of the above. I have, however, had success with both methods and the labour-saving element and the input leftover issues can actually be quite a big deal when you're starting out.

SO HERE ARE SOME TIPS I FOUND HELPED IF YOU DECIDE TO PRE-BLEND SOME OF YOUR COFFEES PRIOR TO ROASTING:

➤ Try to use beans with a similar moisture content.
➤ Try to use beans of a similar size and density.
➤ Try to use beans that will tolerate a similar level of roast depth to achieve their optimal flavour contributions.

EXPERT TIP

My tip to novice master roasters, if still new to blending coffee, would be to post-blend. You will learn a great deal more about the process and the art of blending. You will also have more control over your finished product through more detailed and accurate QA note-taking protocols and analysis.

3
PUTTING TOGETHER YOUR FIRST COFFEE BLENDS

I suggest the following 6-step process when creating a coffee blend:

1. Define your new coffee blend's target market, brewing methods, flavour profile and roast degree.
2. Select your coffee origins based on all of the above criteria.
3. Roast these origins (if post-blending) to their optimal roast levels to achieve their best flavour profiles as single origin roasts. Choose a roast level for mass appeal. I always roasted medium-to-full for my blends. Never too light or too dark.
4. Post-blend your individually roasted single origin coffees to varying ratios to create various blend variations.
5. Cup and evaluate using different brewing methods (eg: filter, espresso, etc.). Take notes and repeat at different ages (1 day – 3 days – 5 days – 7 days, etc., from roast date).
6. Repeat process if unsuccessful with different origin coffees or ratios.

4 SOME COFFEE BLEND RECIPES TO GET YOU STARTED

Here are some coffee blends that I am happy to share with you.
Use them as a base to start with and create your own from there.

ALL-ROUNDER ESPRESSO BLEND

A good all-rounder for milk-based and black espresso-based coffees.

Guatemala Ceylan SHB Washed	50% Roasted to Full Roast
Sumatra Mandheling Grade 1 Washed	20% Roasted to a Medium Roast
Colombia Supremo Popayan Washed	30% Roasted to a Medium Roast

SLIGHTLY MORE CHALLENGING BLEND

Displaying more complex flavours in the cup. Body of the Limu with the sweet Brazil and lemony citrus of the Kimel.

Ethiopia Limu Gr 2 Washed	30% Roasted to a Full Roast
Brazil Daterra Sunrise Pulped Natural	50% Roasted to a Medium Roast
PNG Kimel X Washed	20% Roasted to a Medium Roast

TWO-BEAN EXOTIC BLEND

Sweet, bold and fruity Nicaragua combined with the delicate acidity of berries and dark chocolate from the Kenya Lena. Be careful not to overroast the Lena!

Kenya AB Lena Washed	50% Roasted to a Medium Roast
Nicaragua La Bastilla Santa Luz Washed	50% Roasted to a Medium Roast

These blend recipes are, of course, only suggestions for you to get started. Do your own thing. Don't be afraid to experiment. If it's awful, at least you learn from it! Believe me, you will NEVER stop learning in this business. And if you do stop learning it might be time to do something else …

5

WHAT IS DECAFFEINATED COFFEE? THE PROCESS AND HOW TO ROAST IT

One of the great mysteries of the coffee business is the decaffeination process. There is so much hearsay and, quite frankly, bullshit out there about the process and its results that a lot of master roasters, let alone the general public, have no idea what the process really is. Well, let me try to explain …

Decaf coffee is not sexy. It's like non-alcoholic wine or beer — what's the point, right? From a sales viewpoint (in Australia at least) you will be lucky if it accounts for about 5% of your total coffee sales. There are, however, many reasons to like decaf. "Unleaded coffee" is growing in popularity, as a number of customers have had to make the switch to decaf for health reasons. So while you may ridicule decaf coffee, isn't it better to hold on to these customers rather than lose them altogether?

Modern decaf coffees have improved out of sight in recent years and master roasters are finally learning (or caring enough) how to roast decaf beans properly. The decaffeination process does, however, impact the green bean structure so you need to adjust for that in your roasting profile. We will touch on that aspect in just a bit.

Let's look at two types of caffeine extraction processes:

DIRECT EXTRACTION PROCESS: First of all, let's get one thing clear — coffee is decaffeinated at the green bean stage. It's not something that's done during or post-roasting. Your customers will ask you, believe me …

Using the direct extraction process, methylene chloride and ethyl acetate are the two solvents traditionally used to extract caffeine from coffee beans, with methylene chloride being the most common solvent used.

With this method, the green beans are soaked in hot water or steamed so that the chemical can penetrate the bean. Next, the beans get soaked in a solvent-filled vat. These chemicals are selective compounds and will only bond to the caffeine molecules drawing them out and (theoretically) not impacting the flavour compounds inside the bean.

Once 97.5% of the caffeine has been removed[21] the solvent is discarded and the beans are then steamed yet again to a specific temperature where the solvent evaporates. This leaves a minuscule about 1 part per million solvent residue still within the bean — well within the threshold of USFDA legal limit of 10 parts/million.

Decaffeinated green beans.

FUN FACT
Decaffeination plants using the direct extraction process can extract the caffeine from the solvent and then sell it to pharmaceutical companies and soft drink manufacturers. Red Bull, anyone?

FOOTNOTE
[21] This is the USA guideline benchmark for labelling coffee as "decaffeinated".

WATER EXTRACTION PROCESS: By far the most popular decaffeination method preferred by specialty coffee roasters is the water process. It's the only type of decaf coffee I ever used and would recommend you use. Explaining how it works is a little tricky and voodoo-magic like, but I'll give it a go …

Two companies dominate. Swiss Water Decaffeinated Coffee Company and Descamex with its Mountain Water Process. Both companies pretty much work on a similar principle so I will present a basic hybrid version below of the process.

So the idea is that a solution, or "special sauce" (as I like to call it), is created by soaking a huge amount of Arabica beans in water. All of the soluble components are soaked out of the beans, including the caffeine. The spent beans are discarded, and the "special sauce" is then passed through carbon filters to extract the caffeine, leaving behind a caffeine-free "special sauce". Getting excited yet?

The idea is that a new batch of rehydrated green beans to be decaffeinated using this process and the "special sauce" will be in equilibrium compound-wise, with the exception of one compound – the caffeine! So only the caffeine gets extracted from the coffee beans under controlled conditions of flow, pressure, temperature and vacuum because everything else is in equilibrium – get it? Both companies claim a 99.9% caffeine extraction rate using this process. The beans are then carefully dried, polished and bagged ready to ship.

Don't get me wrong. My description may sound a little tongue-in-cheek, but I have used decaf coffees from both of these companies' water-process methods and the flavour retention of both is remarkable – provided you roast them properly. So let's look at that now.

ROASTING DECAF COFFEE: When you look at decaffeinated green coffee beans they are not actually green anymore. After all, they have been put through the ringer, with all that soaking, high pressure, re-drying and so on – so you can hardly blame them for being a little off colour, can you? In fact, they present as a dull light brown colour. So having this as your starting point you can naturally assume that your final roast colour will be different to non-decaffeinated green beans.

I learned by experience and logic that the decaf green bean is more fragile than the average green bean due to its life experiences to date. Both in terms of the ability to tolerate a deep roast, and its shelf life, after roasting. So please never, ever roast a decaf coffee beyond a medium roast level! Colour-wise a medium roast level will visually look like a full roast anyhow. So when roasting decaf, I recommend you ignore colour and go by length of time elapsed from first crack as your guide.

Another tip I give you for roasting decaf coffees is to charge them around 5°C lower than other coffees at the start of the roast and drop your burners a little earlier than you would for a typical medium roast profile (refer to roast Profile 1 from Part B-2-9 for reference).

Lastly, please roast your decaf coffees with the same respect you would give to your other coffees. Don't be a snob and refuse to taste/cup them. How else will you know if you have nailed the right roast profile?

B5

COFFEE ROASTER MAINTENANCE

Cleaning and maintaining your coffee roaster is critical, from both a coffee quality and safety viewpoint. The following section will outline why you need to have a regular maintenance routine, and give you tips on what to do in a roaster fire situation.

IN PART B-5 WE WILL COVER:

1. WHY YOU NEED TO BE OCD ABOUT CLEANING YOUR COFFEE ROASTER
2. MAJOR BREAKDOWNS/TECHNICAL SPECIALIST ISSUES
3. WHAT TO DO IN A ROASTER FIRE SITUATION

1

WHY YOU NEED TO BE OCD ABOUT CLEANING YOUR ROASTER

Coffee roasting is a messy business. Your roaster will quickly clog up with dust and oil residues, which can rapidly turn into creosote[22] (also known as hydrocarbon residue) if you do not clean both your roaster and flues regularly. Think of it like fatty deposits on your arteries. We don't want Betsy to have a premature heart attack or stroke now, do we?

Lack of regular cleaning is also the major cause of coffee roaster fires. Having experienced several, I can tell you that it's a very distressing and time-consuming experience once the firemen have left. Downtime with repairs, dealing with insurance companies, repairing any other damage to your store, having the landlord and other tenants on your back, paying your therapist's bills – it all adds up both financially and time-wise!

So just get off your bum and clean your roaster regularly! To help, I have put together a scheduled maintenance checklist below, suitable for most retail-sized drum barrel coffee roasters.

Here is a simple regular maintenance checklist that I recommend you follow for your drum barrel roaster:

- [ ] Every month, dress the front and rear bearings with industrial hi-temp bearing grease durable to 300°C/572°F.
- [ ] Once a year check the oil in the gearbox on the drum and mixer motor.
- [ ] The chaff collector must be cleaned after roasting five batches. This is done to prevent possible fire starting in it.
- [ ] Every six months the pipe leading from the exhaust fan to the chaff collector, and flue from the chaff collector to outside or into the afterburner, must be cleaned of creosote build-up.
- [ ] Every six months clean the cooling flue.
- [ ] Clean chaff and ash from the burners section regularly.
- [ ] Clean under the cooling tray regularly.
- [ ] Keep holes in the cooling tray clean and unblocked.
- [ ] Keep fan blades clean.
- [ ] Keep the electrical box clean.
- [ ] Adjust front bearing with hook spanner supplied if drum starts to scrape front plate. Loosen rear-locking collar first, then turn forward collar to move drum away from front plate according to your manufacturer's instructions.
- [ ] If drum gap is too big and chaff is falling under drum, then turn forward collar clockwise to move closer to front plate. Gap should be approximately 0.5mm. Please note: heat the roaster to at least 200°C/392°F when adjusting drum, as the drum expands with heat.
- [ ] The cooling mixer arms need cleaning and greasing if sticking to tray.
- [ ] Every six months remove exhaust motor and fan assembly by removing the screws holding exhaust fan assembly to roaster. Thoroughly clean inside of exhaust housing and exhaust fan including behind exhaust fan. Re-fit exhaust fan assembly.

IMPORTANT SAFETY NOTICE: Always disconnect the power first.

Chaff in the collector.

FOOTNOTE
[22] Creosote is a category of carbonaceous chemicals formed by the distillation of various tars and pyrolysis of plant-derived material, similar to what you'd find in a typical coal or wood-burning chimney. It turns hard and burns slowly but vigorously once it alights.

2
MAJOR BREAKDOWNS/ TECHNICAL SPECIALIST ISSUES

Like a car, your coffee roaster will eventually need replacement parts as they wear out over time. Over time, you will have to replace bearings, motors, gearboxes, belts, brushes, electronic components, shafts and even flues as they start to corrode. In these cases you need to hire either a qualified gas/electrical contractor to assist, a stainless steel fabricator or a mechanical engineer.

As mentioned in Part A-3 of this book most modern roasters use electronic parts that are available "off the shelf" locally. For mechanical parts it can also be more economical, both financially and time-wise, to get a local mechanical engineer to machine and install a new made-to-measure part for you rather than shipping it from your European-based coffee roaster manufacturer.

3
WHAT TO DO IN A ROASTER FIRE SITUATION

You wouldn't wish this situation to happen to your worst enemy. Well, maybe a competitor, but certainly not to your worst enemy …

For reasons already explained above, roaster fires are awful. Avoid them at all costs with good cleaning routines and making sure your roaster has all the latest over-temperature safety devices. But shit happens, and fires still regularly occur in the coffee industry. So here are a few tips on what to do and what not to do should you experience a roaster fire. Oh, and you'll probably notice there aren't many photos in this section. Probably because taking photos is the last thing on your mind when a fire happens.

Coffee roaster fires usually occur due to either poor installation methods or materials used, poor cleaning and maintenance routines or operator error.

INSTALLATION ISSUES: Make sure that the flues and ducting you select are in accordance with what your manufacturer recommends for the temperatures and build-up associated with coffee roasting. Avoid too many elbow angles in your flues to prevent excessive build-up of creosote in these areas, which can block the exhaust and potentially cause a roaster fire[23].

MAINTENANCE ISSUES: The dangers of chaff and creosote (hydrocarbon residues) build-up are very real, as they are a natural by-product of the coffee roasting process. Creosote build-up will affect your roasting by impeding airflow and thereby impact your roast profiles and, ultimately, the quality of the coffee you produce. This build-up can also create traps that can become points for sparks and embers to ignite in the flue as this residue is very flammable. So it is advisable to regularly (at least every three to six months) completely dismantle your flues and scrape the insides of them down to bare metal.

Chaff build-up is equally problematic but can be avoided by regularly emptying and cleaning out your chaff collector (after every five roasts) and cleaning under the cooling tray screen (another area where chaff commonly builds up unsighted).

OPERATOR ERROR: Being distracted, over- or underloading your roaster to its capacity, or electronic equipment failure can all lead to a fire situation. Once a polite chat with a customer near the roaster led to a devastating roaster fire when I forgot to turn down the burners between roasts and walked away thinking I had done so. After that fire I retro-fitted an over-temp gas cut-out system.

FOOTNOTE
[23] http://mailtribune.com/archive/suffaa plant-damaged

Warning Signs of a Fire

As the old saying goes: "Where there's smoke there's fire". So seeing smoke come out of your roaster where it shouldn't be, like the loading hopper, the front or sides of the roaster, or around the fans is not a good sign. It may indicate that your flues are getting blocked, so smoke is now backing out of the roaster as it's got nowhere else to go, but if the smoke level is excessive, it's a sign of a fire. You will also notice a very strong odour of smoke or other burning smells. The roaster may also make a strange chugging/huffing/puffing sound[24] that's quite disturbing. So what should you do?

1. Turn off the gas flow to the roaster immediately.

2. Don't freak out. Stay calm. Calmly ask any customers and non-essential staff to exit the shop.

3. Keep the drum turning but turn off the fan, if you can, to stop oxygenating the fire further.

4. **Do not** open the front door of the roaster to release the beans into the cooling tray. If the beans are on fire, releasing them into the oxygenated cooling tray will spread the fire into your shop.

5. CALL 000 IN AUSTRALIA; 911 IN THE USA; 112 IN EUROPE – AND GET THE FIRE BRIGADE ON THEIR WAY IN CASE YOU NEED THEM.

6. Roasters are built to take a lot of heat and keep the fire self-contained (most fires will eventually burn out inside – like an incinerator) as long as they are not fed any gas or oxygen/airflow. If you see exposed flames, for example, from a seam of a pipe, a joint of the roaster cladding, the damper or fan outlet, spray them lightly with water or a CO_2 fire extinguisher to keep the fire at bay until help arrives.

7. Avoid dousing the roaster with a large amount of water, especially the electronics, as this will probably cause more damage to the roaster than the fire itself. I had to explain this to over-enthusiastic firemen a couple of times.

8. Once the fire really gets going there will be a lot of smoke. This is normal and it will take a few hours to dissipate from your shop. Close the shop for the rest of the day.

9. Once the fire has burnt itself out (and this can take some time) and the roaster has had time to cool down, using fire-retardant gloves remove any beans from the deactivated drum or loading hopper[25] by hand into a steel bucket and have a water spray on hand in case any beans flare up again. Don't dump the burnt beans into the cooling tray as they may still be deceptively hot and could warp the cooling tray, and it will make even more mess for you to have to clean.

10. Have a stiff drink to calm your nerves.

FOOTNOTE

[24] Sorry, it's the only way I can describe that particular sound. It's incredibly scary when it gets to this point.

[25] Bonus Tip: Avoid having beans in the loading hopper before completing your current roast because if you have a fire you will lose both batches, as the extreme heat will also scorch the waiting beans in the hopper – doubling your financial loss.

EXPERT TIP

Having a clear procedure in a roaster fire situation will help you minimise the damage and, in many cases, will have you back up and running in a few days, if not the very next day.

Assessing The Damage

Assuming the roaster is intact, you can start to assess what damage has been done. Often it's quite superficial – such as blistered paint around the outside of the roaster and charred remains of beans/chaff etc. If you are not mechanically minded, I would suggest getting your roaster repair guy out to give it the once-over with you. You will need to do some safety checks before you fire her up again. Here are some recommended checks:

1 Make sure all power is off and disconnected before you proceed.

2 Check all chambers: cooler, drum, chaff collectors, fan housings and all access points for residual water and other mess. Dry and clean out.

3 You will find that the inner walls will be remarkably clean, as the fire would most likely have acted like a "back-burning" exercise and burned off any creosote build-up in the chambers and flues.

4 Dismantle all flues and clean/scrape them back to bare metal.

5 Check that all electronics and switches are dry to touch.

6 Try moving mechanical parts by hand: drive belts, chains and shafts. If they are jammed, have these issues investigated by your mechanical engineer.

7 Re-grease all bearings and moving parts that require high-temp grease, as lubrication may have burned off.

8 Restore power and test all motors and moving parts. If you hear scraping or other strange noises, or your roaster seizes up, then have these issues investigated by your mechanical engineer.

9 Have your roaster's burners and your afterburner checked by a qualified commercial gas plumber.

10 Tumble one or two batches of low grade green coffee with no heat for several hours to clean the drum of any soot and residue.

11 Test-fire your burners and roast a batch of low-grade coffee. Watch that the roaster heats up and cycles as normal, listening for any noises, and test for smoke leaks – mark and patch as required. Watch this first batch like a hawk.

12 Resume normal roasting if you feel confident everything is ticked off and OK.

IN SUMMARY ROASTER FIRES HAPPEN, DESPITE MODERN TECHNOLOGY PROVIDING MEASURES TO MAKE FIRES LESS LIKELY. YOU CAN REDUCE THIS RISK BY:

- Installing your roaster properly and not cutting corners.
- Maintaining your roaster and flues and making sure there is no build-up of flammable material in your roaster or flues.
- Being 100% focused when you roast coffee and training your roastery staff to identify fire warning signs.
- Having a roaster fire protocol you follow, should a fire occur. Address the fire in its early stages, as this could be the difference between closing your business for one day rather than several weeks due to significant damage to equipment and property.
- Ensure that you, your staff and customers remain safe at all times.

B6

THE ECONOMICS OF COFFEE

Understanding how to cost and price your product accurately is critical to running any successful business. In this section we will look at the unique factors that go into producing a kilo of roasted coffee.

IN PART B-6 WE WILL COVER:

1. ROASTING TO A QUALITY/PRICE POINT
2. SHRINKAGE!
3. LEARNING TO COST COFFEE PRODUCTION AND MONITOR MARGINS

1
ROASTING TO A QUALITY/ PRICE POINT

The reality is that you enter business to make money. Working for nothing isn't much fun. Even if it is somewhat exciting in the goggle-eyed romantic start-up phase, it quickly wears off.

Your bread and butter coffees (often your house or signature blends) should be roasted to a certain quality/price point. I purposely join these two words because you must aim for a quality level that represents your brand and your business at a price your customers are willing to pay. It's the simple economic law of supply and demand at work. You need to find that point where price and product quality intersect to maximise the sales potential of a product line.

Obviously, competitive market forces also drive this quality/price point. So don't expect to sell much of a coffee blend that your competitors are selling for $50/kilo if you try to retail it for $80/kilo, if it is of the same perceived quality level.

Sounds obvious, doesn't it? That's because it is. Modern consumers are well researched and savvy. You might fool them for a little while, but good luck in making this your long-term business strategy.

So how do you price coffee? I suggest you work backwards. Know the target price points you need to hit in order to make a profit in your business (see Part C-1-8 of this book where I elaborate more on basic financial accounting for roastery/cafés). It then comes down to the capacity and economies of scale of your production facilities (roaster capacity/packing capacity/storage capacity etc) and product component input prices (green beans, packaging, labels etc).

But first, let's discuss shrinkage!

2
SHRINKAGE!

George Costanza famously cried out his legendary line "Do women know about shrinkage?!" in an episode of the sitcom Seinfeld[26]. Coffee beans suffer from the same fate during roasting I'm afraid. "Like a frightened turtle," as Jerry says, it can shrink up to 20%. Green coffee, depending on the initial moisture level of the beans, its density and the depth of roast you employ, will lose anywhere between 17–20% of its bean weight in moisture loss during the roasting process. So for every 100kg of green beans you buy you will end up with about 80–83kg of roasted coffee that you can sell to your customers. So you have to factor this shrinkage loss into your final retail price point and margin calculations.

We'll examine this next.

FOOTNOTE

[26] George is seen naked by Jerry's girlfriend Rachel, to whom he tries vainly to explain that, having just gotten out of the cold water pool, he is a victim of penile "shrinkage". https://youtu.be/8DoARSlv-HU

3
LEARNING TO COST COFFEE PRODUCTION AND MONITOR MARGINS

Here is a simple costing spreadsheet you can use and reconstruct using spreadsheeting software. You should create one so you can change the variables to recalculate other cells. If you can't, ask your kids. It's highly likely they'll know how.

Let's break down the logic of the spreadsheet below:

YOUR ROAST

ROAST COST PER KG			1KG
Mfg Cost			$4.00
Green Beans inc shrinkage #	$8.85	1	$8.85 #
			$12.85

COST PER KG FOR YOUR ROAST

1kg	1000		
Units /kg	1.0		
Mfg Cost/kg			$12.85
Bag	$0.43	1	$0.43
Carton	$0.15	1	$0.15
Sticker2	$0.10	1	$0.10
Sticker3	$0.02	1	$0.02
Freight	$0.10	1	$0.10
			$13.65
			$13.65
50% GP			**$27.29**
75% GP			**$54.58**

GREEN INPUTS

	% Ratios	Price/Kg	Input cost
Coffee X	50%	$6.77	$3.39
Coffee Y	33%	$7.59	$2.53
Coffee Z	17%	$9.68	$1.61
	100%		$7.53
		minus 17.5%	
		loss	$8.85 #

Revision date 6/12/18

LET'S START AT THE BOTTOM OF THE TABLE WHERE YOU SEE THE WORDS GREEN INPUTS. Here we are calculating the input of three different green coffee beans at their blend ratio and at the individual green coffee's current price to you. The right-hand column calculates the input cost for that recipe input ratio and at each coffee's price. So 1kg of green coffee = $7.53 in this scenario. Here we have factored in an anticipated shrinkage factor of 17.5% (an average I worked out and used in my operations) and added that amount back in to give us the real price of the green coffee required to output 1kg of roasted coffee. Kapish?

OK, SO LET'S NOW GO TO THE TOP OF THE TABLE AND GO LINE BY LINE.
Mfg Cost = your Manufacturing Cost. This is a theoretical cost you work out from what it costs you to roast and pack 1kg of coffee beans. These costs will include the labour, gas, power, rent, etc. per hour you require to roast and pack coffee divided by the number of finished kilos of coffee you can roast in that hour. This is a theoretical number, of course, but for a 15kg shop roaster the cost per kilo will be realistically anywhere between $3.50 to $6.00/kg. Remember, it's always better to err on the high side when estimating. For this example I have gone with the theoretical cost of $4.00 per kilo.

The next line adds your shrinkage-adjusted green bean cost of $8.85 to roast that kilo. So your cost of roasting and packing 1kg of this particular blend is theoretically $12.85.

Then we simply add in the costs of the packaging itself – and I always added in an estimated freight cost to the equation to come to a finished product cost. In this case, the total extras (per kilo of coffee) amounts to $0.80.

This brings our total theoretical cost of producing a packed 1kg bag of this particular coffee blend to the grand total of $13.65.

LASTLY, THE GROSS PROFIT ON YOUR COFFEE IS CALCULATED AS:
➤ Sales - Cost of Goods Sold = Gross Profit.
➤ Gross Profit/Sales = Gross Profit Margin.
➤ (Selling Price - Cost to Produce)/Cost to Produce = Mark-up Percentage.

So to make a 50% GP you would have to sell your coffee at $27.29/kg (an average price in the bulk coffee wholesale market) and to make a 75% GP you would have to sell your coffee for $54.58/kg (a more realistic price point to cover retail volumes and shop overheads).

I will go more into financial literacy in Part C of this book, but I cannot emphasise enough how important it is to have a good understanding of these numbers and concepts for the long-term success of your business.

George from Roastville Coffee sampling a roast batch.

PART C

RUNNING YOUR BUSINESS

TRUE
FICTIONS

Blondie

Blondie was an attractive lady of middle age. She dressed very well and spoke in the manner of someone who had previously had some serious money in her life. Somewhere, somehow, things must have taken a turn for the worse, and here she now was coming to our coffee shop every morning like clockwork.

The strange ones always matched a profile. They always came alone. They always came at the same time every day. They always latched on to other customers. More importantly, they were always obsessed with the newspaper's availability – and this particular obsession is where our problems with Blondie all started.

We purchased two copies of both major Sydney newspapers daily for our shop. Mostly people glanced at them as they waited for a takeaway coffee or read them at a table for about ten minutes as they drank their sit-down coffees. Mostly people were polite about sharing parts of the newspaper or relinquishing it altogether when finished with it. Blondie started to fret when all the newspapers were either in use or had been stolen for the day (another story ...).

She would begin her standover tactics by approaching the table of the unsuspecting customer quietly reading the paper and say, "Have you almost finished with the paper?" in an overly loud and slightly aggressive manner. The more meek customers would quickly offer, "Oh yes, here you go ..." and hand the paper over to avert a confrontation. More confident customers would say, "Well, no actually ...", whereupon Blondie would bristle and move on to her table muttering inaudible obscenities under her breath. The minute the customer got up to leave, however, she'd dash over and snatch the paper from the departing customer's table and hold onto it Gollum-style, muttering, "My Precious ..."

The final straw came one day when a mother with a small child and a baby in a pram were in the café. The small child went to fetch the paper for Mummy to read. Midway between newspaper stand and Mummy, Blondie snatched the paper right from the child's hands and ran off to her table outside, leaving small child in tears and mother and staff open-mouthed in complete and utter shock.

Blondie had officially played her last gig at our coffee shop.

C1

RUNNING YOUR ROASTERY/CAFÉ

Running a retail operation is not easy. Many fail quite quickly for various reasons. In Part C of this book I will look at the numerous facets of running a retail operation and the skills required to do so successfully. The knowledge I will impart here is based on almost 20 years of retail experience. I learnt from my mistakes, survived and prospered.

We'll go over how to operate a retail roastery/café, including marketing/branding and financial accounting basics, look at expansion opportunities and how to take advantage of them and, finally, look at preparing for the end game – a profitable exit.

IN PART C-1 WE WILL COVER:

1. BEING A RETAILER
2. STAFF – THE FACE OF YOUR BUSINESS
3. CUSTOMER SERVICE 101
4. HOW TO SELL COFFEE BEANS TO NON-COFFEE NERDS
5. THE ROASTED COFFEE BEANS DISPLAY, STOCK TURNOVER AND FRESHNESS
6. ONLINE COFFEE BEAN SALES
7. A QUICK MESSAGE ON ESPRESSO AND BREW BAR SERVICE
8. FINANCIAL ACCOUNTING 101

1
BEING A RETAILER

It's easy to get caught up in the coffee roasting bit (and everything else coffee-related) and forget what you're actually in business for – which is, to sell your product to customers who are willing to part with their cold hard cash. The roasting of the coffee is only one part of the equation. You need to provide an excellent retail experience for your customers and manage that experience on a daily basis to make sure it's delivered to plan. Remember that you are a retailer first and foremost!

Once your business gets to a certain volume you simply won't be able to manage the fine detail of running the roastery/café on a day-to-day basis yourself. For that you will need to employ a competent store manager who buys into your customer service philosophy and will act as your willing and able representative. Select carefully and look after this person well, both professionally and financially. If they take ownership of the role you will be paid back in spades, let me assure you. It's important you take a top view management role and don't micro-manage this person otherwise they will quickly lose motivation for the role, and you'll be surprised how quickly any negativity can flow down to your floor staff.

Darren, my wholesale sales manager.

With my assistant roaster Andrew, at the RAS Fine Food Coffee Judging.

A RETAIL STORE MANAGER WILL BE RESPONSIBLE FOR THE DAILY MANAGEMENT OF:
- Shop/stock cleanliness and presentation.
- Stock level and turnover of perishables and other items.
- Pest control and sanitation compliance.
- Customer amenities (toilets/newspapers/Wi-Fi) and comfort.
- Monitoring trading hours.
- Staff rostering and management.
- Condition of fit-out, furniture and equipment.
- Staff customer service and product training/knowledge.
- Security and customer safety.

2
STAFF – THE FACE OF YOUR BUSINESS

Your staff are the face of your business. Never forget that. They are the public image of your brand, of your coffee, of you.

In Part C-2 we will talk about marketing and brand building. Your staff must represent the brand image you develop and project it to the outside world. You can control this image projection with regular and thorough staff training. If you have a clear vision of your brand positioning then it's easier for you to recruit staff, as you know straight away the type of person you're looking for in the job interview. Being a nice guy, it took me a while to work this out, and I hired some real corkers in the early days.

Having a clear marketing plan and system allows you to communicate your personal and brand values with your staff, and if they don't buy into it from the start I strongly suggest not hiring them because it probably won't work out.

Bruno, smiling as always, was my awesome store manager and head barista. The lady customers, in particular, loved him.

Treat and pay your staff well and they will reward you. Don't micro-manage or be a "helicopter boss". When they have been well trained your staff will do their job well and be your brand ambassadors. Don't take advantage of overseas students and pay under-award "cash" rates, even if they ask you to. Once you do that you run the risk of serious repercussions if a disagreement happens or you have to let them go for some reason. If they have the guts to take you to Fair Work[1] then they have you by the balls. Don't risk it.

Occasionally you will employ duds and you have to let them go. If you do everything by the book and follow the Fair Work guidelines you will be protected. Fair Work also protects employers and not just the employees. Fair Work has templates for letters of offer of employment and other guidelines to help you be compliant and save yourself a lot of potential pain should dismissal be required.

Up until 2015 our business transactions were about 90% cash versus 10% card transactions. The advent of tap-and-go style cards has seen this ratio reverse dramatically in the last few years and I believe we will be a cash-free society within the next ten years (fearless prediction here). This will make the issue of cash theft by staff less of a concern. Unfortunately this happens, not just in cafés, but in many cash businesses.

Theft by staff is a difficult thing to deal with, hard to prove and hard to stop unless you have a very advanced POS system that gets around staff entering dummy transactions or being able to open the cash drawer without a transaction. Yes, you can have a surveillance camera pointed at the register, but are you seriously going to watch 12 hours of footage every day to find that moment? The ones that steal normally have personal issues they are dealing with (drugs, gambling, debts, etc.). I found that if I addressed my concerns to the staff as a whole the guilty party would normally resign shortly after as they knew the game was up. It's not a pleasant topic but it is a reality in cash-based retail businesses.

FOOTNOTE
[1] The Fair Work Ombudsman is an Australian government body that helps employers and employees understand and follow Australian workplace laws.

EXPERT TIPS

1. Hire staff who want to work for your brand and love coffee.
2. Create a clearly written staff manual that is accessible and regularly updated.
3. Don't micro-manage staff, especially if you have a store manager.
4. Have clear guidelines on personal dress, grooming, hygiene standards you expect.
5. Provide aprons/protective workwear as required.
6. Provide extensive product and customer service training and role-play various situations in staff training sessions.
7. Have regular team meetings and instill a positive culture.
8. Praise success and thoughtfully mentor any performance issues.
9. Treat your staff with the respect you would expect in return.
10. Pay them well – or at the very least at the award rate.
11. Consult Fair Work to make sure your practices are compliant and use their templates at: www.fairwork.gov.au/how-we-will-help/templates-and-guides.

3
CUSTOMER SERVICE
101

One of the toughest things to manage in retail is customer service. The customer is not always right but issues have to be dealt with in the right manner. You can stop bad situations from escalating by role-playing with your staff and providing them with the tools to cope. One simple but key thing I used to tell my staff was to always acknowledge customers waiting to be served, if for some reason they could not be immediately attended to.

A simple greeting of "Hi Sir, I'll be with you in just a couple of minutes" is all that's usually required to keep waiting customers content. People just hate to be ignored, and it's easy to get that perception as a customer in a retail environment. Simply think to the last time you felt ignored in a store. You got the shits pretty quickly, didn't you?

Often I would step to the other side of the counter or sit at a table for a little while and get the customer's viewpoint of the store and customer service from the staff. You'd be amazed how different your perceived experience is from the other side of the counter of your own shop. You need to do this regularly to understand your customers' perception of your service levels and the presentation of the store.

One simple key to good customer service is to have enough staff on the floor to reflect demand. While this can be difficult to juggle during the early days when you may have some quiet patches, you will benefit in the long run when those busy times occur (think Saturday and Sunday mornings). There is nothing worse than a frazzled barista and an attendant making snide remarks under their breath or, even worse, complaining to customers: "It's just too busy!" FMD!! Is there a better way to destroy your business overnight? I can assure you that next week these customers will not be back for more of the same shenanigans!

In today's social media/share everything environment you can be assured that any disasters like this will be amplified to the masses in no time. So don't be a tight-arse[2] when it comes to all things customer service – it will come back to bite you on the arse[3].

On the whole I'd say 95% of customers are great – courteous and respectful of your staff and to other customers. The other 5% can be challenging. Sometimes they're just not polite (on the phone when they come to the counter, spit out their order with no please or thank you, and look annoyed when they have to interrupt their call to pay for their order). Others have no qualms making other customers wait while they make stupid requests or simply dither around. A lot of it is attention-seeking behaviour and reflects deeper issues within their psyche – or at least that's what I told myself!

So what should you do in the face of these people? Disarming them with a smile and friendly but firm responses while politely refusing their idiotic requests often disorientates them and they move quietly on. Whatever you do, don't get baited into an argument because that's exactly what they want. Train your staff in this subtle art of disarmament – it works (almost) every time!

Over the years I had to deal with a small handful of particularly dreadful customers. Racist or sexist comments made towards staff cannot be tolerated.

FOOTNOTE

[2] An Australian slang term for someone who is overly thrifty with their money.

[3] Arse = Ass for our USA readers (I may have footnoted this one previously).

You need to speak with these customers in a calm and discreet manner away from other customers and firmly but calmly state that you cannot accept that behaviour and that they are not welcome in your store. Best to be rid of such people quickly, but do it in a discreet manner so they don't lose face in front of others. They have probably already made a fool of themselves anyhow by now, but you can't stoop down to their level no matter how upset or tired you may be. Thankfully, on the whole, people like this are few and far between and you rarely encounter them.

EXPERT TIPS

1. Always greet waiting customers so they feel acknowledged.
2. Regularly step over to the other side of the counter to get your customers' perspective on your store.
3. Roster enough staff on the floor during your busy periods.
4. Disarm difficult customers with a smile and friendly but firm responses.
5. Deal with unacceptable customer behaviour firmly but discreetly.

4

HOW TO SELL COFFEE BEANS TO NON-COFFEE NERDS

Back in 1997 you'd be amazed how many people thought that all coffee was instant (soluble). The generations brought up on Nescafé, Moccona (when you splurged out) – or God forbid the evil International Roast (which I'm convinced was not really coffee but, in fact, coffee-infused garden soil). But alas, I digress ...

Thankfully, it's no longer 1997 and mostly the hard work has been done in educating the masses on the joys and techniques of freshly roasted and brewed coffee at home. Many have espresso machines of varying quality or have found their own preferred brewing method. Perhaps it's a filter, a French Press (aka plunger/Bodum) or an AeroPress or the like. Many more are now also buying beans rather than pre-ground coffee, which is fantastic.

The art of selling coffee beans is very similar to selling wine or any other items where people might feel a little uneducated or embarrassed to admit they're clueless. Don't make them feel worse by acting like record store Barry from *High Fidelity*[4]. I found that asking a series of simple questions helped me narrow down the type of coffee they would probably like. See below:

QUESTION: How do you brew/make your coffee at home?
PURPOSE: Filter or plunger-brewed coffees tend to be lighter roasts and more suitable than espresso roasts for this brewing method and vice versa.

QUESTION: What coffee do you mostly drink? Espresso, black filter or plunger, milk-based (cappuccino, flat white, macchiato)?
PURPOSE: Gives you an indication as to what blend to recommend regarding strength and cut-through (for milk-based coffee).

FOOTNOTE
[4] If you watch the movie, can I suggest the scene where Barry (Jack Black) demeans a poor unfashionable dad who comes into the hip record store to buy his daughter a very unhip record for her birthday. A lesson on what not to do when selling coffee: youtube/-ECyX8A3iP0

Explain the narrowed down coffee range to them and why you recommended them, highlighting specific flavour characteristics and aftertaste. Narrowing down the offering helps both you and the customer out, and saves on the transaction time when others are waiting to be served.

A common request (in fact, I wish I had a dollar for every time I was asked) is: "I want a coffee that's strong but not bitter". Initially I would bristle deep down inside that someone had used the "B-word" in my presence, inferring that my coffee could ever possibly taste like International Roast. I quickly came to learn though, that people often confuse stronger or darker roast coffees with overbrewed coffee (which is bitter) – or maybe they had just been drinking International Roast up until now, who knows? – so I would politely say, "No, none of these coffees I've recommended will be bitter, we don't roast that dark here, blah blah blah …"

I would also explain that there was good bitterness (think dark chocolate) and bad bitterness (think International Roast) and that a glorious espresso that tastes like dark chocolate is just like heaven once you get used to it. However, if you drink weak caramel soy lattes all day, well you probably will never know – and you should die in hell.

I would then finish off the transaction by giving them some (free and unsolicited) advice on their preferred brewing technique. Simple things like, "Use a dessert spoon to measure ground coffee into your plunger" (so many people put in 1–2 teaspoons and wonder why it tastes watery), then, "Stir the grounds and the water and let it sit for at least 3 minutes prior to plunging, longer if you like it stronger", and so on. Not only did they appreciate the personalised free advice but very often they couldn't wait to come back next time and tell you how your simple brewing tips had transformed their coffee experience … and guess what? You had a new friend and customer for life!

While it can be a time-consuming exercise, especially if you change your coffee offering often, it's good to have printed coffee description cards and tasting notes that you can give to your customers (for coffee bean and espresso sales). It really lifts the experience for the customer, educates them and makes you look like you actually know what you're talking about as the "coffee expert". Print them on quality cards that reflect your brand image and that will last beyond the trip home.

The cards will also act as marketing collateral when your customers show it to their friends while serving your coffee at home. A secondary benefit is that it will reinforce the cupping regime you follow and help you become a better coffee roaster and coffee taster.

EXPERT TIPS

1. When selling coffee beans to new customers, gauge their interest and knowledge, then ask appropriate questions to ascertain their tastes.
2. Don't make customers feel foolish/uneducated about coffee.
3. Narrow down the coffee options by stealth.
4. Offer personalised tips and advice regarding grind, brewing and storage at home.
5. Remember you are building a long-term customer relationship.
6. Build marketing/educational collateral into your packaging and print material.

5
THE ROASTED COFFEE BEAN DISPLAY, STOCK TURNOVER AND FRESHNESS

Our coffee bean offering in 1997.

Here you will see some images of our coffee bean displays from 1997 and 2012. What a difference 15 years makes in styling; however, in both incarnations the bean displays were situated between the customer and the attendant. When the lids were lifted the customer had the beans right under their noses and in front of their eyes. Their noses smelt freshly roasted coffee and their eyes saw abundance. Coffee is a sensory product, so why would you not display it like this?

I never understood those gravity-fed glass (often dirty) displays that sat on the back wall of coffee shops (and 1970s supermarkets), where the customer would never really see the coffee beans up close until they got home. Who knew how old those beans were? Certainly not the customer. The same goes for pre-packed coffee in bags. Looks great in a rowed display perhaps, but it's the same thing. "How old is that coffee? What does it look like? Nah …"

So from Day 1 we made sure we had an interactive coffee bean display. When serving or post-blending[5] coffee we would do it right under the customers' noses. They saw how fresh it was, and they felt INVOLVED in the process! I can't stress the importance of this sensory interaction enough. Customers enjoyed that experience alone. Some were happy for you to recommend single origins or blends while others liked to invent their own blends – what a great opportunity to talk about coffee and for them to learn from you, the coffee expert!

A display that's as open as this requires a few strategies to manage it well. Our roaster produced 10kg roasted batches and, when cooled, it went straight into our Rubbermaid Brute sealed containers. These were kept under the counter located under the relevant display bins that sat on top of the counter. These customer displays, due to their shape, held only 2kg of coffee, but looked full, while the rest of the batch stayed sealed below. We could easily turn over the customer display several times a day so the coffee always stayed fresh. As you now know, roasted coffees de-gas and peak (especially for espresso) at around 10 days, so by the time the customer got their pack home and was using the coffee it was just about right.

Don't go overboard with available variety. We started with a display of 12 coffees that soon became 10, and finally settled on eight. This number worked well as it allowed for four by then very popular blends (there would have been open revolt if they were not always available) and four rotating single origins or special blends which you could roast lighter for filter etc.

THE PROBLEM WITH HAVING TOO MUCH CHOICE IS THAT:
➤ It's confusing for the customers and the staff.
➤ It's hard to turn over stock, as both staff and customers have their favourites and tend to gravitate towards recommending/choosing the same coffees.
➤ It results in a higher level of wastage if they don't turn over fast enough and have to be discarded.
➤ It's a lot of green coffee stock to carry, as well making inventory/space an issue.

Roasted coffee can be sold as soon as it's cooled down from the roaster. Customers would soon get over their dismay that the coffee they wanted to buy was sold out when I would inform them from my position in front of the roaster that: "Hey, I'm roasting that one right now, come back in 30 minutes and you'll have some fresh from the roaster!" They'd happily take off to the supermarket or wherever with the

FOOTNOTE
[5] The art of blending coffee origins post-roasting.

Our coffee bean offering in 2012.

prospect of picking up some fresh hand-roasted goodness in just half-an-hour's time! Remember that on average customers may keep these beans at home for about two weeks (we always recommended that they never bulk up on coffee, only to buy two weeks' worth max), so to sell it fresh from the roaster was OK. We would, however, always warn them that the coffee would de-gas for a few days, and if they intended to use it for espresso, to let it settle down for a few days before use. They loved it!

On the flip side, you need to turn over your stock within seven days of roast. Holding it any longer to sell to the public was too long, for the same reasons I outline above. So roast enough stock to turn it over within seven days and you should be on the money freshness-wise.

Roasting coffee in-store creates a lot of dust. A daily dust and clean of your coffee bean display lids and all surfaces is required. It's a pain but it goes with the territory. Make it a part of the daily cleaning routine of the store and it can be the chore to do during those quiet moments. Remember this is the vehicle for selling your coffee. Treat it with respect and it will make you a lot of money.

EXPERT TIPS

1. Selling coffee should be a sensory experience for the customer, so get them involved!
2. Make the coffee bean display attractive, interactive and a store feature.
3. Find display containers that hold a maximum of 2kg of beans and store the rest of the roast in airtight pails.
4. Cover your coffee with transparent lids.
5. Label your coffee display containers with informative, easy-to-read information about the coffee on display.
6. Turn over your coffee batch every seven days max.
7. Keep your display clean and free from dust.

6 ONLINE COFFEE BEAN SALES

Online coffee stores have become a big part of any roaster's business and have been following the general online retail trend for most industries. With this though, comes competition. When we started with online sales we were trailblazers, winning the *My Business Magazine* Best Online Store award in 2001.

Today, the Internet is full of coffee bean online stores. You have artisan retail roasters like yourselves, wholesale or contract roasters, and even people who re-sell roasted beans purchased wholesale from other roasters and market it under their own coffee brand. It's getting harder to be seen and rank in Google searches. Inevitably, the bigger coffee brands rank higher in search engines as they outspend the rest on Google Adwords, and today paid advertising has overtaken organic rankings in the search engine provider's priorities (ka-ching! $$$).

Originally our web store coffee bean sales mostly came from regional customers who either could not access good quality coffee locally or were previous city dwellers who had made a sea or tree change. It functioned very much like a modern mail order catalogue business. They would buy in good quantities to make the freight component worthwhile. From my point it was great business as it turned over stock, got the brand out there beyond the Sydney suburbs and equalled more money in the bank.

Today everyone buys online, even if there's a retail shop down the road. This is kinda sad as it means we're not interacting as social beings as much anymore, but it is what it is, and it's an opportunity to sell more product. This has meant a move towards "free freight" as a selling advantage, so costing freight into your product with minimum purchase offerings is essential. Most vendors offer free freight with purchases over $60, for example. Anything less than that amount though will be difficult to absorb the freight profit-wise. Always work out your margins. There is no point in working for nothing unless you're in the very early stage of brand building and just want people to try your coffee. This should be looked at then as a sampling marketing expense.

SO ASSUMING YOU WORK THIS ALL OUT AND YOU HAVE A KICK-ARSE ONLINE STORE HAPPENING YOU SHOULD USE IT EFFECTIVELY AS A VEHICLE TO:

- Sell your coffee beans.
- Promote your coffee brand and values.
- Position your brand through expert advice and resources for your customer.
- Prospect wholesale opportunities if you've started down that line.
- Help turn over your retail coffee stock. But don't use it as a vehicle to sell expired coffee!! There is no benefit to doing this and it's a false economy in the long run.
- Promote your roastery/café, invite people to visit, share it on social media.
- Use it as a BLOG and Social Media hub to educate customers about coffee and brewing techniques.

7

A QUICK MESSAGE ON ESPRESSO AND BREW BAR SERVICE

There are many great and detailed books out there about espresso and brewing coffee technique. While this is not the focus of this book it would be remiss of me not to mention its importance in your coffee roastery/café setup.

The espresso and brew bar part of your roastery is a critical part of your business. It is where your customers will sample your coffee and ultimately/hopefully make the decision to buy your coffee beans to take home. It needs to show your coffee in its best light. It is your ultimate promotional vehicle.

It is also an economic consideration. You cannot survive on selling coffee beans alone in a retail situation. In 1997 we thought that the beans would be the bulk of the sales and the espresso bar would be the support act. How wrong we were!

You see the reality is that a certain percentage of your customers only drink coffee out – they don't brew coffee at home and have no interest in doing so! Our sales pattern eventually settled on a 70:30 percentage split for espresso:beans in dollar (not kg volume) sales. As it turns out after speaking with other artisan roasters around the nation, this was actually an incredibly high proportion of bean sales to espresso sales. We averaged around 80–100kg of pure take-home coffee bean sales per week.

Part A of this book discussed fitting out your coffee roastery. Of course, your coffee roaster will be your dominant capital expense outside of the shop-fitting cost. Your espresso equipment should, however, be your next most important capital purchase. Do not skimp on the quality of this equipment. You get what you pay for. There is a reason that espresso machine brands like La Marzocco and Synesso are expensive. It's because they deliver the best-quality espresso consistently when you're crazy busy and have the best recovery times. Once you get to a certain volume, heat-transfer machines simply can't recover in time to produce consistent espresso pours and steam quality for your milk.

> Professional baristas need to be incredibly focused, organised, patient and dedicated to always wanting to improve their skills. They see it as a career profession and not as a fill-in role. Look after them well and you will reap the rewards.

So my point is, don't skimp on equipment quality here from the start; it will catch up with you and will cost you more down the track to replace your gear.

You need to have dedicated and professional baristas on your team. They need to be well trained and be able to work under pressure. Beware of stereotypes though. Many a bearded tattooed dude walked into my place but couldn't walk the walk when the heat was on, while other unassuming types were absolute beasts behind the espresso machine and pumped out amazingly consistent brews all morning without breaking into a sweat. Professional baristas need to be incredibly focused, organised, patient and dedicated to always wanting to improve their skills. They see it as a career profession and not as a fill-in role. Look after them well and you will reap the rewards.

Of course the coffee world is no longer all about espresso. Pour-over bars and cold drip are very popular and great ways to show off your different origins and roasting techniques to the public. It's also a fantastic way to start a conversation on coffee with your customers and provides an easy entry into coffee tasting that is not as complicated and alien for non-coffee people as the traditional cupping process.

8
FINANCIAL ACCOUNTING
101

"Cash-flow is King" as the old saying goes – and it's so true. You need liquid available cash in your trading bank account to pay your rent, your suppliers, your staff, to meet your other financial obligations and, finally, to pay yourself something. Of course, in the early days it's likely you will burn through some cash savings until you establish your clientele – and this can take some time.

Overnight successes are rare, and you only hear about them in the media because of the very fact that they are so rare (or they're mates with prominent food journos). So don't get sucked into thinking that you'll be rolling in the dosh from Day 1. The key to surviving this period, which could be a few weeks or even months, is to have a realistic start-up capital in your trading account. You may need some other temporary sources of cash, like an overdraft facility, to get you out of trouble until you move to a positive cash flow situation. Inadequate cash reserves are one of the top reasons start-ups don't succeed. I recommend a minimum starting cash reserve position of AU$30,000–$50,000.

An old boss of mine from pre-coffee days, from when I worked as a marketing manager, once said to me: "You bank (net) profit Dave, not sales! Remember that, my son." Those words of wisdom have always stuck with me, and it has been a critical thought that has helped me to always run a profitable business through the good and lean times. To grasp this you need to understand how a profit-and-loss statement works.

The profit-and-loss statement explained

The following Profit-and-Loss Statement graphic shows a typical P&L for a retail café/artisan roastery. Note that I have removed the actual sales dollar numbers from this P&L but have left the % of Sales amount, as this figure is more important to the successful running of your business in the long term. It will form a good platform for you to start and set up your own chart of accounts in your chosen accounting software. So let's start ...

Firstly, you have above-the-line[6] cash inflows in **SALES** less above-the-line production costs (**COSTS OF GOODS**) = **GROSS PROFIT**.

GROSS PROFIT less all the below-the-line expenses (think everything else like rent, staff wages, electricity, gas, communication, staff/customer amenities, insurances, accounting/legal fees, leases/petrol and so on) = **NET PROFIT**, which is what's left to bank, to pay yourself, invest back into the business or save.

On that topic (of paying yourself) I always took the attitude that I was the LAST person to get paid. My staff always came first (including all their entitlements) and my suppliers after them. Nothing riles me more than reading about celebrity chefs who do not pay their staff properly or are left owing them millions of dollars in entitlements when they go bankrupt. This also goes for unpaid, often small, suppliers who are left with a $20K hole in their bank accounts.

Back to the P&L though, let's talk about the **below-the-line** expenses area in more detail, as this is where a lot of people get into trouble. When you're writing your first business plan, even before you open your doors, I recommend working out the expense side of the equation first before you cost your product offering and project sales targets. Why? Because once you have a baseline of outflows you can start to work out a minimum sales and gross profit amount you need to make to Break Even, a very important concept to understand.

Break Even is when Gross Profit = Net Profit. In other words, you're not making a bankable profit but you're not losing money either. Logically, this isn't a bad theoretical financial starting point to work from I think.

Let's start with your two biggest expenses: Rent and Wages. Keep these two beasts under control and you're halfway there towards making a profit. Measuring expenses as a percentage of sales is a proven way to monitor important benchmarks of profitability in a business[7]. Rent should benchmark at around 10–15% of sales or under (in a retail shop situation – it should be way less if you're in a factory non-retail space). Negotiating your lease is covered in Part A of this book and is critical as it will be the starting point of your rent cost base for the next five or so years.

FOOTNOTE
[6] The magical "line" in financial accounting is the gross profit line. Expenses below the line generally are those outside of the manufacturing or purchasing cost of the product you sell.

[7] ATO Café Benchmarks: www.ato.gov.au/Business/Small-business-benchmarks/In-detail/Benchmarks-A-Z/A-C/Coffee-shops

SALES INCOME	4–1100
LESS COST OF SALES	5–0000
	5–1100
	5–2100
	5–3000
	5–9000
TOTAL COST OF SALES	
GROSS PROFIT	
LESS EXPENSES	6–1000
	6–1200
	6–1400
	6–1500
	6–1530
	6–1540
	6–1550
	6–1600
	6–1850
	6–2000
	6–2100
	6–2200
	6–2210
	6–2300
	6–2600
	6–2801
	6–3000
	6–3300
	6–3600
	6–3700
	6–4000
	6–4200
	6–4600
	6–4610
	6–4800
	6–4900
	6–4950
	6–5000
	6–5010
	6–5200
	6–5400
	6–5600
	6–5700
	6–5800
	6–6000
	6–6200
	6–6600
TOTAL EXPENSES	
NET OPERATING PROFIT	

Sales	% Sales
Opening Stock Value	3.7%
Purchases	21.1%
Packaging	2.5%
Equipment Purchases	0.3%
Closing Stock Value	-3.7%
	23.9%
	76.1%
Accounting Fees	1.1%
Advertising/Marketing	2.0%
Bank Charges	0.7%
Cleaning	0.3%
Computer Equipment	0.1%
Consulting Fees	0.1%
Customer Amenities	0.6%
Depreciation	0.0%
Donations	0.0%
Electricity and Gas	1.4%
Entertainment	0.2%
Fees and Permits	0.7%
Filing Fees	0.0%
Freight	0.6%
General Insurances	1.0%
Interest Paid – Bank Loan	1.3%
Internet and Web Hosting	0.3%
Legal Fees	0.2%
Office Supplies	0.0%
Pest Control	0.5%
Postage	0.2%
Printing and Stationery	0.5%
Rent	**10.2%**
Rental – Equipment	0.3%
Repairs and Maintenance	1.0%
Security Monitoring	0.0%
Software Maintenance	0.2%
Staff Amenities	0.1%
Staff Training and Sponsorship	0.8%
Subscriptions	0.1%
Superannuation Expense	2.9%
Telephone	0.3%
Trade Waste Disposal	0.3%
Travel and Accommodation	0.0%
Uniforms	0.3%
Wages and salaries	**31.8%**
Workers Compensation Insurance	0.9%
	61.0%
	15.0%

Wages as a percentage of sales benchmark can vary according to the type of roastery/café you run. If you run a professional kitchen with table service waiters it will be a lot more labour intensive than a café that is purely micro roastery and espresso bar. This is your call, but a benchmark of 25–32% excluding superannuation and Workers Compensation Insurance mandatory requirements above the gross wages is a good starting point.

Without doubt, managing staffing costs is the trickiest area of running expenses to manage as it directly correlates to your customer service levels. I have seen cafés skimp on staff as soon as things go a tad quiet, then they are forever on a vicious downward spiral towards closure as the reduced staff can't cope when customers actually do walk in, service is terrible, and the customers do not return (and tell all their mates on social media how crap your place is).

Of course, a lack of punters coming in is not always solely about your product or service; sometimes you've just got it wrong from the outset planning stage in terms of site location or demographics, so nothing you throw at it will help. I've seen this happen a lot too. Please refer to Part A of this book where research and site selection is discussed in more detail.

Most roastery/cafés are owner-operated to start until the business can support it to be run under management. This is something to consider for the future when your energies as the manager/roaster are better utilised in other areas of the business (such as expansion plans/implementation).

Other expenses to watch out for are marketing/advertising and travel. Having come from a background in corporate marketing, I made the mistake of applying corporate marketing spend ratios to small business. It doesn't work. Spending $200K on print media in corporate will get you some cut-through and targeted reach, but spending $15K in small business does not scale down proportionally and usually results in zero reach and a wasted $15K. We will delve into this a bit more in the next section, but my point here when talking about finances and cash flow is that it's easy to get carried away and burn cash. Also beware of other lavish expenses. Perhaps that trip to the plantations of Brazil should wait until you've actually turned a profit.

Let's now turn our attention to the **above-the-line** areas of Sales/COGS/Gross Profit.

Everyone knows what Sales are so we won't labour this point. Simply, it's what your customers pay you in cash or credit (less fees) for your product or service.

COGS, or Cost Of Goods Sold, is the cost of producing or purchasing the goods you sell. For example, for your roasted coffee it would be the cost of the green beans, the packaging (bags/stickers), etc. For your espresso sales it would be the cost of the beans (although if you roast them yourself you don't want to count this cost twice), the milk, the takeaway cup and so on. For non-coffee packaged goods and coffee hardware it's the wholesale price you paid your supplier for the goods.

My staff doubled as baristas and shop attendants doing other duties. So I accounted for their wages below the line and did not account for the proportion of their time doing barista duties in the COGS of making the espresso coffee.

Equally the labour of roasting the coffee beans themselves was also not costed into the above-the-line coffee bean production cost at the retail level. The same went for the required utilities such as electricity and gas. When I started wholesaling coffee, however, I did calculate a theoretical cost of labour, utilities and so on into my finished coffee cost. However, for ease of accounting in a retail situation it's just easier to group those below the line as expense cost centres. It really depends on what level of costing you require for analysis purposes and how it will benefit your decision making process.

The last piece of this puzzle is to price the goods that you sell. Doing this will allow you to forecast sales and, along with your forecast expenses, you can then work out if you might break even, make a profit or have to fund a temporary loss-making period after you open your doors. Having this financial literacy and intimate knowledge of every cog of how your business makes and spends money is critical to your long-term success in the retail business. You need to know which levers to pull (by either increasing your prices or reigning in your expenses) in order to either survive or make more money.

Although price points are ultimately influenced by what your market will bear (via the laws of supply and demand) do not be afraid to charge a fair price for your goods. I made it a firm policy to NEVER DISCOUNT my coffee (beans and espresso). My coffee was top notch and I had no need to discount. This was an important quality message to send out to my customers. It also stops you getting into a price war where no-one wins. Hold your nerve. Aim to have the best coffee, food and service levels in the area and you will be fine. Customers will pay a fair price for excellent coffee. Life's too short after all …

Remember that profit/loss forecasting, especially before you open your doors, is 50% guesswork. So my advice to you is to employ an accountant or advisor who has had experience with retail coffee businesses (ideally with coffee roasteries and not just cafés) and who can give you benchmark figures/percentages to work with. Be diligent with every cost line, and overestimate expenses/COGS and underestimate sales. As a final sanity check simply halve your sales estimate as a worst-case scenario and see what loss results. If you can fund that loss for, say 3–6 months and survive it may be worth a crack.

GROSS PROFIT is simply your total **SALES** less your "above-the-line" **COGS**.
GROSS PROFIT less your "below-the-line" **EXPENSES** is your **NET PROFIT**.

And remember Dave … **"You Bank NET PROFIT, not SALES!"**

C2

MARKETING AND BUILDING BRAND VALUE

Building your brand image is crucial to your long-term success and business value. An ever-evolving process, you must have a clear brand message and vision to convey to your customers from the outset.

IN PART C-2 WE WILL COVER:

1. FIRST STEPS IN BRAND CREATION
2. TEAM UP WITH A GOOD BRAND DESIGN BUSINESS
3. BRANDING AND PACKAGING – GETTING IT RIGHT
4. DIGITAL AND SOCIAL MEDIA MARKETING
5. ATTRACTING NEW CUSTOMERS AND RETAINING THEM
6. STRATEGIC MARKETING ALLIANCES
7. WEBSITES AND ONLINE STRATEGIES

1

FIRST STEPS IN BRAND CREATION

When you initially wrote your business plan (as discussed in Part A of this book) you should have integrated a marketing plan as a core part of it. Here you may have come up with the name of your business, identified your target market and how you planned to reach and appeal to their coffee-buying sensibilities.

One of the first things people tend to do after choosing and registering a trading name is to design a logo. You'd be surprised how this most important element is often not treated with the respect it deserves. Your name and logo will often be the first thing a new prospective client sees and judges you on. Despite this, most businesses will get a mate or a family member who's "a bit of a graphic designer" to design their logo for them. Many also use exploitative websites like fiverr.com or freelancer.com to take advantage of cheap foreign designers. The results can be varied to say the least.

The Bay Coffee logo underwent three updates over my 19 years. Below is the evolution of the logo over the years I was in charge.

THE BAY COFFEE LOGO RE-BRAND OVER THE YEARS[8]

1997

2008

2013

FOOTNOTE

[8] Please note that from December 2016 Bay Coffee has been under new ownership/management and the overall company branding of its logo, website and packaging has evolved again.

2
TEAM UP WITH A GOOD BRAND AGENCY

Good brand designers are focused on brand design and how it all fits together as a cohesive brand identity that works across all your marketing platforms and communications. Our brand agency at the time was heavily involved in the redesign of our roastery/café in 2012 and our wholesale marketing strategy and packaging redesign in 2015.

The core values of my business were **RESPECT, NURTURE, SUSTAIN.** Every marketing brief I wrote for the brand agency requested that they represent these core value ideas in some way, shape or form. They were very sympathetic to our core values in everything they did for us. What did these values actually mean?

- ▶ **RESPECT:** For the product we were producing and the people who produced it, from the coffee farms right through to the barista who prepared it for you.
- ▶ **NURTURE:** To look after and help my staff to become better at their profession and to nurture as people as they passed through the business as a stepping-stone in their own lives.
- ▶ **SUSTAIN:** I always believed we had to support sustainable agriculture and positive environmental practices in the coffee industry. I was one of the first adopters of the Rainforest Alliance coffees in Australia and always supported fair and sustainable trade practices in the industry.

It is important that the core values of your business are central to your branding and design. Good designers will achieve this without the design being in your face or obvious.

Once your logo and brand graphic design standards are established, all your other design projects – from your packaging, signage, website, store design, social media presence and everything else in between – will flow. It's a skill to make everything tie in seamlessly, but when this is achieved it gives a level of perceived professionalism and style that will forever be connected with your product and service. Branding experts can help you pull this all together and keep it on track as you grow and expand.

Besides values, it's important to always keep in mind your brand positioning in the market. Know the segment you are targeting and drawing on for your sales. Your branding is a key element of your perceived position in the marketplace. Don't try to be or fake something that you are not. Customers are very sophisticated these days and will see through your sham.

Lastly, the coffee industry itself, as well as branding/design tastes, changes over time. Fashions come and go. You need to stay relevant. As the market and your business evolves over the years so too should your branding, design and marketing message.

Marketing campaign promoting our 2012 store renovation and relaunch.

Foldout brochure/poster designed by Creative Order.

Bay Coffee
wholesale and retail
packaging design.

3
BRANDING AND PACKAGING – GETTING IT RIGHT

What a fantastic vehicle to promote your brand and its value message! Of course once you start wholesaling and have the volume to justify it, you have the blank canvas of a printed 1kg bag to work with. When you are in retail though, you normally have to start with printed stickers and apply it to off-the-shelf 250g or 500g plain bags.

To custom-print bags you really need to run around 10,000 bags to make it economically viable in comparison to the plain bag plus sticker option. So most of you will start with the plain bag and sticker option and, hopefully, graduate to the printed bag option down the track.

Either way the same rules apply. My golden rules for bag branding are:

1. Minimalist design is best. Elegant and thoughtful.
2. Convey a brand message through a well thought out graphic image.
3. Use icons to convey instructions (brewing techniques and so on).
4. Avoid excessive text and instructions. Refer customers to your website for more information.
5. Invite ongoing engagement via website or social media links. Tag all your communications with @yourcoffeebrand.
6. Don't go nuts with stickers and add-ons – one will do. Loads of stickers looks cheap and nasty.
7. Consider the artisan handmade look by using Kraft paper coffee bags and hand-written notes. But only if you have elegant handwriting!
8. Remember to always date-code your bags with a 'Roasted On …' date.

4

DIGITAL

AND

SOCIAL

MEDIA

MARKETING

According to a McKinsey Global Institute Study, 85% of consumer and retail companies currently use social technologies for their marketing. Many retailers, however, only use social technologies for marketing and advertising as a sales tool. In reality, it's an incredible tool to build customer relationships and personalise the consumer-seller experience. Social media is valued by customers as it is perceived as transparent and a two-way communication vehicle.

Tip 1: Let's Evaluate A Few Things First

The same basic marketing questions you asked yourself when you wrote your business plan should apply to your digital social media plan.

What are you selling? Will your focus be on coffee bean sales or the espresso/café experience? Identifying your focus will make it easier later on when you decide which social media features to take advantage of.

Who are you selling to? Understanding your target demographic is key. There's more than one social network and it's likely that your target demographic is spread out across several of them. It's also very possible that they'll be more active on some networks over others. Knowing where to focus your energy is vital to success.

How will you measure success? Look beyond vanity metrics such as Likes and Follows and try to find a direct link between conversation and conversion. Focus on influence over inflating a group size or follower base.

What resources should you put into this? This refers to what you are able to realistically afford to dedicate to social media in terms of time and tools. What will your social media team look like? Clearly defined roles and responsibilities will help avoid a digital disaster in the future. The allocation of human resources is by far the most significant cost tied to social media.

Put effort where it's needed. Having a clear understanding of your objectives and available resources will help determine the type of social media strategy to develop moving forward. Where will it allow you to reach the customers who crave a deeper, richer dialogue? Obviously, the more active you are the better. Social media can be very rewarding for retailers, but you only get what you put into it.

Tip 2: Listen to Your Audience

One thing that makes retailers very uncomfortable are uncontrolled comments about their business, products or service on social media. Not all comments will be positive. They dread being the next business to make headlines for a blunder or bad product that took off as a result of Twitter or Facebook discussions.

However, this engagement should be seen as an opportunity to listen, learn, improve and engage with your customers. So it's important to have an effective monitoring system that tracks mentions of your organisation, the good and the bad, across multiple social networks. You can, of course, monitor what's being said about your competition too. Listen methodically and without emotion, and learn what drives your customers' decisions.

Research indicates that people consider a response time to a query of within four hours to be reasonable. However, many brands are willing to let people hang for an average of ten hours. Not every retailer, of course, can afford around-the-clock social monitoring, but it certainly helps to at least make an effort to manage

Even though a lot of attention is placed on negative social mentions, don't let the positive ones go unnoticed either. Be sure to acknowledge the people who took time to share something positive about your brand.

your customers' expectations. Otherwise you run the risk of losing a customer to a competitor.

Learn how to deal with negative feedback and turn it into something constructive. You need to be diplomatic, so if you're too close and take offence easily, it's best to employ someone with these delicate skills to do this work for you. Don't just respond by directing a customer to your contact page and hope that fixes the issue. You really need to hear what consumers are saying and do everything you can to resolve the problem.

Even though a lot of attention is placed on negative social mentions, don't let the positive ones go unnoticed either. Be sure to acknowledge the people who took time to share something positive about your brand (whether they directly mentioned you or not). This practice demonstrates you listen and value what your customers have to say.

Lastly, remember that if your business is not being discussed in the social space, the chances are that people are talking about your competition.

Tip 3: Engage to Build Your Community

There is a lot of detail that goes into building your social presence and it's easy to get distracted. Remember, however, that your ultimate goal is to get people to visit your store. So how do you do that? Think about why people follow and engage with businesses on social media in the first place.

THE TOP FIVE REASONS ARE:
- Promotions and discounts/incentives.
- For the latest product information.
- Customer support.
- Entertaining content.
- Ability to offer feedback.

Offering exclusive deals and discounts to your social media followers is one way to drive social media traffic into your store. It gives you a chance to reward loyal customers and welcome those who are trying you for the first time.

Another option is to hold an offline event like offering exclusive public cupping sessions of new coffee blends. If marketed correctly, an offline event can be a great opportunity to build relationships with both new and existing customers.

Once customers are in your store, it'd be great if they shared their experience with their networks. Getting people to Tweet their locations or upload selfies with their latest purchases isn't terribly challenging. However, you can certainly take advantage of the practice by tossing a branded hashtag # into the mix.

Tip 4: Think Local

It's important for a retailer to always think local in retail. You have to craft your messaging with your particular location in mind. If you're talking to a broad group of people, your message can come across as robotic and not personalised. You should consider personalising your updates based on location if you have multiple stores in different locations. Use built-in targeting features to ensure the right message is delivered to the right place. Even if you just have one location, familiarise yourself with the community you're in.

> Consider holding an offline event like offering exclusive public cupping sessions of new coffee blends. If marketed correctly, an offline event can be a great opportunity to build relationships with both new and existing customers.

Tip 5: Make Your Mobile Advertisements Work Harder

According to Facebook, 49% of in-store purchases are influenced by digital interactions, of which more than 50% occur on mobile. Facebook Ads have long helped retailers promote in-store products, but there wasn't a way to customise creative based on local availability. Marketing out-of-stock products or inaccurate local prices can lead to a poor customer experience.

Dynamic ads for retail help you form better customer experiences and avoid wasted impressions. With this offering, ads are linked to local product catalogues. That means you can customise your ad creative for different stores based on local product inventory, pricing and promotions.

Tip 6: Go Visual

What you say on social media is important, but how you say it is even more critical. What we mean by this is how you deliver your message plays a big role in how it's received. For example, say the same message is published as a text-only update, as a photo and as a video. Which one do you think will receive more engagement? While the exact number might vary, chances are the photo or video will perform the best.

Visual storytelling is a hot trend in marketing right now, and one that many brands are paying attention to. Did you know that including a video on a landing page can increase conversion by 80%? In fact, by 2017 it's estimated that 74% of all internet traffic will be video. And with more support from platforms like Facebook, Instagram and Snapchat, visual storytelling isn't going away any time soon.

Tip 7: Amplify Your Message

Invest in promoted tweets, accounts or trends across social platforms that have already demonstrated the highest yield. Adopt social tools that allow you to scale your programs effectively in order to build social media success into your strategy.

Finally, when creating and executing your social media strategy, focus on the small details. They might seem trivial to you, but to a customer they could mean the difference between a sale and a bail. Strive to deliver excellence in every interaction, be it recognising a loyal customer, answering a question or resolving a customer issue.

5
ATTRACTING NEW CUSTOMERS AND RETAINING THEM

When you first open up your roastery/café you rely a lot on the local community (both business and household) to become your regular customers. "Regulars", as we know them, are the lifeblood of your business, and provide the regular cashflow that pays your wages, rent and other operating costs. Of course, promotion by the media is great to get them there in the first place but this is often short lived, and customers who come to you from outside the area will normally be restricted to weekend visits or as one-offs. The other five days need to have consistent customer flow and for that you will rely mostly on the local "regulars".

My business was in a retail/business/residential hub in Sydney's Neutral Bay. It is an affluent suburb with highly educated people. A prestigious Sydney school known as Redlands was around the corner and, in addition, we were located opposite one of the busiest Woolworths supermarkets in Australia. This wasn't by chance. It was a part of my strategic decision to open the store there (refer to Part A-1 of this book).

Businesses in the area included other retailers and specialty firms such as architects, engineers, software designers and real estate agents – oh, and lots and lots of hairdressers. These people made up the bulk of our espresso customers. Many converted to become regular coffee bean buyers as well over time. The shoppers at the supermarket and the other ancillary fresh food shops in the area (fruit/veg, meats, seafood, deli) were our primary roasted coffee bean clients.

So we had a great base to work off and we built up our client base for both sides of the business one by one. From that initial base you must continue to grow your new customer base constantly as people will drop off the other end over time for varying reasons – new jobs/homes in different areas, had to (God forbid) give up coffee, or simply gone to another coffeehouse for whatever crazy reason!

In small business WORD OF MOUTH referral is everything. I can't emphasise this enough, and it all comes back to having a great core product and excellent customer service. If you get these two things right, I assure you that your business will continue to grow. Theory has it that only one in ten customers will complain to you if they are not happy either with your product or service and that they, along with the other nine, will also tell on average another ten people of their negative experience.

Equally, on the other side of the equation, happy customers will do the same. Having various forms of calling cards they can pass on to their friends as a referral is important. It may be the eye-catching label of the bag of beans they take home: "Hey Steve, this coffee is awesome!"; "Yeah Greg, it's this funky little coffee roaster in Gladesville called XYZ Roasters" (shows Greg bag with your funky label on it). "They're such nice people and watching them roast the coffee in-store is so cool," says Steve. "We've got to go there together for a coffee," responds Greg. Job done.

Local community initiatives like sponsorships with product or espresso service at local schools, junior football clubs and other local initiatives is a great way to become an integral part of your local community and the loyalty you build by doing this is invaluable.

6
STRATEGIC MARKETING ALLIANCES

Always be on the lookout to align yourself with other brands that hold a similar brand value/position to you in the marketplace. It's especially good to leverage the brand value of bigger brands in the marketplace.

A good example of this is to offer an exclusive coffee blend to a major retailer and let them market it as such. You'll be amazed at the extra effort they put into the cross-promotion from their side when they have a story to tell.

I once proposed a joint promotion with a major appliance company to offer a coffee bean subscription with the sales of their domestic espresso machines. At the time we were a fairly small operation, but I sold that fact as an advantage – that we were high end and boutique – and somehow convinced them that they had more to gain by aligning with us than we did with them! Remember that coffee, with its high perceived value, is actually relatively cheap for you to give away as the producer. Much better to use 50kg of coffee for a promotion than hand over $10K in cash! Do the sums ...

Cross-promotional collaborations can also be fun and great for brand equity building. Several coffee and beer companies have collaborated to produce limited edition coffee stouts or variants of such ideas. A recent collaboration between Young Henrys brewery in Sydney and Campos Coffee with a coffee-infused Belgian Dubbel-style beer called Dubbel Skull was heavily promoted and a successful collaboration for both parties. Campos Coffee even released a commemorative hoodie to celebrate the collaboration[9]!

A final word on strategic alliances is to think outside the square with promotional ideas and don't be scared to approach larger businesses. As long as they can see a benefit at their end they are likely to engage and, at the very least, hear you out. Even if nothing comes of it initially it's still a great networking opportunity and puts you out there as a brand thought leader and innovator.

EXPERT TIP
Remember to always think "win:win" when coming up with possible marketing alliances with other businesses.

FOOTNOTE
[9] camposcoffee.com/product/young-henrys-collab-long-sleeve-tee

7
WEBSITES AND ONLINE STRATEGIES

We were early adopters of the webstore idea. Websites and e-commerce were still clunky in those days and nothing like how easy it is now to set one up off the shelf and adapt it to your needs.

All the payment facilities are easily integrated thanks to Paypal and other financial service providers such as Stripe and Square. Integrating major bank-provided merchant systems into websites was such a palaver just 10 years ago. Luckily for you, dear reader, that's all changed for the better.

A website should act as a branding vehicle and an extension of your communication strategy where you can tell your story, assert your values and promote your coffee and wares. It's also a great vehicle for coffee education, especially for the home market, and you can promote exclusive cupping sessions at your store. If you're looking towards wholesale, you can promote that service there too and encourage enquiries, tasting sessions and so on. Integrate a Blog or Vlog to inform and educate, and position your business as experts in the field. Your website should integrate seamlessly with your social media marketing platforms such as Facebook, Twitter and Instagram.

The website must be easy to navigate and use – intuitive I think is the word I'm looking for. In fact UX, or User Experience, has become a buzzword and a profession amongst web professionals and is a very lucrative business these days. A clunky website will reflect poorly on your business, so put a lot of attention into its functionality.

SEO, or Search Engine Optimisation[10], is a mysterious beast and I am no expert in this department, but my advice is to use an experienced web designer to code it for you so that the search engines can find you. Be warned that you will get dozens of spammers with dubious accents who will promise you the world in regards to SEO miracles both via email and via phone spam. Stay well clear of these dudes.

In terms of paid online promotion I found Google Adwords to be the only measurable form of paid advertising where I saw results. It's not cheap though, and you have to weigh up the cost/benefit of the expenditure. The reason it's marginal is that the online coffee business market has become huge and extremely competitive. This has pushed the click-through price (as it's a type of bidding process) through the roof. This means a greater monthly spend to be in the first three-to-four ads on the page, which is important if you want to get click-throughs. If you are promoting a wholesale business then it's definitely worth it, however for retail bean sales it's a marginal punt. It's also a haven for phone spammers, so beware.

FOOTNOTE
[10] Search Engine Optimisation is a methodology of strategies, techniques and tactics used to increase the amount of visitors to a website by obtaining a high-ranking placement in the search results page of a search engine such as Google, Bing or Yahoo.

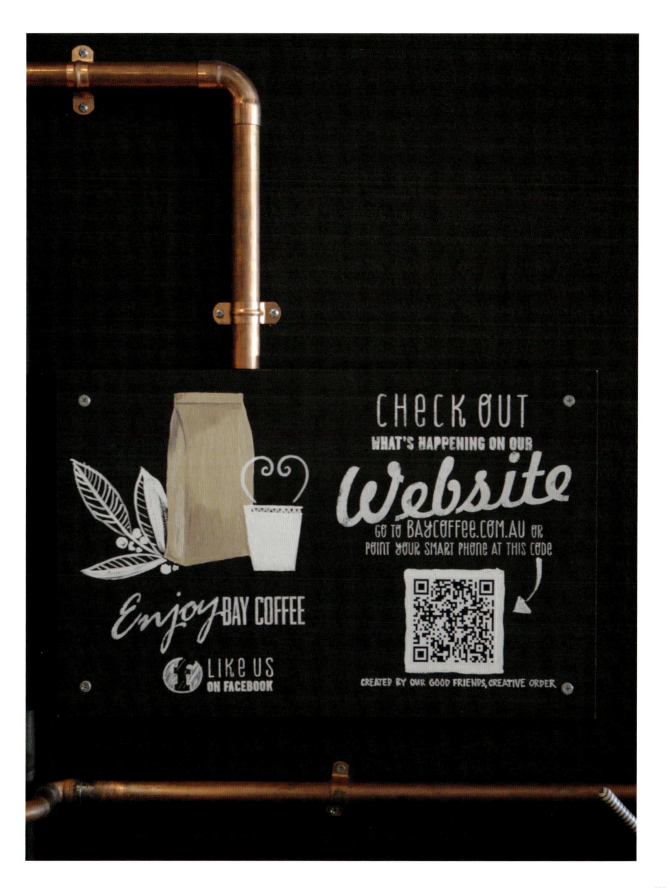

C3

EXPANSION OPPORTUNITIES

There are many ways to expand your business and many appropriate – and some not so appropriate – opportunities will present themselves as you grow and become an established player in the industry. Let's look briefly at some of the common expansion opportunities that can present themselves to smaller coffee companies and examine how you may be able to take advantage of them.

IN PART C-3 WE WILL COVER:

1. OPENING MORE RETAIL SITES
2. WHOLESALE COFFEE – A WHOLE NEW BALL GAME
3. IDLE CAPACITY AND ITS HIDDEN COSTS
4. CONTRACT ROASTERS
5. CHANGE MANAGEMENT
6. OTHER APPROACHES TO EXPANSION

1 OPENING MORE RETAIL SITES

Assuming all is going well with your first flagship store, you may decide that more stores are in order to capitalise on your success. Sales agents (especially from shopping centres) wanting to cash in on your success will approach you. Opening a second or third store is not as straightforward as it seems, however, and there is a history of (especially, for some reason, third store) disaster stories out there.

Where many people go wrong is not putting the same amount of effort into their site location research as they did with their first store, or simply making assumptions that if it worked here it will work there too. You'd be surprised how just a few different social, demographic and location elements can derail your concept.

The first question to ask yourself is: Why does your first store work so well in its current location? Who are your customers, why are they in the area in the first place, and why do they like what you're offering so much? Ask them! A simple market research survey will do the job. Survey at least 100 customers to get a decent sample size. I can't emphasise how important this objective research is. If you feel you can't be objective, hire a good qualitative researcher to help you out. You might think this is expensive but think of the extraordinary expense of a wasted shop fit-out and trying to get out of a lease if the new store is a dud.

Some very successful hospitality operators have done very well by theming their new offerings to the area. Think the Merivale Group (Coogee Pavilion, Newport Arms) and the guys from Applejack Hospitality (shout out to Hamish and Ben!) with The Botanist, SoCal, etc. They put meticulous thought into how they design and launch their new hospitality offerings. Nothing is left to chance and that's one of the reasons they are so successful. "But these guys have mega-bucks behind them!" you counter. That's not the point. It's their research and eye for detail that is the point I'm trying to make here, and it's a critical key to success for all new retail businesses, big or small.

So let's say you've done your meticulous research and it's a goer. You now have to find that perfect site and go through the same processes we discussed in Part A-1 of this book.

What will be different about this site from your first one? Well for one thing, this is an opportunity to adapt your store to the new location/demographic you're servicing. What works and what doesn't in your first store; what have your learned? How can you improve service efficiencies with this store's design and fit-out?

Beyond design, how will the new location demographics affect your product offering? I always found it a great idea to create a new coffee blend to celebrate the new area and name it after the area. You'll be amazed how it resonates and becomes a best seller. Do you need to tweak your food offering? Is it more of a dining-in area (think beachside) than a take-out (think CBD)?

We could go on for days here, but you get my drift. Do your research and your homework. Write a separate business/marketing plan for each new location and develop your strategies based on sound research and logic. Never assume success is a *fait accompli* (pardon the French).

2

WHOLESALE COFFEE – A WHOLE NEW BALL GAME

Cafés and Other Wholesale Markets

Most coffeehouses that develop into coffee brands eventually eye the wholesale coffee market. It's where the volume is and where you can make a shitload of money if you get it right. However, as with all promised lands, there are a million other guys out there thinking the same thing as you. The wholesale coffee market is an extremely competitive and aggressive market to play in. It's also huge. In Australia alone the pure roast coffee sector is estimated to be worth US$218m/AU$302m (+6.6% yoy growth), while in the USA it's estimated at US$9,622m/$AU13,316m in 2018 (+3.1% yoy growth). Of course it's going to be competitive[11].

Just because it's competitive, however, doesn't mean you can't have a piece of it. Even a minuscule percentage share is worth quite a bit of dosh. If you're doing all the right things in your retail space wholesale business normally comes to you, because cafés will want a bit of your success in the retail space. Set a great example with your own roastery/café and they will come.

Moving into the café wholesale supply sector, however, will mean some structural changes for your business.

WHILE IT'S NOT THE FOCUS OF THIS BOOK, HERE IS A LIST OF THINGS YOU WILL NEED TO CONSIDER BEFORE TAKING THE PLUNGE INTO THE CAFÉ WHOLESALE COFFEE MARKET:

- Requirement for specialised sales/relationship managers.
- Roast capacity beyond the volume of your shop roaster.
- Warehousing and additional storage capacity for green, roasted coffee and ancillary products to sell and related equipment .
- Your customer service ability and delivery/fulfillment capability.
- Ability to supply and service espresso equipment on loan or hire.
- Ability to cost product and service offerings and work with finer margins.
- Servicing a B2B market, which is quite different to a retail environment.

There is a lot there to consider and manage. It's quite a specialised area and one you can't go into unprepared and without the necessary structures and systems, as it will quickly catch up with you as you start to grow and add multiple accounts under management. Some of the above points are obvious and all to do with volume and the capacity to produce, store, transport and so on. I'd like, however, to highlight a couple of the bullet points from above and share my experiences with you.

The killer factor in this market is funding and maintaining espresso equipment on loan to your accounts. You will hear some coffee suppliers say, "We don't play that game" and so on, but it's bullshit. They all do it, and if you don't do it you won't win many accounts, especially early on before you've established yourself. Thankfully, it's a tad easier today to fund as there are numerous companies out there doing a nice trade in the finance/rental markets with quite flexible terms.

So, in a nutshell, how it works is that you can rent a machine and grinder/s on a contract and have a fixed weekly cost that you can plug into your costing spreadsheet so you know exactly what your costs are. The other advantage of renting is that it's easily accountable from a financial accounting perspective as it's a below-the-line rental expense and not a capital item you have to depreciate.

FOOTNOTE
[11] Source: The Statistics Portal – *Statista* April 2018.

The other good thing about renting is that you can send the equipment back if the account doesn't deliver the numbers expected, re-deploy it to another account or offer the account to take over the rental contract. So it's extremely flexible. Yes, you will pay a premium on the rental but it's marginal over the risk of having to borrow money to fund the capital of buying numerous machines and risk having idle machinery to store when there is no account to utilise them in. It's a no-brainer really for start-ups and this flows onto my next point.

It's critical to understand the cost of servicing your clients. I developed a spreadsheet that flowed from my finished product (1kg of coffee ready to ship) manufacturing cost analysis through to the bottom line of servicing accounts of varying sizes. I could quite accurately estimate how much each account contributed to the bottom line after servicing costs. Very simply, it functioned like this:

ESTIMATED WEEKLY GROSS PROFIT = KGS X NET $ PROFIT PER KG CHARGED, LESS:
- Weekly cost of equipment supplied (from your rental contract).
- Weekly cost of servicing equipment (I simply worked on a figure of $500/$1000/$1500 p.a. divided by 50 weeks for sml/med/lge accounts).
- Cost of rep servicing: $25 fixed p.w.

Equals Net sum x 50 trading weeks = Net dollar profit return per customer based on volume and price you charge.

Creating a spreadsheet based on this logic will let you play around with various "what-if" scenarios where you can change the variables of sale price per kg and the estimated weekly kg purchases. While the latter can be a little bit of educated guesswork, especially when you supply start-up cafés, once you have some real data to plug in you can make adjustments (e.g. price) and make decisions accordingly. For example, make the decision to pull out of the account or negotiate new terms if they have not lived up to their promise.

Once again, I have come back to the importance of detailed costing analysis and of understanding your numbers. It's probably even more critical in the wholesale market than the retail market as margins are finer. Running a simple spreadsheet based on this logic for every client will make it easier for you to see if you are running an account at a profit or a loss and help make your decisions much easier.

The killer factor in this market is funding and maintaining espresso equipment on loan to your accounts. You will hear some coffee suppliers say, "We don't play that game" and so on, but it's bullshit. They all do it, and if you don't do it you won't win many accounts.

A beautifully laid-out wholesale manufacturing plant in Melbourne – Code Black Roasters.

3
IDLE CAPACITY AND ITS HIDDEN COSTS

Economies of Scale

So you're convinced on the basis of how rapidly you've put on your first fifteen wholesale café accounts that you're absolutely going to kill it in the wholesale market, and it's time to find that factory/warehouse space and buy that 60kg coffee roaster to cope. Whoa, hold on there tiger! Let's do some simple sums first!

Let's assume you're now selling 800kg of coffee per week and your 15kg shop roaster can no longer cope with this volume. It probably could at a stretch, but it's a lot of work and it would be hot and uncomfortable in a shop environment to work the roaster all day long. The step up to a 30kg or 60kg machine will make your life easier and improve batch consistency – but what volume do you need to justify the cost? Let's work that out.

I firmly believe that if you have growth in mind a 30kg machine is a waste of time, as it's only a small step up from your shop roaster. It costs about 75% of the larger 60kg unit and you will quickly outgrow it, requiring yet another substantial investment. So you go with the 60kg machine. This machine can output approximately 50kg of roasted coffee every 15 minutes or 200kg per hour. So in effect you've roasted your entire week's requirement in about five hours. Happy days!

WHAT YOU FORGET THOUGH, IS THAT YOU HAVE TO FUND SEVERAL THINGS TO KEEP IT GOING:

➤ The rental and outgoings on the 150–300+sqm premises you'll require to house your new roaster and associated packaging/processing equipment in – AU$60k +p/a minimum outlay in Sydney.
➤ Funding of your new roasting machine, semi-auto packing line, testing lab, office, pallet racking, forklift, delivery van etc., either via leasing or bank loan facility. Allow a $250–$300K spend.
➤ Staff to run the new factory site.

It adds up quickly and can catch up with you. Idle capacity can kill and you don't know when you'll fill it. Without going into a detailed costing breakdown here, I worked out that you needed to be roasting about 2,000kg per week to make the transition truly viable.

So what's the half-way house of coffee empire expansion production-wise? Contract roasters.

4
CONTRACT ROASTERS

There are two types of contract roasters. Firstly there are contract roasters who are 100% dedicated to contract roasting and do not focus on their own brand, and then there are the branded roasters with excess idle capacity (see opposite) who are desperate to make a few extra bucks to fill in the idle capacity at their shiny new factory. In my experience dedicated contract roasters are your best option. Let's explore the reasons why below.

Contract Roasters and Their Services

So why would I always choose a dedicated contract roaster over another branded coffee roaster? Let me count the ways[12] ...

- Dedicated contract roasters are not conflicted in producing a great coffee for your business as you're not a direct competitor in the same marketplace.
- They have well-maintained equipment and economies of scale – a usual setup will have a 120kg and 60kg roaster for larger clients and a 30kg for small jobs, and they have fully automated packing lines for efficiency.
- They understand and respect the confidentiality of your blend recipes.
- People like you are their core business so they want you to be happy.
- They normally have high-level food product standard accreditation standards such as HACCP.
- Some can provide full marketing services such as packaging, design services and so on.
- Blend development services and QA protocols and standards.
- Logistics and storage facilities for green and roasted coffee/packaging.
- Economies of scale with green bean and packaging purchasing power.
- You'll save money on fixed costs of equipment maintenance, insurances, staff, factory running costs.
- They'll manage the inventory (forecasting) of raw input stock and roasted coffee (aging/turnover).

FOOTNOTE

[12] This saying is not by William Shakespeare, as I too initially assumed. In fact it's by Elizabeth Barrett Browning, *Sonnets from the Portuguese* – Sonnet 43.

Snapshot of a Contract Coffee Roaster

Bruce and Audrey Brawn established Gourmet Gold Coffee Roasters in 1975 in Sydney's leafy north shore. It began life as a micro coffee roastery in Cremorne with a 5kg window roaster. In 1987 the Brawns set up their first factory/warehouse in Artarmon. Their sons, Peter and Geoff, joined the business in the 1980s and subsequently took over its running in 1994.

By 2000 the coffee industry was going through the specialty coffee boom and the demand for high-volume contract roasting started to take off as artisan roasters were beginning to take over the wholesale café market from the traditional large players of the time and needed help meeting demand.

Peter and Geoff decided to change direction with the business and focus entirely on contract roasting. To do this they designed and built their ideal roasting space and warehouse that was specially set up for the unique requirements of contract roasting. They set up a 400sqm factory and warehouse in Lane Cove West and purchased a Joper 120kg roasting system. Coupled with their existing 25kg and 35kg roasters they had dramatically increased their capacity to meet demand.

Of course, roasting capacity is only part of the equation. Packing all this coffee is the other side of the equation. So they added to their semi-automatic hand packer an Italian-made Comunetti automatic bag filler that had an ability to pack 400kg of coffee into 1kg bags in 90 minutes. Compare this to a micro roaster who would have to hand-weigh, pack and seal bags manually at an approximate rate of 80kg per hour.

With 80+ pallet spaces, forklift and truck access, the space is designed for efficiency and large-scale production. Recently they have added a state-of-the-art cupping room for their clients and blend development has become a bigger part of their offering.

Remember that you'll get the best out of a contractor relationship if you actually get involved and participate in the process.

CONFIDENTIALITY IS A HUGE CONCERN FOR ROASTERS WHO DECIDE TO GO DOWN THIS PATH. YOU NEED TO FEEL CONFIDENT ON SEVERAL LEVELS AND SOME QUESTIONS THAT NATURALLY WILL OCCUR ARE:

- Are they roasting the green beans I've specified? Firstly, you own the green beans. They may order it for you, store and manage stock levels, but you should receive the invoice from your green bean supplier – so check! The contractor should also have all your beans, packaging and other raw materials on dedicated pallets that you can inspect at any time.
- Will they keep my blend recipes secret? This is the foundation of being a contract roaster. If you're worried, ask them who within their business knows the blend recipes, and how and where they are stored.
- What are their QA procedures? Before you engage a contract roaster get them to go through their QA protocols. You should be able to access your company file at any time to see your roast logs, cupping logs and QA check lists.
- Are the green beans I'm paying for being used solely for my coffee? Ask to see their order and production log and then do the maths at the standard 20% maximum shrinkage rate.

Clockwise from top: Tom Brawn releasing de-stoned beans; Peter checking out a roast batch prior to packing; a perfectly weighed 1kg of coffee; Geoff operating the Joper 120kg roaster.

EXPERT TIP FROM PETER BRAWN

When looking to choose a contract roaster, look at their experience and longevity in the business. You should have a similar philosophy regarding coffee roasting. Choose a bricks-and-mortar business you feel comfortable going into; it should feel like an extension of your own coffee business. You need to feel a sense of trust in their services, ability and confidentiality.

5

CHANGE MANAGEMENT – HOW A CHANGE OF TACK CAN AFFECT YOUR BUSINESS

If you're a retail coffee roaster and you want to seriously expand beyond the borders of your shop and move into the café, office or any other wholesale supply market it affects more than just your production/supply capability. It will impact your sales and back-room support infrastructure and staffing levels. You may be required to employ specialist staff, employ contractors to certain roles or retrain and educate your existing staff in new knowledge areas and roles. It will also require a change of mindset. This is where some change management skills and knowledge come in handy.

Let's first start with sales and customer support.

Selling to and supporting wholesale accounts is quite different to selling to retail customers. The retail transaction is quite simple really – they pay, and you provide a product or service, usually in the moment.

There are two key areas of wholesale client management: Acquisition and Retention. Both are equally challenging in the ultra-competitive coffee world.

Acquisition can come in many ways – clients come to you because you're such legends, or you go after them by knocking on their doors, advertising your offering or by referral.

Retention is influenced by all the work you do to help your clients, on the coffee side at least, run a great business and be successful themselves. Some companies have specialised reps who just go out there and gain new accounts and others, known as relationship managers, who look after existing accounts only. You'll probably find that until you reach a certain volume size your sales reps will have to multi-task.

Darren loved his Jamaican Blue Mountain coffee and his café clients.

To me the relationship side of client service is the most important and you need the right people in the job. Why? Because these clients will become your brand ambassadors by default. They may not have your brand name on the door but they carry your branded coffee. They can make or break your brand. If their café is awesome and featured in all the food press, you will probably get a mention too. Equally if they are really shitty, not just on the coffee side but overall (service/food) then it can reflect poorly on you as well.

You may have heard of the "snowball effect". If you can get about 10–20 incredibly awesome cafés carrying your brand and demonstrating how fantastic your coffee is to their customers, in time it will generate enquiries from other café owners who want the same level of success. And believe me it can snowball!

This level of relationship servicing is not easy, and you need well-trained sales reps and great training and procedural systems in place. This will involve providing client barista training and workflow training as a minimum. The more you can assist them to thrive, especially in the early days, the greater the potential benefit to you for your coffee brand. As coffee wholesaling is not the focus of this book I won't elaborate further here on customer service as there is another whole book on this topic, but I think I've highlighted the fact that it's critical to your success in this area.

Next let's look at the financial side. Margins are tighter in the wholesale area. Everyone needs to make a margin, of course. The trade-off is that you have volume. Cafés can purchase anywhere from 10kg per week in a sleepy suburban location to 200kg+ in a busy CBD location with three espresso machine bays.

Personally I don't know how a café can survive financially on less than 20kg of espresso coffee sales per week, but that's another story. You want to get the averages up. Each account gives you work to do – and believe me, a crappy 5kg or 10kg account can give you way more trouble and suck up more time than a large, efficient account doing 50kg+ per week. You don't want too many crappy accounts.

The other implication is that they are also likely to be late or poor payers on invoices. Unlike retail the transaction usually isn't in the moment of providing the product or service (COD). These accounts probably have another dozen suppliers chasing them for payment, as well as their landlord chasing overdue rent as weeks of poor sales figures stack up against them.

So it snowballs for them too, but in a very bad way. They do a runner[13] and the landlord impounds your loaned espresso equipment. This is why you must always get a signed loan agreement itemising EVERYTHING you loan and noting the serial numbers. I've had several awful experiences of having to retrieve loan equipment – so don't go there. It's not fun, especially if shopping centres are involved. As I have noted previously, they are ruthless knobs[14].

> Change Management is the collective term for all approaches to prepare and support individuals, teams and organisations in making organisational change. Done properly, it can be a very rewarding and motivating process.

The "runner scenario" is extreme, but late payments and the time it can take out of your day to chase payment is just dead time and soul destroying if you have several. There will always be one, but you don't want to have many on your books. Remember, you are not a financier. If they need a line of credit, they should see their bank, not you. I always requested COD for the first couple of months and then a 7-day account. They have, after all, used your product within the seven days to turn a profit so they can pay you. No excuses.

Change Management is the collective term for all approaches to prepare and support individuals, teams and organisations in making organisational change.

This process can be made easier by having separate functional teams (retail and wholesale) but this, at least initially, may be hard to justify financially. You will, therefore, need to retrain staff to become sales reps, relationship managers, machine technicians, training managers and so on. However, it can a be very rewarding and motivating process to up-skill dedicated staff and good employees will repay your faith in spades.

I was very proud in my time that I only had to bring in one outsider from the organisation (a specialist sales representative). All my other staff who worked in the wholesale division started in our retail roastery and learned their craft there.

FOOTNOTE

[13] An Aussie term for locking the doors and disappearing into the night.

[14] Something you will find attached to a door.

6
OTHER APPROACHES TO EXPANSION

Mergers and Acquisitions

There are essentially two kinds of mergers and acquisitions: strategic and financial.

A financial merger or acquisition is pursued, as the name implies, for financial reasons – often to pick up some quick cash or as an investment. But I'm not really interested in financial M&As for this particular discussion.

Strategic mergers and acquisitions offer a solution to a different business problem. Perhaps the acquirer is looking to grab a new product line, add some additional facilities, enter a new market, or gain expertise and intellectual property. For professional service firms, a strategic M&A is often about gaining credibility, adding intellectual firepower or changing the balance of power in a particular market. The bottom line is a strategic merger yields value for both the acquired and the acquiring firm.

SOME ADVANTAGES OF MERGERS AND ACQUISITIONS ARE TO:

- Fill in gaps in product or service offerings or client lists.
- Efficiently acquire talent or IP.
- Leverage cost and revenue synergies such as accessing new markets, expanding customer base and reducing competition.
- Save time and money on long learning curves.

Joint Ventures

When two companies invest funds to create a third, jointly owned company that new subsidiary is called a joint venture. Because the joint venture can access assets, knowledge and funds from both of its partners, it can combine the best features of those companies without altering the parent companies. The new company is an ongoing entity that will be in business for itself, but the profits are owned by the parent companies.

Strategic Alliance

A strategic alliance is a legal agreement between two or more companies to share access to their technology, trademarks or other assets. A strategic alliance does not create a new company.

EXPERT TIPS

1. Expansion opportunities will arise if you're a success with your retail coffee roastery. Assess each opportunity logically and without ego.
2. When opening a new retail store be as meticulous with your research as you were with your first store.
3. Retail stores can fail in different locations for various demographic reasons. Don't assume a successful store will automatically replicate its success in a new location.
4. Supplying cafés in the wholesale coffee market is a great opportunity to scale up in volume sales. It can, however, be a rocky road, extremely competitive and specialised.
5. Be meticulous with your costings and understanding of numbers.
6. Expansion of your roasting facilities can have hidden costs and idle capacity can kill.
7. Consider the services of a dedicated contract roaster as a transition strategy until you have the roasting volume to support your new factory and a larger coffee roaster.
8. Study change management principles. Changing markets can have a big impact on how you run your business and your staff.
9. Look at possible partnerships, acquisitions and mergers as a way to expand your business. Seek expert advice when looking into this.

C4

THE END GAME – CASHING IN THE CHIPS

This is, once again, potentially an entire book topic on its own. I can only touch the surface here. I hope, however, that this overview will give you some perspective on the process involved in successfully selling your business and, as they say, cashing in the chips when the time comes to realise your investment.

IN PART C-4 WE WILL COVER:

1. PLAN THE END GAME FROM THE START
2. THE RED FLAGS FOR POTENTIAL BUYERS/INVESTORS
3. FIVE CRITICAL STEPS FOR GETTING YOUR BUSINESS SALE READY
4. ARE BUSINESS BROKERS WORTH IT?
5. A NOTE ON WELL-BEING FOR WHEN YOU EXIT STAGE LEFT

1
PLAN THE END GAME FROM THE START

This may sound a bit counter-intuitive, but you should have some idea about an exit strategy when you write your initial business plan. Of course, you won't know why, when or how you will be exiting the business before you even start, but I always swore that I would not be carried out in a box[15].

If you're not planning on a long-term return on your investment, then you could be selling yourself short. Remember that when you invest in your business you are foregoing another investment opportunity. The stock market has averaged about 8–9% over the ten-year cycle, property a similar growth number in the major cities, and even keeping your money in the bank will at least earn you around 2% pa (but where's the fun in that?)

My point is you must see this as an investment and an employment opportunity. If you see this solely as a job, the dream is likely to end in tears. You don't have to become a huge player in the market to be a success. Your strategy may be to divest and bring in investors to achieve growth, or build it to a certain point and then sell it for someone else to carry things on. If this is your plan, and you're happy with that, then good on you! Cash in the chips and move on to the next adventure! The latter is exactly what I did and I was very satisfied with the outcome.

So if you have a trajectory in mind and a target exit point then you can plan for it and steer the business in that direction from Day 1. It helps you set targets to achieve and it motivates you. Of course, your plans may change as things pan out over time. You might decide that the idea of a coffee empire really sits well with you and you keep going. The very fact you have a plan with targets to aim for will help you become successful. Having no vague plan is the real issue.

> "Often when you think you're at the end of something, you're at the beginning of something else." FRED ROGERS

FOOTNOTE
[15] http://bit.ly/2GvaCDm

2

THE RED FLAGS FOR POTENTIAL BUYERS/ INVESTORS

When the time comes – and if you're on top of your game – you will receive approaches, be it directly or through a third party like a business broker. The difference between getting a good price and a great price for your business depends a great deal on how prepared your business is to hand over. There are many red flags that potential buyers and investors look out for, and while they may not turn them off entirely, these red flags will impact the money they are prepared to offer you.

So what are some of the key red flags that will put off potential buyers or investors? You may already be in business and be reading this book. The following buyer red flag checklist will help you decide if your business is sale ready or in need of some remedial work before going to market.

See how many of these buyer red flags currently apply to your business:

1 The business is overly reliant on the owner for its continued success on a day-to-day basis.

2 There is a lack of clear systems and procedures in place making the transition to a new owner difficult for all concerned (including your staff, clients and suppliers).

3 The owner is in a hurry to sell, and wants a quick exit.

4 Does the business have verifiable financial claims? Is there unreported income, payroll or do the numbers just not add up?

5 The business plant and equipment is not in good condition or accurately valued.

6 Does the business show a steady increase in sales and/or profit over the last three years?

7 The business is showing a drop in sales and/or profit in the last 12 months. Are the declared profits real?

8 The buyer is unable to negotiate a favourable lease with the landlord.

9 How likely is the landlord to grant transfer of lease to a new owner?

10 The seller refuses to sign a non-compete clause.

11 The business is carrying a high percentage of unexplained bad debt.

12 The seller's accounting system is dodgy or unreliable.

13 The seller is behind in filing his annual statements and tax returns with the ATO.

If you already own a business, even if it's not a coffee business, tell me … how did you go? These are the same questions that any savvy (and good) buyer will ask of any seller. Most of you will only have a few areas of concern in your business. In most cases these can be fixed and will instantly make your business stand out as a great buy, especially in a market full of other questionable offerings.

I believe that having your business prepared for sale could make the difference between not just a successful sale, but hundreds of thousands of dollars in your pocket. Why? Because a buyer will pay a premium for a business they can feel confident in to risk their cash. The easiest way to think about this is to put yourself in the buyer's shoes (and please try to be completely unbiased here). Would you buy this business from someone you don't really know in its current shape?

3

FIVE CRITICAL STEPS FOR GETTING YOUR BUSINESS SALE READY

I am indebted to the authors of the book *Small Business Big Exit* for the structure and the ideas presented that I have essentially reworked with my own thoughts and experiences for the following section of the book. I highly recommend you read this book if you are thinking of selling your business at some stage[16].

Following is a summary of the steps you will need to go through in order to achieve the best possible sale of your business. I will explore these in a bit more detail after the summary.

INTENT: Why do you want to sell? What will you do next?
VALUE: What's your business worth on the market in its current state? What do you need to sell it for to make it viable for you?
PREPARE: This is how you make your business attractive to the right buyers – by putting in the systems and fixing any "buyer red alerts" in your business. By doing this you close the gap between what you want/need dollar-wise and what the market currently values your business at dollar-wise.
MARKET: Who and where are your buyers? When is the right time to list? What platform is most appropriate and cost effective? Your buyer could be a competitor, or even an existing employee.
CLOSE THE SALE: Find the right buyer and close the deal.

Now let's briefly look at each of these preparation stages in a bit more detail.

Intent: Should I Stay or Should I Go?

This is, without doubt, the single hardest decision you will make in your professional life. It's hard because it has a lot of implications. What will you do afterwards? You will normally have a non-compete period so your safety net of working in coffee will be gone. In fact, I could write an entire chapter on this one question as it's very complicated. So let me say it again, if you have a clear exit plan in place (the one you started working on all those years ago), the decision and the passage through the sale process will be made a lot easier. You should, as a result, also secure the best possible price for your business. This will make the transition process to your new life venture a heck of a lot easier too.

Remember that the best time to sell your business is when you WANT to and not when you HAVE to. The key to achieving this goal is through preparation.

It helps to understand why you want to sell and what you want to do next. This will help clarify how much your business will need to sell for so you can do what you want to do next comfortably. You can then work out if the current market value of your business aligns with your financial needs and, if not, what you have to do to get your business into shape to achieve your goals. This is called exit planning and it can take years to get your business positioned to meet your exit plan goals.

Of course, shit happens in life and you may have to sell for various reasons such as ill health, life trauma, conflict with business or personal partners, greedy landlords and so on. You may have run out of capital or simply misread the market/location – or just generally stuffed things up big time and you've run out of cash. The sad reality of small business is that 80% fail in the first five years, although coffee roasteries seem to fair better in the longevity stakes.

FOOTNOTE
[16] Please refer to the Book, Article and Web References at the end of this book.

Value: So What's it Worth to You, Dear Buyer?

It's not just the internal state of your business that will impact its market value at any given point in time. Many external factors can affect what your business is worth. From the state of the economy (recession/downturn), rising interest rates or tighter monetary lending policy (impact on financing ability of buyers), right through to "are coffee roasteries hot in the market right now?" or, is the market flooded (supply and demand factors)?

Timing is everything in business. From when you open, to when you invest in expansion into new market sectors, and especially when you decide to sell. In my experience I got this both right and wrong at various times and the impact can be long lasting if you do get it wrong. Get it right though, and the rewards can be considerable. Even if you screwed up at times during the journey – and you will – remember that as long as you sell at the right time you will do OK.

Of course, getting approached to sell presents as a great opportunity as you feel that you are in the position of power. This can be a double-edged sword, however. You may indeed get lucky and your Alan Bond[17] may appear on the horizon; however, opportunists who have nothing to lose might also approach you. They are banking on the fact that you either have no idea what your business is really worth now or down the track, or that you've done all the hard work and are about to reap the rewards in a few years' time, but you're exhausted and fragile of mind. A bird in the hand, after all ...

You will be amazed at how much the valuation of your business will vary depending on who values it. An accountant will always be super-conservative (especially the buyer's accountant). You will always be the opposite ("Oh, it has to be worth millions!"). The business will be worth what the market dictates at that point in time. Yes, there are industry standard methods for valuing a business (and we will explore these shortly), but they are guides only and many factors within and outside your business will impact the actual price at any given point in time. So it's not really a surprise that you may not know what your business is really worth on the open market.

Knowing who your potential buyers are will help you work out the value as well. Strategic buyers may want to buy your business to expand their customer base – for example, a large food-based conglomerate may want to add a coffee brand to their portfolio or tap into the premium coffee segment they do not currently occupy. This is a great opportunity, as they will often pay over the odds to acquire a brand, especially if the buyer is a large multi-national. They may also just want to purchase just a part of your business – say, your wholesale operation, to tack onto theirs.

On the other end of the scale, you could sell to one of your employees, or there may be cashed-up individuals looking for a lifestyle change away from corporate life, or you may have investors who want the business purely as an investment and for it to be run under management. Each of these potential buyers has their own positives and negatives in terms of the price you achieve and the ease of exit on your part. Do you want to remain a part of management of the business at a reduced shareholding (smaller piece of a much larger pie) for an agreed time, operate it on a wage on behalf of the new owners without the headaches of ownership, or just get the hell out of there and do the next thing in your life?

FOOTNOTE

[17] The late Kerry Packer famously quipped: "You only get one Alan Bond in your lifetime, and I've had mine", referring to when he bought back his television station from him for AU$250 million after having sold it to Bond for a then record AU$1.02 billion just three years prior in 1987.

So what is a coffee roastery worth according to benchmark figures? There are many ways to value a business and I will not go into them all here. Often you will use a combination of methods to reach a valuation. A common method, and the easiest one to explain here, is to value the business as a multiple of EBITDA + SOH with a factor added in for assets and goodwill. Let me explain these terms:

EBITDA = **Earnings Before Interest and Tax with Depreciation Added Back.** Essentially this is your net profit figure before interest earnings are added in and any tax is taken out. A year-end P&L statement will have depreciation deducted for assets, so this needs to be added back into the profit line as it's an accounting measure.

SOH = **Stock On Hand**, calculated on the day of the settlement by both parties conducting a stocktake and verifying together the value of the business-owned stock on the day of handover.

ASSETS: **Tangible assets** like buildings have a market value and need to be factored into the business sale price. Many business owners prefer to retain the building and become the landlord. If you're in a position to do this, having been lucky enough to own the building you operate in, then that's your choice. It really depends on how much you and the buyer value it at. Everything is, after all, for sale at the right price, isn't it? Most other tangible assets in general have little worth if you are a small business. Shop fittings, manufacturing equipment, cars, etc., are either usually depreciated to the hilt or under financing arrangements, so they can count for little in the final sale price.

Intangible assets like your brand's goodwill, systems, intellectual property and business model are harder to value.

GOODWILL: the established reputation of a business regarded as a quantifiable asset and calculated as part of its value when it is sold.

In reality, the value of your business amounts to a number that represents future earnings potential, assets and goodwill. These factors can vary a great deal and the best person to value your business is a reputable business broker. They have thorough valuation systems and generally have their finger on the pulse. Find a broker that has experience in selling coffee businesses. This is crucial both in terms of valuation and finding the right buyers.

If you operate a retail coffee roastery with a café component like I did, you sit between two benchmarks. At the time I sold, wholesale coffee roasting businesses were selling at up to 3–4 x EBITDA and cafés between 1–3 x EBITDA. The difference in multiple is explained by the risk of retail situations being more exposed to market downturns and other external market factors, and the number of under-performing traditional cafés in the market. Distressed sales are common in the café market and, unfortunately, drag the overall EBITDA benchmark multiple factor down.

So let's use a quick "back of the envelope" type look at what your business MIGHT be worth on paper. Remember though, that this is just a benchmark. As I have explained already and will explain further in the next section, your final price is influenced by numerous internal and external factors at any given time and the market will ultimately decide what it is worth. Remember, a business is usually sold on profit and valued on potential.

	SCENARIO 1	SCENARIO 2	SCENARIO 3
EBITDA	$200,000.00	$400,000.00	$600,000.00
2 x multiple	$400,000.00	$800,000.00	$1,200,000.00
3 x multiple	$600,000.00	$1,200,000.00	$1,800,000.00
4 x multiple	$800,000.00	$1,600,000.00	$2,400,000.00
plus			
SOH	$25,000.00	$25,000.00	$25,000.00
2 x multiple	$425,000.00	$825,000.00	$1,225,000.00
3 x multiple	$625,000.00	$1,225,000.00	$1,825,000.00
4 x multiple	$825,000.00	$1,625,000.00	$2,425,000.00

THEREFORE, SCENARIO 2 VALUES YOUR BUSINESS AT APPROX. $1,225,000.00 AT 3X EBITDA + SOH FACTOR.

EXPERT TIPS

1 Valuing a business properly is complicated. Find someone to help you who has a thorough knowledge of selling businesses and understands your industry.

2 Know your possible buyers, what they are looking for, and what could possibly scare them off.

3 It's the intangible assets of your business that will give you the price premium over your P&L and balance sheet book value.

Prepare – Doing the Hard Yards to Make Your Business Irresistible

Let's talk about the intangible assets of your business. It's these babies that you need to focus on if the numbers already stack up pretty well in your financials.

Think of it from the buyer's perspective. If you had a choice between a business that falls over every time the owner or key manager walks out the shop door, and another business that runs flawlessly even when the owner's not there, which one would you feel more inclined to purchase, all other things being equal? It's a buyer's market, and while established coffee businesses are hard to find, they do have choice, if nothing else but to wait a little longer until a suitable business comes on the market or can be approached. In fact, the buyer may pay a premium to snap this business up. See where I'm going with this?

Buyers are terrified of buying a lemon, especially if it's a family or an individual buyer and not another company. They know that there will be a steep learning curve. They can't afford for the wheels to fall off the minute you leave. There is a lot at stake for them financially and personally. So even more important than the financial returns, you need to present a business that is well run with comprehensive and easy-to-understand systems in place, and that is therefore easy to transition to a new owner. If you go back to my red flag checklist you will see that most of the red flag questions cover a lot of these factors. The table opposite highlights some key intangible assets to focus on.

EXPERT TIP

The importance of having clear documented systems as to how your business runs is critical. If your business is already running seamlessly and is consistently profitable then it's highly likely you have these systems in place in some shape or form already. If not, document your systems pronto. It's of no value to anybody if it's all in your head as, thankfully, your head is not usually part of the sale. Remember, it will give potential buyers a much higher level of comfort when deciding to buy your business and many buyers will pay a premium for this level of confidence that, unfortunately, very few businesses offer.

INTANGIBLE ASSET	WHY IS IT IMPORTANT?
Reliance on the Business Owner	While non-compete clauses are the norm, customers can be fickle and are not bound by any agreements to stay on. Equally, if the business knowledge is all in the owner's head things can falter quickly.
Brand Name	A strong brand has great value, especially to corporate buyers. Equally, a brand with poor market perception can be very hard to turn around for a new owner.
Systems and Processes	Clear systems that show how to operate the business are critical for an easy transition to a new owner. Everything – customer service, how to roast the coffee, how to do the pay runs and other obligations. It needs to all be systematised to be able to function even if you dropped dead. Critical.
CRM Systems/ Customer Retention/ Loyalty	Customer Relationship Management (CRM) is a strategy for managing all your company's relationships and interactions with your customers. Customer retention/ loyalty is critical for future growth.
Supplier Relationships	Having great relationships and pricing agreements are critical, especially with your green bean and packaging suppliers on pricing and supply.
Staff Agreements/ Stability/Retention	Stable, well-trained and loyal staff are critical to both your sales success and a successful handover and transition to a new owner.
Marketing and Sales Plan	A clear strategy with proven success will give a new owner a lot of confidence in taking over the reins.
Intellectual Property	Your blend recipes are key and have a value. This is critical in coffee businesses.
Lease	It can be argued that this is a tangible asset as it's a fixed contract. It's more than that though. In retail, a good relationship with your landlord is important. In Australia the landlord can refuse to assign a lease to a new owner if they have reasonable concerns about the business's ongoing ability to pay the rent. A long lease also gives the new owner a level of comfort in that they know what the rent will be for the next few years.

Market – Tell Them the Price Son!

Marketing your business for sale will vary depending on whom you have identified as a potential buyer. Strategic sales to larger coffee or food companies, other current competitors or management buyouts require a direct approach. If you are not confident in this type of approach it may be better to do it through a specialist such as an experienced business broker, accountant or advisor. You really only get one chance to make a good first impression and you need to make it count.

You need to put together an impressive prospectus document that covers all the bases. It needs to highlight the business's successes, its strengths and a three-year financial snapshot as a minimum. It should also address any key areas that may be of concern to a potential buyer so as to reassure them your business is a safe and wise investment for them. You may also want to highlight why it would be such a good opportunity for them to buy your business out. Remember, eliminate the red flags!

If you are going on the open market you will need a multi-pronged approach to marketing your business. Local and international online sales/advertising platforms are essential these days. Once again, this is where a business broker with an established qualified customer database will come in very handy. They can direct-mail qualified buyers with your business sale details and utilise their expansive buyer network to best effect. A good broker will qualify the buyer for you. Are they tyre kickers, or competitors who just want to look over your books? Do they have the financial means to buy your business? Are they a good fit for you and your business in terms of ease of handover and so on?

Business brokers will tend to confidentiality agreements for you prior to releasing information about the identity of the business and your top line financial figures to interested parties. At this stage you need to be judicious about what information you hand over to a prospective buyer for their perusal. It has to be enough to answer their questions adequately, but you can't hand over detailed client lists with sales figures as the prospective buyer may be a direct competitor. You need to maintain control over this marketing process. You need to also get something in return from these potential buyers, such as a deadline for an offer to be made.

One difficult part of marketing your business is keeping it quiet, for obvious reasons. It's very easy to spook your staff, customers and clients if they get wind of the potential sale. It's important you keep things operating as normal and you don't stop running your business. If shop inspections are required, do it after hours and have meetings off-site where possible. Coffee industry types are pathetic when it comes to working the rumour mill, so for God's sake, keep it quiet.

It's always best to have at least three interested parties to get some competitive bidding action happening. This is the ideal situation to be in. Selling a specialty business, however, is not as easy or as straightforward as selling a house. It will take some careful maneuvering and good negotiation skills to find the right buyer for your business. Remember that the best buyer may not be the one that offers the most money up front.

Close the Sale – Job Done!

There is a process that follows and the deal can fall over at any point along the line. You must provide a Letter of Intent that will become the basis of the Sales Contract, which will need to be drafted by your solicitor. Once agreed and signed, a 10% deposit is paid and held in trust. The prospective buyer can then do what's called Due Diligence to go over your financial statements and look at any documents they require to make sure everything you've told them is kosher and above board. If all the conditions are met then Settlement occurs (remaining payment is made and the stock sale is sorted). Then the agreed handover and training period will commence.

Then you say bye-bye …

4
ARE BUSINESS BROKERS AND ADVISORS WORTH IT?

On the whole I would say yes, but with a very big proviso that they have a track record of recent experience in your industry and have a good range of contacts and potential buyers on their books. Good business brokers are very hard to find. The broker I used approached me as he had recently sold several roasting businesses like mine for phenomenal prices and had keen buyers. Of course I was interested to hear him out. Over the years, complete idiots whose only experience was in selling distressed cafés also approached me. You do not want to deal with these people. They will waste your time and stress you out. Don't do it.

A good business broker will go through all the steps I have outlined with you. They will also honestly tell you if your business needs more work to get a better price at market. They will grill you on your financials. They will make an effort to understand your business inside out. They do not want to sell a lie or a dud to buyers and damage their reputation. They are great negotiators and aim for a fair win:win result for both sides. They encourage you to keep running your business during the time it can take to market and sell (usually 6–12 months on average from listing). They talk sense to you when your emotions get the better of you and you start to lose perspective.

A good broker will qualify the buyer for you. Are they tyre kickers, or competitors who just want to look over your books? Do they have the financial means to buy your business? Are they a good fit for you and your business in terms of ease of handover and so on?

5

A NOTE ON WELL-BEING FOR WHEN YOU EXIT STAGE LEFT

A friend of mine, Gordon, who ran the shop next door to me for 20 years, sold his successful deli business a few years before I sold mine. I bumped into him one day in Mosman. We chatted and I told him I had interested buyers and mentioned the turmoil I was going through about the prospect of selling. He looked me straight in the eye and said: "Know exactly what you're going to do next before you sell". My reaction was to feel incredulous. "Really?" I thought. "I know exactly what I'm going to do ... have a huge holiday and do nothing for 12 months." You know what, though? Twelve months after the sale I realised he was absolutely right!

If you've worked intensely for many years on and in your business it's all-consuming. It becomes part of your identity. You make great friendships with customers and staff. You hand all of this over, as well as the keys to the shop, to the new owners when you sell. I stayed away from the shop after I did my three-month handover. I was ready to go and did not feel any pangs of regret at all when I drove home for the last time.

I had a couple of great overseas trips. I started studying a post-grad course in a field I'd always been interested in. I took up playing music again after a long absence and made some new friends doing this. I also, however, cut myself off from all things coffee for a while, turning down work when offered and withdrawing from coffee judging competitions I was invited to attend.

I had a two-year non-compete clause in my sale contract, although this didn't worry me as I had no desire to start again so soon after selling. I also did not return to the roastery/café as I'd always hated it when old owners would hang around like bad smells talking to customers and staff. Creepy stuff. It also stings a little to see things you had worked hard on in the business changed by the new owners keen to put their own stamp on the place (and rightfully so!). Sounds silly I know, but it does sting – a little.

My self-imposed withdrawal from the industry meant that the phone eventually stopped ringing. It doesn't take long before you are forgotten. I started to feel a bit lonely and depressed. The house-husband novelty was wearing off. I was losing my coffee identity and it was difficult to process. So I started ringing around some old coffee colleagues to let them know I was still alive. I found that it was good to talk "coffee" with them again. It was great to see my old industry friends.

It was during one of these catch-ups at Cofi-Com that John Russell Storey brought up the book idea again with me. I'm so grateful he did.

EXPERT TIPS

1. Before you sell, have an idea of what you want to do next work-wise if you're too young to retire.

2. Keep busy and active. Volunteer, get fit, study, play music – do things you haven't had time to do for a long time.

3. See the time between career gigs as an opportunity to grow and plan the next part of your life's journey.

4. Stay well.

A Parting Story

My breakout stories in this book have thus far featured the odd-ball and amusing customers that I encountered over the years. I'd like to leave you with a heart-warming story of how some customers genuinely become your friends and make it all worthwhile.

Stuart Wagstaff AM was a well-known Australian television personality and theatre actor in Australia from the 1960s into the 1980s. He was a long-time customer of ours. I loved our chats about the golden years of Australian TV and theatre. Stuart was in his 80s by then. I had not seen him for a while and one day his PA came in to buy some coffee. I asked him how Stuart was and he told me that he was gravely ill (he had pulmonary fibrosis). I immediately packed up two bags of coffee and asked him to give them to Stuart as a tiny gift from me and wish him well.

A few days later I got a call on my mobile. On the other end was Stuart, wheezing as he could barely breathe without his oxygen tank. He had rung me to thank me for the coffee. I was staggered at his thoughtfulness. I was too choked up to say much, but thanked him for his friendship and wished him well. When I put the phone down I burst into tears. I saw on the morning news a few weeks later that Stuart had passed away. A true gentleman and friend. A friendship made possible through a mutual love of coffee.

AN ARTISAN ROASTER'S DICTIONARY

A

ACIDITY: Typically seen in high-altitude coffees, acidity is a pleasing piquant quality that gives liveliness to the cup. Acidity levels can vary in different coffees.

AFTERBURNER: A device attached to a coffee roaster used to filter exhaust air at very high heat (600°C+) that eliminates smoke, odour and particulates.

AFTERTASTE: (aka finish). The lingering flavour impression of a coffee on your palate.

AGTRON SCALE: The measuring system used to estimate the degree of roast using a numbering system scale as measured using an AGTRON Reader.

ALKALOID: Any of a class of nitrogenous organic compounds of plant origin that have pronounced physiological actions on humans.

ARABICA: (aka Coffea Arabica). The most widely planted commercial coffee species. Considered to be of the highest quality.

AROMA: The distinctive, usually pleasant, smell of a brewed coffee.

ASTRINGENT: Classified more in relation to its effect on the tongue than its actual taste. It creates a puckering sensation in the mouth or a dry, chalky feeling.

B

BAGGY: A smell or off-taste in coffee similar to that of a burlap/hessian coffee bag.

BAKED: A roast defect that results in a cereal-like flavour and reduces the coffee's sweetness. Usually experienced in coffee roasted too slowly or at too low a temperature.

BALANCED: When you have a pleasing combination of two or more key taste sensations.

BATCH: A quantity of coffee roasted in each roast cycle.

BEAN TEMPERATURE: The external temperature of the coffee, used to control the temperature of the roaster during the roasting process.

BITTER: A strong, unpleasant taste detected on the back of the tongue. Moderate bitterness balanced with sweetness in the cup is a good thing.

BLACK: A physical defect in green beans where 50% or more of the external bean is black in colour, usually due to extended fermentation or an infection during the bean's development.

BLEND: The process of mixing two or more coffees of differing growing regions/farms, varieties, processing methods and roast levels to create a new drinking coffee.

BODY: (aka mouthfeel). A spectrum of how big and heavy a coffee feels in your mouth.

BOURBON: A botanical variety of Arabica coffee known for its sweet and distinct cup profile.

BURLAP: (aka hessian). This is the jute fibre material used in the traditional bag that green coffee is packed and shipped in.

BUTTERY: A full and rich coffee flavour with an oily texture/body in the mouth.

C

"C" MARKET: The commodities exchange in New York where coffee futures are bought and sold. This price is considered the base price for coffee trading.

CAFFEINE: The stimulating, bitter alkaloid that coffee is famous for.

CARAMELISATION: Sugar-browning reactions in the coffee roasting process. Similar to cooked/brown sugar, it can be a desirable flavour in roasted coffee if managed during the roasting process.

CERTIFICATION: Guidelines set to a specific set of social or environmental guidelines. These guidelines may cover where and how a coffee is grown, harvested or processed. There are numerous certification bodies.

CHAFF: (aka silverskin). The thick skin that's left on the coffee bean/seed after processing and which comes off as the beans expand during roasting.

CHARGE: The act of loading the green beans into the roasting chamber of your coffee roaster.

CHARGE TEMPERATURE: The air temperature of the empty roaster before loading your batch of green beans into the roaster.

CHERRY: The fruit where the coffee seeds (beans) live. Will usually have two seeds or one peaberry.

CINNAMON ROAST: A very light roast level that occurs at the start of the first crack. In tasting terminology this refers to a flavour nuance in light roasts and a particular spice-like aroma.

CITY ROAST: A light-to-medium roast level.

CLEAN: A coffee free of taints and faults.

COCOA: An aroma generally associated with stale coffee.

CONDUCTION: The flow of internal energy (heat) from a region of higher temperature to one of lower temperature.

CONVECTION: When a fluid, such as air, is heated and then travels away from the source, it carries the thermal energy along with it.

CONTINUOUS ROASTER: A high-yield roaster that roasts coffee continuously rather than in batches.

COMPLEX: A term that describes the balance and intensity between a coffee's flavour and characteristics.

CREOSOTE: (aka hydrocarbon residue). The organic compounds deposited in the exhaust ducting of the coffee roaster. Highly flammable and slow burning.

CUPPING: A sensory evaluation of coffee for flavour and aroma profiling that should follow a systematic procedure.

CURRENT CROP: Green coffee beans from the most recently available harvest.

D

DATA LOGGER/LOGGING: Equipment used to record time and temperature data during the roasting process in order to assist the master roaster in profile roasting.

DECAFFEINATION: The complex process of removing caffeine from green coffee beans.

DEFECTS: Faults detected in green beans. Commonly caused by problems during picking, processing, drying, sorting, storage and transportation.

DEGASSING: When coffee releases CO_2 naturally after being recently roasted.

DEMUCILAGE: (aka water process, wet process). Process where the fruit pulp (aka mucilage) is removed from coffee beans by scrubbing in machines.

DEVELOPMENT: A measure of the degree of breakdown of the coffee bean's cellulose structure during the roasting process.

DIRTY: An undesirable flavour in coffee cupping that can imply that a defect is present.

DOUBLE DRUM: (aka double walled, double barrel). A coffee roaster where the drum is made of two layers of steel separated by a small gap in between.

DOUBLE ROASTING: A process where a batch of coffee is roasted to the yellow stage, allowed to cool, and then roasted again to the desired final level.

DRAW: The natural draw of air created by the chimneystack/flue that draws smoke out.

DROP: To release the roasted coffee from your drum barrel into the cooling tray.

DRUM ROASTER: A type of coffee roaster where batches of coffee beans are continuously tumbled as they roast in a rotating cylindrical steel drum.

DRY MILL: Facility where coffee is hulled, sorted and graded.

E

EARTHY: Considered a taint in washed coffees and in some dry process coffees. Reveals a mustiness picked up by coffee sometimes when dried on the ground.

EMMISSIONS CONTROL: The control of emissions through the use of afterburners in accordance with smoke and odour regulations.

ENDOTHERMIC: A process that requires or absorbs energy from its surroundings, usually in the form of heat.

ENVIRONMENTAL TEMPERATURE (EV): The air temperature of the roaster.

ETHYL ACETATE: A chemical used in the decaffeination process.

EXOTHERMIC: A chemical reaction that releases energy through light or heat. It is the opposite of an endothermic reaction.

EXTRACTION: The process of dissolving soluble flavours from coffee grounds in water.

F

FAIR TRADE: Certification by organisations that guarantee that minimum wages and environmental conditions have been met.

FERMENT: Microbial green coffee defect that gives an acrid or sour taste and smell.

FERMENTATION: A part of the wet process method where natural enzymes loosen the pulp as the skinned beans soak in water tanks.

FIRST CRACK: Characterised by loud popping noises and is a significant phase in the roasting process. When pressure and water vapour are released from the inner coffee beans as a result of complex chemical reactions inside the bean.

FLAT: See Stale.

FLAVOUR PROFILE: The total impression of the coffee. The sum of aroma, acidity, body, sweetness and aftertaste.

FLOATER: Green bean defect. Characterised by fermented, bitter or straw-like flavours.

FLUID BED ROASTER: (aka air roaster). A coffee roaster that uses hot air to agitate and roast coffee simultaneously.

FRENCH ROAST: Very dark-roasted coffee, oily surface. Characterised by dark and pungent, smokey flavours.

FRUITY: Can be a flavour taint in line with fermented taint. However, mostly used to describe a citrus/berry sweetness in certain coffees.

FULL (CITY) ROAST: US term for a medium espresso roast. Most popular commercial espresso roast level.

FULLY WASHED: Green beans that are pulped, fermented and washed clean before drying.

G

GEISHA: A popular Arabica wild coffee that has been achieving remarkably high prices at auction.

GRAINPRO: Hermetically sealed bags used for the storage of green coffee beans.

GRASSY: A herbal-like flavour taint found in green coffee not dried properly in processing, as well as in under-roasted coffee.

GREEN COFFEE: Unroasted raw processed green coffee beans. The form in which coffee is internationally traded.

H

HARD BEAN: See Strictly Hard Bean (SHB).

HEIRLOOM VARIETY: Coffee that is genetically closer to the wild varieties of Arabica coffees.

HONEY PROCESS: (aka miel process). Similar to the pulped natural process, the coffee is pulped but a good amount of the fruit flesh is left on during the drying phase.

HULLING: The process of removing the parchment and silverskin on washed coffees prior to the milling process.

I

INTERNATIONAL COFFEE AGREEMENT: A quota system in place between many coffee-producing countries and importers to prevent supply and demand swings and keep prices relatively stable.

IMPERFECTIONS: Physical defects present in green beans such as shells, quakers and broken beans. Green coffee is graded according to a limited number of the imperfections being present.

ITALIAN ROAST: A dark roast often taken into the second crack and displays some oil on the surface.

L

LEAF RUST: A disease spread by spores on the underside of the plant. Originally found in Brazil it is now present in many coffee-growing countries.

LIGHT ROAST: A roast level that preserves a coffee's acidity and fruitier flavours. In roasting terms it is a coffee where the beans are dropped before, or just after, the end of the first crack.

M

MACHINE DRIED: A coffee that has been dried mechanically.

MAILLARD REACTION: A browning reaction resulting from a chemical effect between amino acids and reducing sugars. Also contributes to a coffee's "roasty" flavour.

MARAGOGYPE: (aka Maragogipe, Elephant Bean). An Arabica coffee characterised by its large size and low yield.

MEDICINAL: A flavour taint found in coffee described as chemical or astringent.

MEDIUM ROAST: When a coffee is dropped during the roasting process right on, or just before, the second crack.

METHYLENE CHLORIDE: A colourless chemical used in the decaffeination of green coffee beans.

MICRO-LOT: Typically a volume of 10 x 60kg/132lb bags or less, of a green bean selection from one producer or farm.

MILLING: The mechanical removal of the dried fruit husk from a dry process green coffee bean or the dry parchment skin from a wet process bean.

MONSOON COFFEE: The practice along India's south-west Malabar Coast where harvested beans, having been processed to the 'green' coffee state, are then subjected to a lengthy period of exposure to the humid sea air in order to increase the body and reduce their acidity.

MOULDY: Usually caused by damp storage conditions, this is a flavour or visual defect in coffee beans.

MOUTHFEEL: (aka body). The tactile attributes of how the coffee feels in your mouth when drinking it.

MUCILAGE: See Pulp.

N

NATURAL PROCESS: The drying of picked ripe coffee beans in the sun until the entire cherry is dry. The dried cherry is then milled to remove the coffee beans. This process can result in a complex and fruity flavour profile.

NEW CROP: (aka current crop). Processed green coffee from the most recent harvest.

O

OILY: Seen in dark roasts, this term describes the surface of the coffee bean after a deep roast.

OLD CROP: Green coffee from the latter half of the harvest year.

ORGANIC: A third-party certified coffee that has been grown and processed without the use of pesticides or herbicide chemicals.

ORGANIC ACID: An organic acid is an organic compound with acidic properties.

P

PARCHMENT: A thin paper skin surrounding wet process coffee beans after they have been de-pulped and dried.

PARCHMENT COFFEE: As above. Keeping this layer on the bean prevents deterioration of the coffee before milling for export.

PAST CROP: Warehoused green coffee that is from the previous harvest year.

PEABERRY: When a single seed forms inside the coffee cherry instead of the usual two seeds.

PROBE (TEMPERATURE): Can measure/estimate temperature during the roasting process. Most machines will have an environmental (EV) air temperature probe and a bean temperature probe.

PROFILE/ROASTING: A time and temperature path analysis of the roasting process. Roasters try to replicate profiles that deliver the optimal roast flavour for a particular coffee by controlling the rate of heat transfer to the bean during coffee roasting.

PULP: (aka mucilage). The fruit of the cherry removed during pulping.

PULPED NATURAL: (aka semi-washed, wet hulled). Post-harvest process where the beans are mechanically removed from the cherry and then dried on patios or raised beds.

PUNGENT: Defined as having a sharply strong taste or smell.

PYROLYSIS: The chemical breakdown of fats and carbohydrates into delicate oils during roasting that provides aroma and flavour.

Q

QUAKER: An underdeveloped/unripened coffee bean, often with a wrinkled surface. Quakers do not darken well when roasted.

R

RAISED BED: Typically seen in Africa, this is a raised, flat-bed structure on which parchment coffee is dried. The raised structure allows more air to flow through the coffee during the drying phase.

RATE OF RISE (ROR): A progression of bean temperature rise against elapsed time.

REFRACTOMETER: Used in coffee lab analysis to measure a coffee's refractive index related to its density and concentration as a solution.

ROAST PROFILE: See Profile/Roasting.

ROBUSTA: A coffee species that is high yielding and more disease resistant than Arabica but maligned for its inferior flavour and higher caffeine content.

S

SCORCHING: Early-stage roasting burning of the bean surface, usually due to an overly-hot roaster barrel.

SCREEN SIZE (CLASSIFICATION): A sorting procedure of green beans by size. The beans have to pass through a set of screens with holes of various dimensions. Screen sizes typically range from the smallest (13) to the largest (19).

SECOND CRACK: A phase of the coffee-roasting process where CO_2 released from the roasting beans creates loud, rapid popping noises. Roasts taken beyond this roast are considered dark roasts.

SHRINKAGE!: In *Seinfeld*, this referred to what happened to George when he got out of the cold pool. In the coffee world, however, it refers to the weight lost by coffee during roasting.

SILVERSKIN: See Chaff.

SINGLE ESTATE: (aka estate-grown, single farm). A coffee produced by a single farm, mill or group of single farms and marketed as such.

SINGLE ORIGIN: An unblended coffee from a single country, region or crop.

SMOOTH: A term often used to describe a full-bodied, low acidity coffee.

SOFT BEAN: Coffees grown at a lower altitude tend to have a softer structure. These beans cannot tolerate deep roasts very well.

SPECIALTY COFFEE: A term used for a certain quality level by the entire coffee industry, from producers to roasters.

STALE: (aka flat or dead coffee). A flavour detected in old and deteriorated roasted coffee either by excessive storage or exposure to air. Lacks intensity, flavour and acidity.

STRICTLY HARD BEAN (SHB): Coffee grown above 1350m in altitude.

STRIP PICKING: A harvesting technique where cherry pickers run their hands down the branch to strip off large amounts of cherries. Unfortunately, this results in beans of various ripeness which have to be sorted later with varying degrees of success.

SUN-DRIED: Coffees that are dried in the sun on patios or drying racks and not mechanically dried by machines.

SUSTAINABLE COFFEE: Coffees that are grown and sold in an environmentally and socially sustainable way.

T

TAINT: A negative issue with a coffee occurring anywhere along the line.

TASTE: The overall sensory impression of a coffee as perceived by the tongue.

TERROIR: The overall impact of a coffees origin's geography on its overall taste.

TIPPING: Burn marks on the tips of the coffee beans.

TRACEABILITY: The transparency of the supply chain so that one knows exactly who produced a particular coffee.

TROWEL (aka tester). The small scoop mounted on the faceplate of the roaster for sampling roasting coffee beans at various stages.

TYPICA: Widely considered as being the oldest and original Arabia variety.

U

UNDERDEVELOPED: When coffee is roasted too slowly or at too low a temperature the breakdown of the coffee bean's structure may be insufficient to produce the desired flavour.

UTZ: A certification that is based on guidelines geared towards responsible coffee production and sourcing.

V

VACUUM SEALED: A method of packing coffee that removes air prior to sealing.

VARIETY: The genetic subspecies of coffee based on a location.

VOLATILE AROMATICS: The soluble gases that contribute to a coffee's aroma.

W

WASHED PROCESS: (aka aquapulp, demucilage, wet process, lavado). A post-harvest process where the seeds (beans) are pulped (separated) from the fruit. The beans are then put through a process of controlled fermentation to break down the remaining sticky fruit flesh still on the bean. They are then washed off and the bean is either mechanically or naturally sun-dried.

WASHING STATION: (aka wet mill). The facility where the washed process occurs.

WATER PROCESS DECAFFEINATION: A trademarked decaffeination process. The best-known versions are the Swiss Water Process and the Mountain Water Process.

X, Y & Z

The coffee industry does not seem to like words starting with these much-maligned final letters of the alphabet.

BOOK, ARTICLE AND WEB REFERENCES

PUBLISHED BOOKS

Goodfellow, S., Harrop, S.: *Small Business Big Exit*. Published by Michael Hanrahan Publishing 2015.

Hoffman, J.: *The World Atlas of Coffee*. Published by Mitchell Beazley, an imprint of Octopus Publishing Group Limited 2014.

Puro, E. (editor): *Book of Roast*. First Edition. Published by JC Publishing, Inc. 2017.

Rao, S.: *The Coffee Roaster's Companion*. Self-Published 2014.

Thurber, J.: *Coffee: From Plantation to Cup*. First published in 1881. Current edition by Franklin Classics 2018.

Yi-Fang Chu, C. (editor): *Coffee: Emerging Health Effects and Disease Prevention* (First Edition). Published by Blackwell Publishing Ltd 2012.

PUBLISHED ARTICLES

Boot, W.: *Blending The Rules*. Published in July/August 2006 issue of *Roast* magazine (USA).

Boot, W.J.: *In Hot Pursuit*. Published in September/October 2010 issue of *Roast* magazine (USA).

Caspersen, B.A.: *A Focus on Flaws*. Published in May/June 2016 issue of *Roast* magazine (USA).

Frederiksen, L.: *The Pros and Cons of Mergers and Acquisitions as Part of Your Growth Strategy*. Published in November 15 2016 issue of *Iris* magazine.

Klebba, K.: *Making Sense of Certifications*. Published in *The Book of Roast* 2017 (USA).

Larkin, J.: *Fire Fighters*. Published in May/June 2007 issue of Roast magazine (USA).

Mullins, B.: *Roasting Through the Ages – Exploring the Roots of American Craft Roasting*. Published in May/June 2009 issue of *Roast* magazine (USA).

Rivera, J.A.: *Alchemy in the Roasting Lab: Parts 1 & 2*. Published in May/June 2005 issue of *Roast* magazine (USA).

Rivera, J.A.: *The Science of Coffee Roasting*. Published in May/June 2008 issue of *Roast* magazine (USA).

Roche, D., Osgood, R.: *A Family Album. Getting to the Roots of Coffee's Plant Heritage*. Published in November/December 2007 issue of *Roast* magazine (USA).

Stewart, K.: *Deconstructing Decaf*. Published in March/April 2011 issue of *Roast* magaine (USA).

Taylor, L., Roelofs, J.: *Machinery, Ingenuity, Discovery – A History of Roasting Equipment*. Published in May/June 2010 issue of *Roast* magazine (USA).

WEB REFERENCES

www.driftaway.coffee/the-history-of-cold-brew: Cold Brew History.
https://mck.co/2yHQabT: Social Media Data Insights.
www.sproutsocial.com/insights/social-media-for-retail: Social Media for Retailers.
www.sproutsocial.com/insights/data/q2-2016: Social Media Data Insights.
https://bit.ly/2OhqdYD: Selling Before It's Too Late.
https://bit.ly/2Dwkmvp: Coffee Plant Upgrade Tips.
www.emis.vito.be/nl/node/19473: Thermal Afterburning.
www.emis.vito.be/en/techniekfiche/catalytic-oxidation: Catalytic Oxidation.
https://bit.ly/2MyRo0g: Small Business Contribution to Economy & Employment in Australia.
https://bit.ly/2VkLQhO: Record Geisha Auction Prices.
www.coffeeresearch.org: The Coffee Research Institute.
https://bit.ly/2KVCHIt: Green Bean Chemistry.
www.coffeechemistry.com: Roasted Coffee Chemistry.
www.descamex.com.mx/2_proceso_naturali.html: Water Based Decaffeination Process.

SUPPLIER DIRECTORY (AUSTRALIA ONLY)

GREEN COFFEE BEANS
NAME: Cofi-Com Trading Pty Ltd
WEB: www.coficom.com.au
CONTACT: Dariusz Lewandowski/John Russell Storey
PHONE: +61 2 9809 6266
EMAIL: info@coficom.com.au
ADDRESS: 73 Ryedale Road, West Ryde, NSW 2114
PRODUCT: All origin green coffee beans, green bean blending service, teas, chocolate powders and syrups.

COFFEE ROASTING EQUIPMENT
NAME: Roastquip Pty Ltd
WEB: www.roastquip.com.au
CONTACT: Will Notaras
PHONE: +61 404 879 107
EMAIL: sales@roastquip.com.au
ADDRESS: 11 Fred St, Lilyfield NSW 2040
PRODUCT: IMF Coffee Roasters.

NAME: Roastmax Roasters
WEB: www.roastmaxroasters.com.au
CONTACT: Will Notaras
PHONE: +61 404 879 107
EMAIL: sales@roastmaxroasters.com.au
ADDRESS: 11 Fred St, Lilyfield NSW 2040
PRODUCT: Roastmax Coffee Roasters

CONTRACT COFFEE ROASTERS
NAME: Gourmet Gold Coffee
WEB: www.gourmetgold.com.au
CONTACT: Peter Brawn
PHONE: +61 2 9420 0186
EMAIL: peter@gourmetgold.com.au
ADDRESS: 15/12 Mars Road, Lane Cove West, NSW 2066
SERVICES: Contract coffee roasters – specialising in wholesale, retail and private label coffee.

NAME: The Indie Coffee Project
WEB: www.indiecoffeeproject.com.au
PHONE: +61 407 665 250
EMAIL: indiecoffeeproject@gmail.com
SERVICES: Private label coffee, blend development, quality management, café training and advice.

GRAPHIC DESIGN
NAME: King Street Press
WEB: www.kingstreetpress.com.au
CONTACT: Melissa Mylchreest
PHONE: +61 412 144 964
EMAIL: info@kingstreetpress.com.au
ADDRESS: 402 Parramatta Rd, Petersham, NSW 2049
SERVICES: Logo, web design, photography, print, styling and book design.

COFFEE ROASTER TRAINING AND CONSULTANCY
NAME: The Artisan Roaster
WEB: www.theartisanroaster.com
CONTACT: David Rosa
PHONE: +61 407 665 250
EMAIL: info@theartisanroaster.com
SERVICES: Coffee roaster training, coffee courses and consultancy.

INDEX

A

accounting. *see* finance
acidity, 130, 131, 147, 149, 240
acquisitions, 222
advertising. *see* marketing
aeroPress, 47
Africa, 90
afterburners, 66, 67, 71, 240
aftertaste, 240
AGA (Australian Gas Association), 64, 71
Agtron scale, *128,* 129–130, 240
air roaster, 60, 241
airflow control, 62, 118
alkaloid, 88, 113, 240
Allen-Bradley, 68
approvals. *see* legislation
aquapulp, 102, 244
Arabica species, 80, *81,* 84, 85, 240
    chemistry, 87–88, 113–114
    origins, 89–91
Argentina, 136
aroma
    blending, 149
    brewed coffee, 113
    caramelisation, 114
    cupping, 142, 143
    defined, 240
    green coffee, 106
    roasting, 87, 88, 122, 125, 130, 136, 139
Asia, 91
asset finance, 51
astringent, 240
Australia, 91, 105
Australian Gas Association (AGA), 64, 71

B

baggy, 240
baked, 124, 139, 143, 144, 240
balanced, 240
ball roasters, 18, *22*
bank guarantees, 36, 51
baristas, 43, 186, 220

batch, 240
batch size, 17, 23, 61, 117, 119
Bay Coffee Roasters
    design, 39
    house blend, 148
    logo, *194*
    marketing, 195, *196, 198*
    opening of, 10–11
    refurbishment, 38, *42,* 195
bean temperature, 240
beans, green. *see* green coffee
Bennett, Darren, *174,* 220
Best Online Store award, 184
bitter, 88, 130, 144, 149, 181, 240
black, 240. *see also* defects of green coffee
    blending, 148–152, 240
    post-blending, 149–150
    pre-blending, 149–150
    process, 151
    recipes, 152
    species used, 80
Blue Mountain hybrid, 84
body, 240
Bolivia, 136
Boot, Willem J., 62
Bourbon variety, 82, 83, 240
branding, 194–205
    as an asset, 233
    core values, 195
    image projected by staff, 175, 220
    packaging, 199, 204
    promoting, 184
    websites, 206
Brawn, Geoff, 216, *217*
Brawn, Peter, 216, *217*
Brazil
    coffee characteristics, 90
    harvesting, 94, 105
    processing, 102, 103
brew bar, 43

brewing systems, 46–49, 131, 185–188
BRIGAS, 65
brokers, business, 229, 234, 237
browning, 122. *see also* caramelisation; Maillard Reaction
burlap, 106, 134, 240
Burns, Jabez, 17–18, *18,* 23
Burns coffee roaster, *17, 18,* 23
business brokers, 229, 234, 237
business plan, 32, 194, 225
buttery, 240
buying direct, 109

C

C market, 240
cafe. *see* retail operations; roastery
Café Procope, 15
Caffè Florian, 15
caffeine, 88, 112, 113, 240
Campos Coffee, 205
Canephora species, 80
capacity. *see* batch size
caramelisation, 88, 113–114, 240
Carmody, Andrew, *174*
Cassen roaster, 23
catalytic oxidisers, 66
Catuai variety, 83
Caturra variety, *82,* 83
Central America, 90
certification, 108, 109, 112, 116, 240
chaff, 118, 157, 158, 240
change management, 220–221, 223
characteristics of coffee from different origins, 90–92
charge temperature, 119, 120, 125, 133, 240
Charles II, *15*
Châtelet, Emilie du, *15*
chemistry
    of green beans, 87–88
    of roasting, 112–114

cherries, coffee
  anatomy, 85
  defined, 240
  harvesting, 85, 94–95
  processing, 96–97
  varieties, 82
cinnamon roast, 121, 122, 130, 139, 240
city roast, 241
clean coffee, 241
cleaning, 43, 68, 134, 136
Clover brewing system, 48, 49
cocoa aroma, 241
Code Black Roasters, 212
Coffea genus, 80
coffee characteristics, 90–92
Coffee: From Plantation to Cup, 16
coffee houses, 15
Coffee Quality Institute (CQI), 101, 112
coffee species
  Arabica, 80–84, 81
  Canephora, 80
  Eugenioides, 80
  Robusta, 80
Cofi-Com Trading, 11, 98, 101, 238
cold brew machines, 47, 128, 186
Colombia
  coffee characteristics, 90
  harvesting, 94, 105
  processing, 102
combustion chambers, 66
complex, 114, 241
computer-controlled profiling, 23, 62, 65, 68
Comunetti bag filler, 216
conduction, 241
consistency, 133, 134, 148
continuous roaster, 241
contract roasters, 215–217, 223
convection, 241
cooling, 62, 132
cooling trays, 17, 23, 132
core values, 175, 184, 195
Costa Rica
  coffee characteristics, 90
  harvesting, 105
  processing, 103
  Torrefacto roasting, 136

costing. *see* pricing
costs
  equipment for roasting, 31, 32
  espresso equipment, 185–186
  production, 165
  roastery, 31, 32
creosote, 157, 158, 160, 241
cultivars, 82
cup quality, 87
cupping, 140–143, *142–143*, 181, 202, 241
current crop, 241
customer amenities, 44, 174
customer education, 180–181
customer relationships, 181, 200, 202, 233
customer service, 178–179, 204, 220

D

dark roast, 128, 130
data logger/logging, 241
data-logging software, 65, 138
date codes, 199
decaffeination, 153–154, 241, 244
defects of green coffee, 99, 100, 241
degassing, 241
Deidrich roasters, 57
deliveries, access for, 33, 41
demucilage, 102, 241
density of beans, 119
Descamex, 154
designing a roastery, 38–43
de-stoners, 67
de-stoning, 135
development, 118, 124–125, 128, 129, 131, 241
development time, 124–125, 126–127, 131
Di Bartoli Coffee, 61, 117
Diodato, Johannes, 15
direct trade, 108
dirty flavour, 241
display, 182–183
Ditting KR1403 grinder, 71
Dominican Republic, 105
double drum roasters, 56, 57, 58, 62, 241
double roasting, 241
draw, 241
drinking coffee, history, 14–15

drop, 241
drum roasters, 18, 56, *57–59*, 241
drum speed control, 64
dry mill, 241
drying, 97
dry processing, 102
dust, 40, 43, 183

E

earthy, 241
education, of customers, 180–181, 206
El Salvador, 105
Elephant bean, 242
Emmericher Maschinenfabrik und Eisengießerei, 18, 21
emmissions control, 23, 44, 58, 59, 60, 241
endothermic, 124, 125, 132, 241
England, first coffee houses, 15
environmental temperature (Ev), 65, 116, 120, 138, 241
equipment
  bean sales, 45
  brewed coffee, 47, 185–186
  cost, 31, 51
  drum roasters, 18
  espresso coffee, 46, 185–186
  history, 16–23
  leasing, 51
espresso coffee, 128
estate coffee, 147
Ethiopia
  coffee characteristics, 91
  harvesting, 105
  processing, 102
ethyl acetate, 241
Eugenioides species, 80
Europe, first coffee houses, 15
events, 43
exit strategies, 225–238
exothermic, 241
expansion, 209–223
  acquisitions, 222
  contract roasters, 215–217
  joint ventures, 223
  mergers, 222
  more sites, 209

strategic alliance, 223
   wholesale, 210–213, 220
extraction, 241

F
facilities, toilets, 44
Fair Trade, 108, 241
Fair Work Ombudsman, 176
faults, 144
ferment, 241
fermentation, 96, 241
filter light, 128, 130, 131
finance
   production costs, 164–165
   profit and loss statements, 189–192
   set-up costs, 50–51
   value of the business, 228–230
   wholesale, 211, 220–221
fires, 134, 158–160
first crack, 121, 122, 124, 125, 130, 131, 241
flat. *see* stale
flavour profile, 241
flavours
   blending, 24, 148
   chemistry, 88, 113–114
   describing, 24
   effect of processing on, 102–103
floater, 96, 100, 241
flue, 72
fluid bed roasters, 60, *60*, 241
France, 136
French Press brewing system, 49
French roast, 128, 241
freshness, 88, 106, 107, 182. *see also* seasonality
fruity, 241
full (city) roast, 241
full espresso, 128, 130
fully washed, 242
functionality, 39, 40–43
futures, 84

G
gas burners, 62
Geisha variety, 84, 242
Giesen roasters, 57
Gimborn, Carl, 21

Gimborn, Theodor von, 18, 21
Gimborn-Abbing, Tina von, 21, *21*
Globe roaster, 18
Google, 184, 206
Gothot Company, 23
Gourmet Agtron scale, 129
Gourmet Gold Coffee Roasters, 216–217
grading, 98–101
GrainPro bags, 106, 134, 242
grassy, 242
Green Arabica Coffee Classification System (GACCS), 99
green coffee, 79–109
   chemistry, 87–88
   consistency, 134
   defects, 99, *100*
   defined, 242
   grading, 98–101
   harvesting, 94–95
   processing, 96–97
   samples, 138
   as seeds, 85
   storage, 33, 41, 106, 107, 134
   water content, 88
grinders, 45, 46
Guatemala
   beans, 126
   coffee characteristics, 90
   harvesting, 94, 105
Gülpen, Alexius van, 18

H
Hacienda La Esmeralda, 84
hard bean. *see* Strictly Hard Bean (SHB)
Harrar hybrid, 84
harvesting, 85, *93*, 94–95, 104
Hawaii
   coffee characteristics, 90
   harvesting, 105
heat transfer, 56, 88
heirloom variety, 242
hessian, 106, 134, 240
history of coffee drinking, 14–15
history of roasting equipment, 16–23
Hoffmann, James, 89
Honduras, 105

honey processing, 103, 242
hot air recycling, 23
hot air roasters, 60, *60*
hulling, 242
humidity, 107, 134
hybrids, 82

I
IMF roasters, 59
imperfections, 242. *see also* defects of green coffee
India
   coffee characteristics, 91
   harvesting, 105
Indonesia
   blending, 148
   coffee characteristics, 91
   harvesting, 105
installation of roasters, 30, 68, 71–72
insurance, 52
intellectual property, 149, 222, 229, 233
International Coffee Agreement, 242
International Roast, 180
Italian Roast, 128, 242

J
Jamaica, 105, 106, 220
James Carter, 17
joint ventures, 223
Joper roasters, 57, 58, *62*, 65, 216

K
kahwah, 14
Kaldi berry legend, *14*
Kenya
   coffee characteristics, 91
   harvesting, 105, 106
Kenyan Ruiru 11 variety, *86*
Kolschitzky, Georg Franz, 15

L
La Marzocco espresso machines, 185
Larsen, Vanessa, 38
lavado, 102
Le Nez Du Café, 143
leaf rust, 82, 242
leases

of assets, 51
as assets, 233
of sites, 34–37
legislation, 30, 31, 44, 71
Lensing, Johann Heinrich, 18
Lewandowski, Dariusz, *98*
light roast, 130, 131, 242
lighting, 41, 44
loans, 50
logo, 194, 195
Loring roasters, 59

M

Macagi de Seabra, Bruno, *175*
machine dried, 242
Mackay, Andrew, 9, 11, 98
Maillard, Louis Camille, 113–114
Maillard Reaction, 88, 113–114, 242
maintenance, 68, 157, 158
Maragogype (Maragogipe) variety, 83, 242
Market Lane Coffee, *53, 73, 123, 141, 180*
marketing
    alliances, 205
    as an asset, 233
    costs, 191
    to customers, 181, 185, 204
    digital, 200–203
    online, 184
    sale of the business, 234
    set-up, 194
    social media, 200–203
    websites, 206
M-Basic Agtron scale, 129. *see also* Agtron scale
medicinal flavour, 242
medium espresso, 128
medium roast, 242
mergers, 222
methylene chloride, 242
Mexico
    coffee characteristics, 90
    harvesting, 105
    Torrefacto roasting, 136
micro-lot coffee, 147
milling, 242
Moccona, 180

Mocha Java blend, 148
moisture meter, *100*
monsoon coffee, 242
mouldy, 242
Mountain Water Process, 154, 244. *see also* wet processing
mouthfeel, 242
mucilage, 96, 242
Mundo Novo variety, 83
My Business Magazine, 184

N

natural processing, 102, 242
Nescafé, 148, 180
Neuhaus Neotec roasters, 23, 60
Neutral Bay, 10
new crop, 242
Nicaragua
    harvesting, 105
    processing, 103
North America, 90
Notaras, Will, 59, 72

O

Oceania, 91
oily, 125, 136, 242
old crop, 242
online sales, 184, 206
operating hours, 44
organic, 101, 108, 109, 242
origins of coffee, 89–91, 147
Ottoman Empire Turkish coffee house, 15
over temperature sensors, *64*
overdrafts, 51
oxidiser technologies, 23

P

packaging, 199, 204
Panama
    coffee characteristics, 90
    harvesting, 105
Papua New Guinea
    coffee characteristics, 91
    processing, 102
parchment, 85, 99, 242

parts for roasters, 68
past crop, 243
peaberry, 243
Penny Universities, 15
picking. *see* harvesting
pollution control, 30, 66
Portugal, 136
post-blending, 149–150
pour over, 47, 128, 186
pre-blending, 149–150
pre-owned roasters, 70
preparation, 133
pressure switches, 64, *64*
pricing, 163, *164–165*, 184
Probat, 18, 21, 23
Probat Museum of Coffee Technology, 21
Probat roasters, 18, *19, 20, 22, 40, 54, 57,* 138
probe (temperature), 62, 65, 116, 119, 120, 138, 243
processing, 96–97
    effect on flavour, 102–103
    effect on roasting temperature, 119
Procopio dei Coltelli, Francesco, 15
profile roasting software, 23, 62, 65, 68
profiles, roasting, 126–127, 131, 243
profit and loss statements, 189–192
promotion. *see* marketing
pulp, *96,* 243
pulped natural, 243
pulped processing, 103
pungent, 243
purchasing equipment. *see also* equipment
    espresso, 185–186
    roasters, 55–72
pyrolysis, 243

Q

qahwa, 14
quaker, 99, 243
quality control, 138–146

R

Rainforest Alliance, 195
raised bed, 243
Rapid Roaster, 18, *19, 20, 22*

rate of rise (ROR), 125, 243
Ready to Roast – From Old-School Artist to Modern Artisan, 62
recipes, 152
recirculating heat roasters, 59, *59*
Reed, Margo, 38
refractometer, 243
retail operations. *see also* roastery
    accounting, 189–192
    branding, 194–205, 220
    brewing techniques, 185–188
    customer education, 180–181
    customer service, 178–179
    display, 182–183
    espresso equipment, 185–186
    expansion, 209–223
    marketing, 181, 194–205
    operating hours, 44
    selling the business, 226–238
    social media, 200
    staff, 175, 186
    stock turnover, 183
    store manager role, 174
    systems, 232, 233
    wages, 189–192
Rivera, Joseph A., 112
roast profiles, 126–127, 131, 243
roasters (the machines). *see also individual names*
    batch size, 17, 23, 61
    cleaning, 43, 68, 157
    continuous, 241
    features, 61–68
    fires, 157, 158–160
    history, 16–23
    hot air, 23
    installation, 30, 68, 71–72, 158
    maintenance, 68, 157, 158
    parts, 68, 158
    pre-owned, 70
    purchasing, 55–72
    sample, 138–139
    types, 56–60
    Yang-Chia 500g roaster, 138
roastery. *see also* retail operations
    aesthetics, 39
    branding, 39, 194–205

    design, 39–43
    expansion, 209–223
    finance, 50–51
    functionality, 39
    marketing, 194–205
    operating hours, 44
    retail operation of, 171–186
    selling point, 39
    selling the business, 226–238
    setting up, 30–37
    systems, 232, 233
roasting. *see also* sample roasting
    airflow control, 118, 121
    as an art, 24, 139
    batch size, 117, 119
    books on, 11
    browning, 122
    chemistry of, 112–114
    consistency, 133, 134
    cooling, 62, 132
    curve, 65, 121–122, 124, 126–127
    decaffeinated coffee, 154
    de-stoning, 135
    development times, 126–127, 131
    faults, 144
    levels, 128
    powering down, 136
    preparation, 133
    process of, 117–136
    profiles, 126–127, 131, 138
    sampling, 124
    as a science, 24, 139
    stages, *120–121,* 122
    temperatures, 119, 120, 122, 133
    times, 17, 23, 56, 119, 124–125, 126–127
Roastmax roasters, *57, 61, 62*
Roastville Coffee, *37, 44, 166*
Robusta species, 80, 85, 243
    chemistry, 87–88, 113–114
Rosa, David, *10, 54, 98, 174*
Rosée, Pasqua, 15
Rubbermaid Brute containers, 144, 182
Rubiaceae plants, 80
Russell Storey, John, 11, *98,* 238
Rwanda
    coffee characteristics, 90
    harvesting, 105

S

safety devices, 64, 71
sales and service, 41, 43
sample roasting, 138–139. *see also* roasting
sampling, 124
scales, 45
Schnell Roaster, 18, *19, 20*
Scolari, Antonio, 23
scoops, 45
scorching, 132, 243
screen size (classification), 98, 243
screens for grading, *98*
sealers, 45
seasonality, 104–105, 107. *see also* freshness
seasoning drums, 116
seating, 43, 44
second crack, 114, 125–127, 128, 130, 243
second hand roasters, 70
selling the business, 226–238
sensory experience, 182, 183
setting up a roastery, 30–37
    business plan, 32
    designing, 38–43
    entry barriers, 31
    entry costs, 31
    finance, 50–51
    functionality, 40–43
    research, 31, 32
    sites, 31, 33–37
shrinkage, 163, 165, 243
Sidamo hybrid, 84
signage, 44
silverskin, 118, 157, 158, 240, 243
single estate, 243
single origin coffee, 147, 243
sites, 33–37, 223
    leases, 34–37
    location, 33
Sivetz, Michael, 23
SL-28 variety, 83
SL-34 variety, 83
Small Business Big Exit, 227
smooth, 243
social media, 178, 184, 200–203, 206
soft bean, 243

software, 65, 68
sorting beans, 97
South America coffee characteristics, 90
Spain, 136
specialty coffee, 12, 80, 84, 98, 106, 144, 154, 216, 243
Specialty Coffee Association of America (SCA)
   defect handbook, 99, 100
   Green Arabica Coffee Classification System (GACCS), 99
   Joseph Rivera, 112
Specialty Coffee Association of America (SCA) Defect Handbook, 99, 100
species of coffee. *see* coffee species
sphere roasters. *see* ball roasters
staff, 175–176, 186, 233
stale, 243
Starbucks, 49
stinkers, 99, 100
stock turnover, 183
storage, green beans, 33, 41, 106, 107, 134
storage, roasted coffee, 144, *145*
store manager role, 174
strategic alliance, 223
strictly hard bean (SHB), 243
strip picking, 243
sun-dried, 96, 103, 243
sustainable coffee, 108, 195, 243
Swiss Water Process, 154, 244. *see also* wet-processing
Synesso espresso machines, 185
Syphon brewing system, 48, *49*
systems, 232, 233

T

taint, 243
Tanzania
   coffee characteristics, 90
   harvesting, 105
target market, 195, 200
taste, 243
taste testing. *see* cupping
temperatures, 119, 120, 122, 133
terroir, 243
tester, 118, 243

The Grand Café, 15
The World Atlas of Coffee, 89
theft by staff, 176
thermal oxidisers, 66
Third Wave, 10, 24, 108, 128
three-phase power, 71
Thurber, Francis, 16
tipping, 56, 243
toilet facilities, 44, 174
Toper roasters, 57
Torrefacto roasting, 136
traceability, 243
trowel, 118, 243
true fictions. *see* customer stories
Turkish coffee house, *15*
turnover of stock, 183
Typica variety, 82, 83, 243

U

Uganda, 105
underdeveloped, 124, 128, 131, 138, 244
used roasters, 70
UTZ, 108, 244

V

vacuum packing, 106, 107, 134, 244
Vacuum Pot brewing system, 49
values. *see* core values
varieties, 82–84, *82*, 244
ventilation, 72
volatile aromatics, 66, 87, 244

W

Wagstaff, Stuart, 239
washed process, 102, 244
washing station, 244
Water Process Decaffeination, 244
websites, 184, 206
   The Artisan Roaster, 138
   coffeechemistry, 112
Welcome Dose Specialty Coffee, *63*, 151, 172
wet mill, 244
wet processing, 102, 241
wholesale, 210–213, 220–221, 223
work zones, 41–43
workflow, 40

Y

Yang-Chia 500g roaster, *138*
Yemen, 102, 148
Yirgacheffe hybrid, 84
Young Henrys, 205

Z

Zimbabwe, 105

ACKNOWLEDGEMENTS

First of all I'd like to thank John Russell Storey and Andrew Mackay who suggested that I write this book and encouraged me throughout the process. Andrew has been a mentor to me and is truly an icon of the Australian coffee industry. He also likes Paul Weller and The Cure, which makes him a pretty cool dude in my eyes.

I'd also like to thank Will Notaras for his expert knowledge and guidance on all things coffee roasters-related. His technical engineering expertise has been invaluable in the detail of this book. To Peter and Geoff Brawn, you are both a font of knowledge in the art of roasting coffee, and I also thank you for your encouragement and support of this book. You will not meet a nicer family in the coffee industry than the Brawns. A big man-hug goes out to Paul Mannassis for his review of my book drafts and general roasting advice over the years.

In addition I'd like to thank Tina von Gimborn-Abbing from the Museum für Kaffeetechnik in Emmerich, Germany. Tina is the great-granddaughter of Probat's founder and inventor Theodor von Gimborn. Tina was so generous in sharing her knowledge of the history of modern industrial coffee roasting machines and in providing rare archival photos and images of roasters and promotional material from the 19th and 20th Centuries.

I'd like to thank my wonderful book designer Melissa Mylchreest from King Street Press, who was called in very late in the piece to put it all together in the format you see before you. We clicked straight away design-wise and the process was made so easy by Melissa's expert eye and sense of style.

I am by no means a coffee expert. I learned a lot about coffee roasting by trial and error and from the writings of international legends in the coffee industry. In particular I would like to mention Willem Boot, Joseph A. Rivera and Scott Rao, whose articles and books have guided me over the years to become a better coffee roaster and develop my own roasting style. I truly stand on the shoulders of giants.

I'd like to thank the Australian-based coffee roasters who supported me with images or let us photograph their artisan roasteries. Fleur Studd from Market Lane Coffee and Allan Yeh from Code Black Coffee Roasters in Melbourne, thank you for supplying beautiful images of your roasteries. The same goes to my Sydney-based roaster friends: George Choutis from Roastville Coffee, Kit Cheong from Welcome Dose Specialty Coffee, and finally Ofra Ronen and Renzo Castillo from Di Bartoli Coffee. I would also like to thank and credit Mark Bean and Ian MacPherson for their photography, which appears throughout this book. Lastly, a big thank you to Brenda from Hacienda La Esmeralda, for letting me use the beautiful images of her awesome coffee farm in Panama.

Personally, I owe a big debt of gratitude to some of the people I have worked with at Bay Coffee over the years. I simply can't thank everyone who worked with us over the 18 years but I must single out a few. To Andrew Carmody, Store Manager and then Assistant Roaster, your wicked sense of humour, hard work and encouraging words will never be forgotten. To Bruno Macagi de Seabra,

Store Manager/Head Barista and the son I never had. The customers loved you (some literally) and the staff loved you (some literally). Your Brazilian positive energies and general good vibes made going to work fun every day. To Darren Bennett, my main man in the wholesale area. Together we built something from nothing and our ongoing friendship is treasured. I would also like to thank from the depths of my heart the loyal customers of Bay Coffee during my time at the helm. You supported an unknown prospect from day one, you helped me put my kids through school and to realise one of my dreams in life.

I'd like to thank the Sydney Writers' Room for providing such a wonderful space to write in. It was great to be surrounded by such brilliant people. I often felt like a fraud next to such accomplished writers when I was in there, but hey, I managed to pop a book out myself in the end!

Lastly, to my wife Elizabeth (someone who can really write), and to my beautiful and super-talented daughters, Zoe and Bella. Thank you for always believing in me and for your continual encouragement during this journey. Your love and support mean the world to me.

DAVID ROSA

NOTES